The Peer Guide to Applie Sport Psychology for Con in Training

Successful sport psychology professionals have benefitted from stimulating conversations, challenging questions, support, camaraderie, guidance, and advice offered by their graduate school classmates. Peer relationships are vital and valued aspects of professional development, with many of the relationships formed during school serving as the closest confidences and strongest friendships throughout careers and lifetimes. Yet, the voices and experiences of fellow graduate students are sparsely reported in the sport psychology literature, and profoundly silent in textbooks. *The Peer Guide to Applied Sport Psychology for Consultants in Training* provides a platform for the influential voices of peers, with whom graduate students relate and connect on a visceral level.

Mimicking the environment of a thriving classroom, each chapter within the *Peer Guide* is primarily authored by graduate students, or in some cases recent graduates, with an academic mentor serving a secondary role. The chapter topics were selected by the editors—all of whom are experienced graduate instructors and have taught and mentored many young professionals—as areas where graduate students are commonly challenged, and, correspondingly, where peer support and guidance are most valued. These topics include developing a theoretical orientation to performance excellence, utilizing science to guide practice, ethics, getting the most from supervision, initial experiences in consultation, working with both individuals and groups, and multicultural considerations. The chapters are written in a personal, relatable tone and provide science and practice, challenge and comfort, humor and vulnerability, and insights and anecdotes that are particularly meaningful and accessible coming from peers. A unique addition to the sport psychology literature, this volume is a key resource for developing and established consultants alike.

Mark W. Aoyagi, Ph.D., is Director of the Sport and Performance Psychology program and Founder and Director of the Center for Performance Excellence at the University of Denver. He is a certified consultant for the Association for Applied Sport Psychology (CC-AASP), is a licensed psychologist (CO), and maintains a group practice, Sport and Performance Excellence Consultants, which provides performance psychology consulting services.

Artur Poczwardowski, Ph.D., is a Professor and Director of Field Placements for the Master of Arts in Sport and Performance Psychology program at the University of Denver. He is a Certified Consultant—AASP (Association for Applied Sport Psychology)—and is listed in the USOC Sport Psychology Registry.

Jamie L. Shapiro, Ph.D., is a faculty member and Assistant Director of the Master of Arts in Sport and Performance Psychology program at the University of Denver. She is a Certified Consultant of the Association for Applied Sport Psychology (CC-AASP) and is listed on the United States Olympic Committee's Sport Psychology Registry. She is part of a private practice, Sport & Performance Excellence Consultants, where she provides mental training to athletes and performers.

The Peer Guide to Applied Sport Psychology for Consultants in Training

Edited by
Mark W. Aoyagi,
Artur Poczwardowski
and Jamie L. Shapiro

UNIVERSITY OF DENVER

Routledge
Taylor & Francis Group

NEW YORK AND LONDON

First published 2017
by Routledge
711 Third Avenue, New York, NY 10017

and by Routledge
2 Park Square, Milton Park, Abingdon, Oxon, OX14 4RN

Routledge is an imprint of the Taylor & Francis Group, an informa business

© 2017 Taylor & Francis

Library of Congress Cataloging-in-Publication Data
A catalog record for this title has been requested

ISBN: 978-1-138-86030-8 (hbk)
ISBN: 978-1-138-86031-5 (pbk)
ISBN: 978-1-315-40406-6 (ebk)

Typeset in Sabon
by Apex CoVantage, LLC

Dedication

We dedicate the Peer Guide to all the professors, classmates, students, colleagues, friends, and family that we have had the honor of calling peers.

MA: To my classmates and friends at Georgia Southern and Missouri who taught me so much, in particular about the value of peers, and to all the students at the University of Denver who have allowed me the privilege to be part of their professional and life journey—thank you for establishing a peer community so strong that the SPP family is not a cliché.

To the MHC—I am fortunate to call you peers and friends; all that I am as a professional and person is better because of you.

To Artur and Jamie—thank you for making this book a reality and even more for your daily peer guidance and support.

To my peerless wife, Staci, and my favorite peers Big K and Little K—thank you for bringing more love, joy, and fun into my life than I thought possible.

AP: With thanks and appreciation that nurture my daily joys of professional activity—I have embraced the tradition of supportive mentorship and mutual sharing and learning among established professionals and aspiring performance psychologists. To all of the chapter authors and the many colleagues and friends: your selfless service to the field guides the current and future generations of students, professionals, and leaders—thank you for allowing me to learn from your rich experience. Thanks so very much, Mark and Jamie—you have made this project very fulfilling and fun to contribute to. And to my family—love.

JS: I would not be where I am today without the support and guidance of my mentors, family, friends, colleagues, and students—thank you to each and every one of you that has impacted me along my career path all across the country (and beyond!). To the Springfield College and West Virginia University crews—thank you for providing the professional and ethical foundations to my career and fostering the value of collaboration; I especially want to recognize Dr. Judy Van Raalte for being a strong female role model for me in this field (and for being part of this project!). To my University of Denver colleagues, students, and alumni, and especially Mark and Artur—this job is a dream come true, specifically because of the mentorship, support, collaboration, and bidirectional learning I have had the privilege of receiving. To mom and dad—thanks for always being there for me and for putting up with me living across the country to pursue my dream—I love you!

Contents

Preface

The classroom has played a central role in each of our lives and the lives of all the contributors to this text. Our time as students, classmates, and professors has shaped a critical component of who we are as people and professionals. With the typical hierarchical nature of classrooms, it is easy to fall into the assumption that the direction of learning and influence flows from the teacher to the novices. Indeed, the vast majority of textbooks follow this format (i.e., a learned teacher/author writing for an audience of students). While learning and influence assuredly do flow from teachers to novices, teacher to novice is not the only direction that learning and influence occur. Our experiences as professors have supported the maxim that teachers learn as much from the instructional process (including numerous contributions from students) as students do from teachers. The purpose of *The Peer Guide to Applied Sport Psychology for Consultants in Training* is to capture the guidance of an additional aspect of the classroom dynamic: that of classmates.

Classmates, peers, and fellow students have played at least as large a role in our growth and development as professionals and people as professors and mentors have. In our roles as professors, we have seen this trend thrive as younger generations of students respond less to hierarchy and more to collaborative approaches. As vital a role as the voice of our peers has played in our development, the voice of peers is silent in textbooks. We are not aware of a single textbook in sport psychology that offers students the guidance and insights of their fellow students. *The Peer Guide* is intended to address this gap and facilitate conversations in the classroom that are guided and informed by the experiences and advice of fellow students from various training programs and backgrounds. To preserve the authenticity of these voices, and consistent with our previous editorial approach (see *Expert Approaches to Sport Psychology: Applied Theories of Performance Excellence* [Aoyagi & Poczwardowski, 2012]), we limited our role as editors to providing initial formative feedback and general guidance for the chapter contributors.

In addition to the student-centered approach that we take to education and training, perhaps the most significant impetus for *The Peer Guide* was our experiences as supervisors. In our program, the faculty serve as primary supervisors, and we also have multiple layers of supervisory oversight. These layers of oversight include second-year students offering advice to their first-year shadows, doctoral students supervising master's students (with the doctoral students receiving supervision of their supervision from faculty), and alumni supervising graduate students (under supervision unless they are credentialed to do so independently). In observing and supervising these layers of supervision, we have been able to observe how differently students participate in supervision based upon who the supervisor is. Not surprisingly, students often report that it is much easier for them to be vulnerable and talk about what they do not know or situations that make them uncomfortable with supervisors closer in age and experience to them. Furthermore, students may implement guidance from peers more flexibly and less dogmatically than that coming from professors whom they may more easily defer to. All of these factors contribute to a different dynamic than often occurs between students and faculty supervisors.

Certainly, "different" does not inherently mean better or worse, and indeed we are not suggesting *The Peer Guide* as an alternative or replacement to the many excellent textbooks and resources already in print. Instead, the students' voices contained herein are a supplement and augmentation to what exists. To emphasize this point, we have also included faculty members on each chapter to simulate the environment we have found so enriching in our classrooms—namely, that faculty provide the situational context in which the discussion occurs, students shape the conversation with their comments and questions, and faculty then provide yet another perspective that is potentially more informed by experience and the broader literature. Thus, in *The Peer Guide*, we as the editors have offered the framework for each chapter, the students have taken this structure and made it their own based on their experiences and what they felt would be important to share with their peers, and the faculty members have then supplied their insights.

We hope you gain as much from reading this text as we have in compiling it. The wisdom and advice of the student authors is both inspiring and attainable—a unique blend of uplifting and achievable. Their authentic voices come through clearly and offer a connectedness, normalization, and, when necessary, empathic lifeline during the inevitable (and necessary) struggles and tribulations of being a sport psychology trainee and neophyte sport psychology practitioner. We owe a debt of gratitude to the contributors of this book, our own students, and our peers for helping us to arrive at this point in our journey. We trust that *The Peer Guide* will serve as a valuable companion on your journey toward professional competency.

Mark W. Aoyagi, Artur Poczwardowski,
and Jamie L. Shapiro
University of Denver

Reference

Aoyagi, M. W., & Poczwardowski, A. (Eds.). (2012). *Expert approaches to sport psychology: Applied theories of performance excellence*. Morgantown, WV: Fitness Information Technology.

Contributors

Mark W. Aoyagi: Mark Aoyagi, Ph.D., is the Director of Sport and Performance Psychology and Associate Professor in the Graduate School of Professional Psychology at the University of Denver. He is also the founder and Director of the Center for Performance Excellence. Mark is a recognized sport psychology consultant and has worked with several professional and Olympic teams and athletes as well as NCAA athletic departments and developmental athletes. The practice he co-founded is Sport & Performance Excellence Consultants (spexconsultants.com). He is a licensed psychologist in the state of Colorado, a Certified Consultant, AASP (Association for Applied Sport Psychology) and is listed in the United States Olympic Committee (USOC) Sport Psychology Registry. Along with Artur Poczwardowski, he coedited the book *Expert Approaches to Sport Psychology: Applied Theories of Performance Excellence*. Mark earned a Ph.D. in Counseling Psychology with an emphasis in Sport Psychology from the University of Missouri and was the Sport Psychology Post Doctoral Fellow at the University of Southern California. Prior to that, he completed a B.S. in Exercise and Sport Science and a B.S. in Psychology from the University of Utah and an M.S. in Kinesiology, Sport Psychology emphasis from Georgia Southern University. Mark also completed a Graduate Business Certificate in Management from the University of Denver Daniels College of Business. He was the recipient of the 2005 Student-Practitioner Award from the Association for the Advancement of Applied Sport Psychology and the inaugural Early Career Professional Award from Division 47 (Exercise and Sport Psychology) of the American Psychological Association in 2013. He was appointed a Fellow of AASP in 2016.

Alex Auerbach: Alex Auerbach is a 3rd year doctoral candidate in Counseling Psychology at the University of North Texas. He currently works as a graduate sport psychology consultant with the University of North Texas football program. His research interests include grit and sport performance, mindfulness, athletic intelligence, and behavioral economics in sport.

Jessica D. Bartley: Dr. Jess Dale Bartley earned a B.A. in government and sociology as well as an M.S. in Social Work from the University of Texas. She went on to complete an M.A. in Sport and Performance Psychology as well as a Doctorate in Clinical Psychology with an emphasis in sport and performance psychology and behavioral therapy at the University of Denver. Jess is currently a licensed psychologist as well as a licensed clinical social worker in the State of Colorado. She is also Certified Consultant with the Association for Applied Sport Psychology (CC-AASP) and is listed in the United States Olympic Committee (USOC) Sport Psychology Registry. Jess works primarily with teams and athletes in the high school and collegiate settings as well as Olympic teams and athletes. Her areas of expertise include mental health with athletes—specifically depression, anxiety, eating disorders and body image, substance use, performance, motivation, and sport transition/retirement after sport.

Leigh A. Bryant: Leigh A. Bryant is a Ph.D. candidate in West Virginia University's Sport and Exercise Psychology program. She holds a Bachelor's degree in Psychology from Bucknell University and Master's degrees in Sport and Exercise Psychology and Counseling from West Virginia University. Bryant's primary research interests include stress and coping, injury prevention, professional ethics, and gender issues. A former gymnast, soccer player, and dancer, she enjoys staying active and spending time with family and friends.

Megan M. Byrd: Megan Byrd is a Research Director and assistant professor in sport psychology at John F. Kennedy University. She is also a Ph.D. candidate in Sport and Exercise Psychology at West Virginia University. Additionally, she has a Master's degree in counseling from West Virginia University, a Master's degree in Sport Sciences from Miami University, and a Bachelor's degree in Psychology from Eastern Kentucky University. Megan's research interests include anger and aggression in sport, perfectionism, emotional effects of concussion, and professional ethics.

Jeb Clay: Jeb received his undergraduate degree from Northern State University where he was a part of the wrestling program, and he obtained an M.A. in sport and exercise psychology from Minnesota State University, Mankato. Jeb is a Master Resilience Trainer—Performance Expert for the United States Army. As an MRT-PE he provides sport psychology consultation services as well as resiliency training for soldiers and civilians that carry out the Army mission. Research interests for Jeb are emotional intelligence and performance, mental toughness, and resilience. Jeb is an avid mixed martial arts fan and has worked with numerous professional fighters.

Trevor A. Cote: Trevor Cote, M.A., is a doctoral student studying counseling psychology on the sport and performance psychology licensure track at Boston University. Trevor received his M.A. in sport and performance psychology from the University of Denver. He has enjoyed a wonderful blend of consulting and clinical work. On the path to be a certified consultant, AASP (Association for Applied Sport Psychology), Trevor has worked extensively with high school and Division I and III college student-athletes. As a clinician, Trevor has developed his counseling skills in the fields of community mental health and college counseling. His main goal is empowering others to access their full potential through an integrated approach of mindfulness, acceptance, strength-based interventions, and cognitive-behavior therapy. He has several publications and scholarly presentations on topics of athletic transitions, bullying, and mindfulness in sport. Currently, he is actively engaged in mindfulness and performance research under advisement of Dr. Amy Baltzell. Trevor resides in Boston with his wife, daughter, and lovable dog.

Chad Doerr: Chad is currently a graduate student in James Madison University's Combined-Integrated Doctoral Program in Psychology. He is the Assistant Director for the Challace J. McMillin Center for Sport Psychology at JMU. Chad received his M.A. in Sport and Performance Psychology from the University of Denver in 2014, and B.A. in Psychology from the University of Nevada—Reno. Chad played college baseball at Feather River Community College in Quincy, CA, where he received his Associate's Degree. Previously, he has worked with teams at Regis University in Denver, CO under the mentorship of Dr. Jeni Shannon. He has also worked with various male and female high school and college programs. Chad's current research interest involve the links between well-being and performance, and the development of theories of performance.

Jessica Eichner: Jessica Eichner grew up in Germantown, WI, which is about 25 minutes north of Milwaukee. She attended Germantown High School and was a four-sport athlete (volleyball, cross country, basketball, and softball) where she first realized her love for sport psychology. She played softball at Lakeland College in Sheboygan, WI and graduated with a double major in Psychology and Sport and Exercise Studies. In 2015, she graduated with a Masters of Arts in Sport and Exercise Psychology from Minnesota State University, Mankato. She current lives in the Milwaukee area and is building her consulting business for athletes.

Edward F. Etzel: Ed is a Licensed Psychologist in the state of West Virginia. Since 1990, he has served as a psychologist for the West Virginia University Department of Intercollegiate Athletics and is a half-time staff member of Well WVU and the WVU Carruth Center for Counseling and Psychiatric Services. Ed is involved in the provision of counseling services for personal, career, and sport performance enhancement concerns, and consultation with WVUIA staff on mental health issues. Ed serves as a Professor in the Department of Sport Sciences within the WVU College of Physical Activity and Sport Sciences. Ed is listed as a consultant on the U.S. Olympic Committee's Sport Psychology Registry. He serves as Chair of the Association for Applied Sport Psychology's Ethics Committee, and did so from 1998 to 2007. Ed is a Fellow in the Association for Applied Sport Psychology and received the American Psychological Association's Division 47 Distinguished Contribution to Education in sport and exercise psychology award in 2009.

Joanna M. Foss: Joanna Foss is a current doctoral student in Counseling Psychology with a subspecialty in Sport Psychology at the University of Missouri. She currently works as a Mental Performance Coach in the Athletic Department, where she delivers individual and group performance enhancement services to athletes and coaches. Prior to Missouri, Joanna received her M.A. in Sport and Performance Psychology from the University of Denver and her B.A. in Psychology from Marist College. Joanna has consulted with teams at a variety of levels including Division I, II, and high school teams. Joanna also received the 2012 AASP Student Diversity Award for her work with underprivileged youth while in her Master's program. Born in Michigan, Joanna grew up swimming and playing soccer before ultimately pursuing volleyball in college.

Thomas Fritze: Thomas (Tommy) Fritze is a Colorado native who grew up enjoying and playing a variety of sports. His experience of studying the human body and mind as a student interested in physical therapy and psychology coupled with his experiences as a collegiate athlete led him to the field of sport and performance psychology. He seeks to continue these themes via a career as a clinical sport psychologist in a college athletic department. Engaging in sport and performance psychology consulting as a neophyte graduate student solidified for him the importance of supervision at all levels. Additionally, he is drawn to teaching sport and performance psychology as well as clinical psychology subjects.

Nicole T. Gabana: Nicole Gabana is a certified sport psychology consultant (CC-AASP) and Ph.D. student in counseling and sport psychology at Indiana University Bloomington. She is completing her predoctoral internship at the Ohio State University Counseling and Consultation Service. During her time at IU, Nicole was an Associate Instructor of Sport Psychology and Positive Psychology. From 2013 to 2016 she served as sport psychology consultant to the IU Athletic Department, completing her final practicum at IU Counseling and Psychological Services. Nicole's research centers on the integration of positive psychology and sport, specifically the effects of gratitude on student-athlete wellbeing. Nicole graduated with a B.A. in psychology in 2011 from the College of the Holy Cross (Worcester, MA) where she rowed for the Division I crew team. In 2013, she obtained her M.S. in counseling from Springfield College (MA), where she worked as an athletic counselor for Division I–III collegiate teams, high school, and youth sport.

Kensa K. Gunter: Kensa K. Gunter is a licensed psychologist in the state of Georgia and is designated as a Certified Consultant by the Association for Applied Sport Psychology (AASP). In her Atlanta based private practice, she provides individual and team-based sport and performance psychology services, individual counseling for athletic and nonathletic populations, and consultation services. She also facilitates educational workshops and provides lectures locally and nationally. Kensa received a Psy.D. in Clinical Psychology with an emphasis in Sport-Exercise Psychology from Argosy University in Phoenix, Arizona. She completed her internship and postdoctoral fellowship at the University of California, Davis—Counseling and Psychological Services. She is a member of the American Psychological Association and the Georgia Psychological Association, and she is listed on the United States Olympic Committee Sport Psychology Registry.

Aaron W. Halterman: Aaron Halterman is a sport psychology consultant to the Indiana University athletics department where he has provided individual counseling, team performance enhancement sessions, team process sessions, coach consulting, crisis management, and program planning. He is finishing his Ph.D. in counseling psychology with a minor in sport. He has been counseling student-athletes at the high school and collegiate level for 6 years. Before counseling Aaron played collegiate football at Indiana University where he earned a B.A. in psychology, from there he went on to play professionally in the NFL for four years before a back injury ended his career. In 2012, he earned his M.S. in counseling from Indiana University. Aaron and his wife Lora live in Indianapolis with their son (Nolan—1).

Robert J. Harmison: Robert J. Harmison is the Kibler Professor of Sport Psychology in the Department of Graduate Psychology at James Madison University and the Director of Sport Psychology for JMU Athletics. He teaches courses and conducts scholarship in applied sport psychology, provides sport psychology services to JMU athletes and coaches, and delivers educational outreach programming to the surrounding athletic community. Robert received a Ph.D. in Counseling Psychology from the University of North Texas in 2000 and an M.S. in Exercise and Sport Sciences from the University of Arizona in 1994. He is a member of the U.S. Olympic Committee Sport Psychology Registry and is designated as a Certified Consultant and Fellow by the Association for Applied Sport Psychology. He was a member of the U.S. Olympic Committee sport psychology staff from 1997 to 1999, provided consultation to the U.S. Snowboarding national and Olympic teams from 2000 to 2011, and has worked with athletes at four NCAA Division I universities.

Adisa Haznadar: Adisa Haznadar is a doctoral candidate in the Psy.D. program in Counseling Psychology, with an athletic counseling concentration, at Springfield College. Adisa earned her M.S. in Sport and Exercise Psychology (European Master in Sport and Exercise Psychology) from the University of Thessaly, Greece and Leipzig University, Germany. Adisa's research interests are related to mental warm up, motivational climate, self-talk, and self-efficacy. She is a member of the International Relations committee of the Association for Applied Sport Psychology (AASP) and works actively on promoting sport and exercise psychology outside of North America.

Shu Jiang: Shu Jiang earned her M.S. in Athletic Counseling at Springfield College and a B.S. degree in Sport Psychology from Xi'an Physical Education University, Xi'an, China, in 2013. She became a Certified Counselor in China in 2013. Her research interests include language and perceptual learning in speech recognition, second language acquisition, and behavioral change. She also provides athletic counseling services for teams and athletes.

Cindra Kamphoff: Cindra Kamphoff, Ph.D., CC-AASP, is a professor at Minnesota State University, Mankato and the Director of the Center for Sport and Performance Psychology. She has published more than 18 research manuscripts, 7 book chapters, and has received more than $175,000 in grants. Her work has been published in *Journal of Applied Sport Psychology, The Sport Psychologist*, and *Research Quarterly for Exercise and Sport*. Her podcast, The High Performance Mindset, is available on iTunes and has been downloaded in more than 70 countries. Dr. Kamphoff received the Dorothy Harris Award from AASP and also served as the Research and Practice Division Head. She also has a private practice where she works with elite and NFL athletes as well as championship teams. She practices performance psychology herself as a marathoner competing in 13 marathons, and in 2012, she won the Omaha Marathon. A summary of her work can be found at cindrakamphoff.com.

Michael D. Lewis: Michael Lewis is a Mental Conditioning Coach at IMG Academy. Michael received his Masters in Sport and Exercise Psychology from Argosy University and a Bachelors in Sports Management from the University of New Haven. Michael's background is in performance training. He is a provisionally certified consultant through the Association for Applied Sport Psychology. Michael is responsible for the Men's Post Graduate programs in Basketball and Baseball as well as the Academy Track and Field and Football teams. He also supports IMG's NFL combine, NBA and MLB pre draft programs as well the Elite Track and Field Athletes. Michael works with more than 125 athletes from varying ages and backgrounds on a weekly basis, supporting them in achieving their athletic dreams.

Annamari Maaranen-Hincks: Annamari Maaranen-Hincks is completing her Psy.D. in Counseling Psychology with a concentration in Athletic Counseling at Springfield College. She earned her M.S. in Athletic Counseling from Springfield College. Annamari's applied interests include integrated behavioral medicine, particularly in pain management and rehabilitation, and fear, anxiety, and mental blocks in artistic sports. Her research focuses on mental blocks on backward moving and twisting skills in gymnastics. Annamari has presented her research at sport psychology conferences, coauthored an article on eating disorders for *Sport Psych Works*, and published research on mental blocks in performing backward moving skills in gymnastics in *Technique: USA Gymnastics Official Publication*. She is also a gymnastics coach and has worked internationally with youth, collegiate, and elite athletes.

Megan K. Marsh: Megan Marsh grew up in Southern California with a background in competitive figure skating. Megan moved to Denver to pursue a Master's degree in Sport and Performance Psychology and has since chosen to continue her education by pursuing a doctoral degree. Megan is currently in the Clinical PsyD program at the University of Denver. Some of Megan's specialties include performance consulting, exercise adherence, LGBT issues, specifically gender identity, as well as complex trauma. She also has experience working in college counseling centers, which she feels ties many of her passions together. Megan both enjoys and appreciates the supervision and consultation processes, similar to those outlined in the chapter she authored.

Emily Minaker: Emily was born and raised in Kelowna, British Columbia, Canada. She attended the University of British Columbia during her undergraduate degree and majored in Psychology. Emily stumbled upon sport psychology while on exchange at the University of California Santa Barbara. Combining psychology with her love of sport, Emily decided to pursue graduate studies at the University of Denver's Masters of Arts in Sport and Performance Psychology program. Growing up, Emily was a competitive hockey and soccer player and now enjoys running and hiking. Emily loves to go home during the summer and waterski on Okanagan Lake. Upon graduation from the University of Denver, Emily plans to pursue doctoral studies in Industrial Organizational Psychology.

Taryn K. Morgan: Taryn Morgan is the Assistant Director of Athletic and Personal Development (APD) at IMG Academy in Bradenton, FL, where she helps oversee a staff of 40+ specialists in athletic training, physical therapy, physical conditioning, mental conditioning, leadership, nutrition, and vision training. Daily, the APD staff works with more than 1,000 athletes of varying sports, ages, and levels. Her background is in sport psychology, and she received her Ph.D. from the University of Tennessee. Taryn is an Association for Applied Sport Psychology (AASP) Certified Consultant and is the Vice Chair of the AASP Certification Committee. She has coauthored book chapters and journal articles, and has spoken nationally and internationally on the High Performance Mindset. She has worked with Olympians, professional athletes, and collegiate teams, as well as the youth athletes at IMG Academy to assist them in reaching their potential both in and out of sport.

Angus L. Mugford: Angus is the Director of High Performance, for the Toronto Blue Jays Major League Baseball team. This role oversees the integration of an interdisciplinary performance team to support the development and performance of players, coaches and support members. His background is in sport psychology, with a PhD from the University of Kansas, after which he worked for more than a decade at IMG Academy overseeing mental conditioning programs and work with junior and professional athletes, as well as U.S. military and other high performers. In 2015 he was elected by his peers as the president of the Association for Applied Sport Psychology (AASP), the leading professional organization for applied sport psychology consultants in the world. He continues to present at professional conferences, publish in academia and popular press, as well as sought after for interviews in magazines and media outlets, like ESPN, CNN, and the BBC.

Adam M. O'Neil: Adam works with athletes at the Olympic, Paralympic, professional, collegiate, and high school levels; with TV, film, stage and recording artists; and with executives in a range of fields. He believes that in order to perform at an elite level one must be able to optimize thoughts, emotions, and behaviors. He holds board certifications in applied sport and performance psychology (CC-AASP) and in neurofeedback brain training (BCN-BCIA), and he is a peer-reviewed published author, and is currently conducting large and small-scale research under the supervision of Dr. Michael Gervais. Adam received his bachelors degree from Lake Forest College, his masters degree from the University of Denver, and he is studying clinical psychology at Fielding Graduate University (Ph.D.). Adam is happily married, and the father of two awesome boys.

Trent A. Petrie: Trent A. Petrie, Ph.D. is a Professor and Director of the Center for Sport Psychology, Department of Psychology at the University of North Texas. He is a licensed psychologist (Texas), Certified Consultant, Association for Applied Sport Psychology (AASP) and a Fellow in both AASP and Division 47 of the American Psychological

Association. His research interests include eating disorders and body image among athletes, psychological antecedents and consequences of athletic injury, achievement motivation and athletic performance, and professional issues in applied sport psychology. His research has been funded by grants from the NCAA and AASP.

Artur Poczwardowski: Artur Poczwardowski, Ph.D., is a Professor and Director of Field Placements at the University of Denver. Artur has supervised student-consultants in their delivery of sport and performance psychology services for the past 12 years. Artur has more than 40 publications (in professional journals and as book chapters) and has delivered more than 80 professional presentations and more than 70 invited and educational lectures and workshops. His scholarly work focuses on sport psychology practice for performance enhancement and psychological well-being, coach–athlete relationships, and coping strategies in elite performers. He served as an Associate Editor for *The Sport Psychologist* (2004–2006) and currently serves on its editorial board. He is a Certified Consultant, AASP (Association for Applied Sport Psychology) and is listed in the *USOC Sport Psychology Registry*. Artur and his wife, Kasia, live in Denver with their two children.

Steve Portenga: Steve Portenga, Ph.D. is the CEO of iPerformance Psychology, working with elite, professional, and Olympic athletes. As the former director of sport and performance psychology for the USA Track and Field Team, Dr. Portenga worked with Olympic athletes onsite during the 2012 London Games. He was the founding director of the Sport and Performance Psychology in the Graduate School of Professional Psychology at the University of Denver. His areas of expertise include: Psychology of elite performance; neuroscience and performance; technology and behavior change; leadership (coaches and peer) and team development; and the psychology of injury. Due to his expertise as a scholar, scientist, and practitioner, Steve was invited to be a founding member of the American Psychological Association's Coalition for the Psychology of High Performance.

Joey Ramaeker: Joey Ramaeker is a 6th year doctoral candidate at the University of North Texas (UNT) and is completing his doctoral internship at Iowa State University's (ISU) Student Counseling Service. His passion for performance psychology emerged from his experiences as a collegiate baseball player and youth baseball coach. Throughout his training, Joey has had the honor of providing consultation services to numerous teams and individual student-athletes at both ISU and UNT, community based athletes, and professional organizations. His current research interests include the intersection of masculine ideologies, athletic participation and mental health, psychological service utilization among athletes, stigma associated with professional help-seeking, and the provision of supervision. His research has been funded by the Association for Applied Sport Psychology.

Laura Reutlinger: Laura Reutlinger is a 2015 graduate of the Master of Arts program for Sport and Exercise Psychology at Minnesota State University, Mankato. She has consulted with tennis, volleyball, football, basketball, and softball teams and individuals at the collegiate and high school level. She is a Certified Consultant with the Association for Applied Sport Psychology. She graduated with a BA in Psychology and Health from Luther College. Currently, she works as a health coach, providing behavior change and motivation consulting to clients looking to embrace a healthy lifestyle.

Jamie L. Shapiro: Dr. Jamie Shapiro is a faculty member in the Master of Arts in Sport and Performance Psychology program in the Graduate School of Professional Psychology at the University of Denver. She earned a Ph.D. in Sport and Exercise Psychology from West Virginia University (2009), an M.A. in Community Counseling from WVU (2008), and an M.S. in Athletic Counseling from Springfield College (2005). She earned a B.S. in Psychology from Brown University, where she was on the gymnastics team for four years. Dr. Shapiro is a Certified Consultant of the Association for Applied Sport Psychology (CC-AASP), listed on the United States Olympic Committee's Sport Psychology Registry, and a National Certified Counselor (NCC) by the National Board of Certified Counselors. Dr. Shapiro is a consultant for Sport and Performance Excellence Consultants based in Denver, CO. She has consulted with youth, collegiate, elite, and Paralympic athletes from a variety of sports. Dr. Shapiro's specific interests include psychology of sport injury, learning life skills through sport, psychological skills training, psychology of performing arts, exercise psychology, and ethics and training in sport and performance psychology.

Shelly Sheinbein: Shelly Sheinbein is a 5th year doctoral candidate in Counseling Psychology at the University of North Texas (UNT). She previously worked as a graduate sport psychology consultant with the UNT Tennis team for one year, followed by a year of outreach with coaches, parents, and personal trainers from the local community, and the UNT Track and Field program for two years. Her research interests include examining the impact of mindfulness and imagery based interventions on athletes' psychological and physical response to sport injury, funded through a UNT research grant, as well as exploring the psychosocial benefits of exercise. Her passion for sport psychology grew from being an avid exerciser and NCAA Division III collegiate women's lacrosse player.

Jesse A. Steinfeldt: Dr. Jesse Steinfeldt is an Associate Professor of Counseling Psychology at Indiana University as well as a certified Sport Psychologist (CC-AASP). He created and directs the Indiana University Sport and Performance Psychology program, wherein he trains and supervises graduate students who provide Sport and Performance Psychology and consultative services to student-athletes, teams and coaches at Indiana University and at local high schools. Dr. Steinfeldt recently completed a year-long clinical sabbatical in Seattle where he was a Senior Fellow at the University of Washington, providing Sport and Performance Psychology and consultative services to Husky student-athletes, coaches, and teams, while also serving as a Senior Fellow in Neurosurgery, providing neuropsychological testing and treatment recommendations at Seattle Children's Hospital to adolescents who suffered sport concussions (mTBI). A Yale graduate and former multisport collegiate and professional athlete, Jesse and his wife Erica live in Bloomington with their children (Aaron—13, Addison—12, Aidan—10).

Alexandra J. Thompson: Alex Thompson is a 4th year doctoral candidate in Counseling Psychology at the University of North Texas (UNT). She began her tenure as a graduate sport psychology consultant with the UNT Track and Field program for two years, after which she worked with the UNT basketball programs for two years. Her research interests include examining the developmental trends of disordered eating behaviors in female collegiate athletes, and include projects that have been funded by the NCAA and the Association for Applied Sport Psychology. Her passion for sport psychology began as an athlete, when she competed as a NCAA Division I collegiate basketball player.

Emily A. Tonn: Emily Tonn is a high school teacher at La Joya Community High School in Avondale, Arizona. She teaches courses in Advanced Placement Psychology, Psychology, and Sociology. Emily has coached numerous sports throughout her teaching career, including volleyball, basketball, and track. Emily received her M.A. in Sport-Exercise Psychology from Argosy University in 2002. She was a supervisor for multiple Argosy

University graduate students as they completed practicum experiences in sport psychology where she would provide guidance in consultation and team dynamics.

Erika D. Van Dyke: Erika D. Van Dyke is completing her Ph.D. in Sport and Exercise Psychology at West Virginia University. She earned her M.S. in Athletic Counseling from Springfield College. Erika coauthored a book chapter regarding sport and exercise in health psychology and has presented at national and international sport psychology conferences. In 2016, she received the American Psychological Association's Society for Sport, Exercise and Performance Psychology Master's Thesis Award for her research exploring relationships among collegiate gymnasts' use of self-talk and balance beam performance in competition. Erika is also a certified group exercise instructor through the Aerobics and Fitness Association of America.

Julie Vieselmeyer: Julie Vieselmeyer, M.S., M.A., is currently completing a doctoral degree in clinical psychology at Seattle Pacific University. She is a graduate of University of Denver's Sport and Performance Psychology program. Her research interests are in health psychology, developmental psychopathology, cognitive emotion regulation, positive character traits as protective factors, and sport-based youth development programs as prevention for mental health outcomes. Julie has supported athletes as through her role as a USA Triathlon and USA Track and Field coach and now provides sport psychology consulting for high school and collegiate athletes in the Pacific Northwest. She has taught undergraduate programs at Western Washington University and provides continuing education at Seattle Children's Hospital. Julie serves on the executive board for American Psychological Association (APA)—Division 47 and is an Association for Applied Sport Psychology (AASP) certified consultant.

Judy L. Van Raalte: Judy L. Van Raalte, Ph.D. is professor of psychology at Springfield College, Certified Consultant, Association for Applied Sport Psychology, and listed in the United States Olympic Committee Sport Psychology Registry. Dr. Van Raalte has presented at conferences in 18 countries, published more than 90 articles in peer-reviewed journals on topics such as self-talk and professional issues in sport and exercise psychology, and produced more than 20 sport psychology videos. The National Institutes of Mental Health has funded her research on eating disorders. The National Collegiate Athletic Association (NCAA) funded her work developing and evaluating a multimedia website for student-athlete career development and student-athlete mental health. Dr. Van Raalte served as President of the American Psychological Association's Society for Sport, Exercise and Performance Psychology and as the Vice President of the International Society of Sport Psychology. She is a fellow of the American Psychological Association and the Association for Applied Sport Psychology.

Jack C. Watson II: Dr. Jack Watson is a Professor of Sport and Exercise Psychology and Chair of the Department of Sport Sciences at West Virginia University. Dr. Watson completed his Ph.D. in sport psychology and postdoctoral respecialization in counseling psychology at Florida State University. Dr. Watson is a Certified Consultant with the Association for Applied Sport Psychology, is listed on the United States Olympic Committee Sport Psychology Registry, and is a licensed psychologist in the State of West Virginia. Dr. Watson served as President of the Association for Applied Sport Psychology (2012/13). He continues to provide services to athletes in his community and supervise doctoral students who are providing sport psychology services. Dr. Watson's research revolves around the topic of professional issues in sport psychology, including ethics, supervision, and mentoring. He has edited a book, written more than 75 articles and book chapters, and has given numerous presentations and keynote addresses.

1 Developing a Theoretical Orientation to Performance Excellence

Joanna M. Foss, Emily Minaker,
Chad Doerr, and Mark W. Aoyagi

People have moments in their lives when they feel like they were able to perform at their best, when it mattered most. These fleeting moments are often labeled peak experiences or optimal performances. Performance excellence captures these moments but also broadens the perspective and encapsulates performing at a consistently high level over time and enjoying the process of performance. The field of sport and performance psychology (SPP) has dedicated itself to understanding what underlying mental and emotional factors contribute to a performer getting the most out of his or her ability in those important moments as well as in the moments training outside of the spotlight and developing capability. Professionals in the field of SPP have developed effective and complex theoretical understandings that guide their work. These theories help consultants conceptualize and understand why performers may experience a peak performance, perform consistently well over time, and, as is bound to happen, perform less than desirably at times. They also inform and provide rationale for the use of interventions targeted at training specific mental skills that will help their clients perform to their highest abilities.

Although many would argue for the importance of practicing from a theoretical orientation, a gap exists within the SPP literature around this issue. Steps have already been taken to remedy this gap (see for example Aoyagi & Poczwardowski, 2012), and continued attention within the literature will support this foundation of SPP practice. Thus, the purpose of this chapter is to identify the current state of theory within SPP, to discuss the importance of developing and of working from a theoretical orientation, and to propose a model to guide students and other practitioners through the process of developing their own theoretical orientation to performance excellence.

Theoretical Paradigms in SPP

When examining the state of theoretical paradigms in SPP, it is first important to define what is meant by a theoretical paradigm. Terms such as theory, model, philosophy, and frameworks are often used semi-interchangeably within the SPP literature. This has led to confusion as each of these terms has a particular nuance (Aoyagi, 2013). A theoretical paradigm refers to a framework with a high level of abstraction (Prochaska & Norcross, 2010), which guides practitioners in attaining a global understanding of the area of interest (e.g., performance excellence) and is typically built from several theories (i.e., explanations of specific phenomena). Additionally, theoretical paradigms enable practitioners to understand and to explain why certain characteristics or interventions impact clients in the ways that they do (Aoyagi, 2013). Thus, a theory is abstract enough to allow practitioners to make sense of vast amounts of information or to generate hypotheses based on incomplete information.

Currently, SPP literature tends to rely on models as opposed to overarching theoretical paradigms. These models may be based on theoretical paradigms; however, they often lack the depth or the ability to predict behavior that is expected when utilizing a theoretical paradigm. For example, the psychological skills training (PST) model often utilized in SPP reflects aspects of cognitive-behavioral therapy; however, it lacks the ability to explain behavior inherent in its parent theory (Tod, Andersen, & Marchant, 2009). In addition to models, specific theories are sometimes confused with theoretical paradigms. An example here is Self-Determination Theory (SDT [Ryan & Deci, 2000]), which has been widely adopted within the SPP literature to explain motivation due to its well-researched and practical applicability. However, SDT is a theory, as opposed to a theoretical paradigm, and therefore is not at a high-enough level of abstraction to explain overall behavior, performance excellence, or areas outside of motivation. SDT may be a component of a theoretical paradigm but is not one itself. Rather, theoretical paradigms can inform practitioners to intervene on a wide range of issues with performers as opposed to specific subsets of their presenting concerns. The limited scope of information coverage that models and theories provide clearly does not allow for practitioners to make sense of large amounts of information from various contexts.

Furthermore, the theoretical paradigms that are utilized in SPP are often taken from general psychology. These general psychological paradigms have been developed to "explain and understand pathology, and to assist practitioners in preventing, eliminating, or assessing, symptomatic, maladaptive, or undesired behavior" (Aoyagi, Portenga, Poczwardowski, Cohen, & Statler, 2012, p. 33). However, the needs of the populations with whom SPP practitioners work are often different from the needs of populations experiencing psychopathology. General psychology theoretical paradigms can certainly provide a framework for practitioners to support athletes, and in many cases may contribute to performance excellence; however, theoretical paradigms specific to understanding and facilitating performance excellence would better guide practice for the provider seeking to offer performance excellence services and even more importantly for clients seeking performance excellence consultation (rather than therapy).

Performance psychology was defined by the American Psychological Association Division 47 Practice Committee as "the study and application of psychological principles of human performance in helping people consistently perform in the upper range of their capabilities and more thoroughly enjoy the performance process" (2011, p. 9). Although this is the definition of SPP, it is clear that there is a distinct lack of theoretical paradigms describing the underlying constructs behind performing to the upper range of their capabilities (Aoyagi & Poczwardowski, 2012). This is not to say that practitioners are atheoretical in their approaches to working with athletes; however, few practitioners directly working with performers in the field have articulated their theoretical paradigms in the literature and exposed them to scientific scrutiny. In an age of accountability and evidence-based practice, further attempts to address this gap would enhance the scientific credibility of the field.

It is from theoretical paradigms that practitioners develop their Theoretical Orientation to Performance Excellence (TOPE). A TOPE is a "consistent perspective on human performance, psychological facilitators and inhibitors of performance, and the mechanisms of influencing performance excellence" (Aoyagi, 2013, p. 142). This is comparable to practitioners within the field of psychology working with clients from the lens of specific theoretical orientations (e.g., cognitive-behavior therapy, acceptance and commitment therapy); however, the TOPE is meant to inform reaching performance excellence and high-level functioning, rather than the reduction of psychopathology.

Why Develop a TOPE?

Developing a TOPE is a task that should be embraced by future professionals in SPP, as it provides support and guidance for understanding issues and proactively informs service delivery (Christensen & Aoyagi, 2014; Henriksen & Diment, 2011; Stambulova & Johnson, 2010). We believe that a TOPE gives you a framework from which to build on for the remainder of your career and challenges you to engage in a process of lifelong learning. However, developing a TOPE can often be seen as difficult, and sometimes tedious. "I am only a first year student with little experience, so why am I developing a TOPE?" is a question I (EM) asked myself before developing my own TOPE and one that was frequently echoed by my classmates. I soon realized that this was precisely the reason why, as a novice consultant, I needed to develop a TOPE. With my lack of experience in SPP fieldwork, it was imperative that I had a foundation of theory to guide future service delivery. This strong theoretical underpinning provided a basis for determining the best strategies or interventions to use with my clientele. By embracing the uncertainty and realizing the task was not as daunting as first thought, I was able to see the increased confidence it would bring me in working with a client for the first time. It also made service delivery personally meaningful and more enjoyable (and less stressful!). Answering the question of "why" made the process more sensible, and I was able to see the benefits in guiding my applied work. (See Chapter 7 for in-depth exploration of initial practicum experience.)

Developing a TOPE represents a sophisticated approach to service delivery. It allows you to proactively conceptualize how to move a client toward performance excellence, as opposed to reactively responding to issues by eclectically selecting interventions. As a novice consultant, I (JF) found myself trying to cater to coaches' desires or "in the moment" problems rather than stepping back and viewing client concerns from a wider lens. I picked interventions that would alleviate the current problem as opposed to considering the "real issue" behind the problem. I recall one of my first consulting experiences working with a high school soccer team where this issue was particularly present. During that time, I had no overarching plan for what I intended to do with the team. Instead, I would take observations from practice or from the game and then do a session on related topics the following week. For example, there was a game where the team became very angry and frustrated with an opponent, so I followed with a session on composure. In approaching from this angle, I missed social and cultural considerations that impacted the athletes' emotional states. Other times the coaches or I would notice players going through the motions in practice, so I would follow with a session on commitment or on the benefits of deliberate practice. Reflecting on that experience, there seemed to be two main factors working into the style of my consulting: lack of big picture planning and lack of confidence in my own consulting. It was much more comfortable to respond to immediate concerns and to feel like I was addressing topics the coach wanted rather than taking a more long-term approach to my work.

This is much different than the way I (JF) approach my consulting today. I currently begin with the end in mind (Covey, 1989) for my work with teams and with individuals. Rather than react to problems, I try to conceptualize what is needed for performance excellence in specific domains and then proactively build those skills throughout the off-season and season. For example, I more recently worked with an individual closed sport. I began by observing practice and ultimately decided that the performance excellence goal was to "win" each individual skill execution by giving each instance full focus, intensity, and trust. With that end goal in mind, I created a general plan for which sport psychology concepts and applications would be needed to reach that ability based on my TOPE. This plan was general to allow for flexibility within the season while still serving as a guide for my work. In general, operating from a TOPE required that I step back and practice my skills in conceptualization about both what was occurring and why it might be, and then to proactively address the concern. This critical thinking ability is a skill that I continue to develop when working with clients and teams.

Taking into account a wider view of client concerns also can help develop strategic mental programs when working with teams. In developing my TOPE, I (EM) was able to understand why I was selecting particular interventions and to formulate a program that allowed me to address issues before they arose. Despite the planning, my formulated program was never executed perfectly, due to unforeseen circumstances that naturally arise when working with SPP clients. However, my TOPE still gave me a direction to work toward and something to fall back on when presented with unique challenges within the sport and performance domain (Poczwardowski, Sherman, & Ravizza, 2004). Focusing on the process (versus the outcome) during the development of my TOPE allowed me to understand the importance of maintaining a flexible mindset. When unexpected circumstances arose, I was able to be proactive in choosing interventions to inform future practice. An example of this was during my first term as a novice consultant when I was brought in to work with a team because they were having a lot of issues with player attitudes and team cohesion. I was aware of the unpredictable environment that I was walking in to, as before I conducted my first session I had spent two weeks observing practices and games and getting to know the players. In my third session with the team I was leading an activity about creating a team vision. The session did not go as planned, as the players turned the session into an opportunity to discuss the issues they had with each other and the coach. It was in this moment when my session was quickly turning into an unproductive, anger-fueled conversation that I realized my TOPE had already proactively informed my service delivery. Due to the time I had taken to get to know the team, I was able to create a space where they felt comfortable openly discussing issues. My TOPE allowed me to know in that moment the most beneficial intervention was not for me to follow my own agenda. Therefore, I was able to move the session along to better suit the team's needs in discussing team issues and allowing them a safe space in which to do so. I quickly learned that having a flexible mindset and being proactive in choosing interventions were key to helping this team and informing my future practice. In the end, we did end up developing a team vision, and it greatly increased cohesion within the team; however, if I was not grounded in a theoretical foundation, my relationship with this team would have been more self-serving and less beneficial to the client.

Focusing on learning major theories and theoretical integration at the beginning of my training was frustrating at times. I (CD) felt a strong urge to simply learn a set of interventions, and I wanted to be told exactly what to do in order to "fix" any problem that arose with a team. I was impatient, in that I wanted to know the secret formula to peak performance and teach that the same way to all my future clients. However, as great athletes know, a deep internalization of fundamentals is the key to high performance. Therefore, initially focusing my education on pre-existing theories and models of human mental behavior, and deeply reflecting on what high performance personally meant for me, allowed me to develop a strong ability to understand and conceptualize. While I was not the best at presenting and providing interventions for athletes at the beginning of my training, the fundamental ability of conceptualization through my developing TOPE fostered my creativity and allowed me to understand, connect, and provide the appropriate interventions for the performers I was working with. Instead of my initial question ("How do the best consultants work with their clients, and how can I imitate them?"), I began to ask how the field of SPP can be better and think in new ways to develop more effective services.

Figure 1.1 Model for Developing a Theoretical Orientation to Performance Excellence

In sum, future professionals in the field of SPP would benefit from developing a strong TOPE. It informs applied work and provides a sense of security and direction in the often nebulous and sometimes chaotic world of consulting. We suggest that novice consultants developing their own TOPE take a sense of fulfillment in that not only are they benefiting their own future service delivery but they are also contributing to the advancement of SPP by fostering new and creative methods to intervene with performers that are theoretically and scientifically based.

Model for Developing a TOPE

As individuals who have developed our own TOPE, we understand that the process of developing a TOPE can seem overwhelming. The remainder of this chapter will discuss a proposed model that will help guide students and novice practitioners in formulating their own TOPE (see Figure 1.1). These sections will discuss both the process of succeeding within each stage and personal themes that emerged for us authors while undergoing the process ourselves. These will serve to normalize some aspects of the experience and to offer advice for students that we believe would be useful to know earlier in development. However, this is not to say that these experiences are exhaustive or typical of all students who undertake this process.

Personal Experiences and Beliefs

We suggest that your personal experiences and beliefs form the foundation of your theoretical orientation to performance excellence. What are your own thoughts on how to achieve performance excellence? What makes sense to you based on your history and the knowledge you have already accumulated? Novice consultants developing a TOPE with no applied SPP field work may experience difficulty when first facing the task of writing a theoretical orientation, which was a task in one of the early courses in our graduate program. After we read *Expert Approaches to Sport Psychology: Applied Theories of Performance Excellence* (Aoyagi & Poczwardowski, 2012) and examined highly regarded SPP professionals' theoretical orientations, it was encouraging to see how a TOPE can evolve over the years. However, the realization that the basis of these highly regarded professionals' TOPE stemmed from their own personal experiences and beliefs made the task of writing my (EM) own theoretical orientation more enjoyable. By incorporating my own personal experiences and beliefs, I was able to self-reflect and to realize how these could inform my theoretical orientation. This made the process very meaningful to me and allowed the task to resonate on a deeper level than just one of a course "assignment."

I first revisited Newburg, Kimiecik, Durand-Bush, and Doell's (2002) resonance performance model (RPM), as this was an article that I had read earlier in the term that was able to greatly inform my writing. In revisiting the dream (Newburg et al., 2002) I was able to ask myself the question of "why it is I do what I do." Why am I a graduate student in SPP? Why do I want to be a future professional in this field? In answering these questions, I began to formulate my theoretical orientation and realized that taking from my own personal experiences and beliefs was an important way to ground myself within my theoretical orientation. Incorporating and reflecting on your values and beliefs allows your TOPE to be unique to you and allows you to better incorporate this into your own consulting style. This ensures you are operating from a perspective that feels authentic to you, rather than trying to adopt styles, techniques, or interventions that do not fit with your style or personality. As you grow and gain more personal experiences and beliefs within SPP, you will find that your TOPE grows too.

Developing a theoretical orientation is extremely unique to the individual. In SPP, what works for one client may not always work for another; therefore, it is also important to realize that the way every consultant works is different. In recognizing these differences, we encourage you to think about your values and beliefs, as not only does this make the process more enjoyable and personally meaningful but also it makes your consulting style unique. By beginning with my own values and beliefs, I was able to be a self-reflective learner and think critically about how these fit into my theoretical orientation. In doing so, I felt engaged when writing and eager to revisit it when I learned new material.

Acquire Theoretical Knowledge

Once you have an understanding of how your personal experiences and beliefs could impact performance excellence, the next step is to acquire theoretical knowledge of both human behavior and performance excellence. Acquiring this knowledge can help provide terminology to aspects highlighted within your personal beliefs and values. Importantly, grounding yourself within the SPP literature will provide a strong working knowledge to inform your practice.

Understanding Human Behavior

An important aspect when developing a TOPE is to develop your theoretical orientation to human behavior. As you develop your theoretical orientation, it is important to have a foundation in one (or more) of the major psychological paradigms, as this allows you to describe and to explain human behavior and enables you to predict and control behavior change (Poczwardowski et al., 2004). While SPP has perhaps inappropriately relied on general psychological theories and models to try to understand performance excellence, it is wholly appropriate and necessary to draw from psychology paradigms to understand human behavior. Additionally, it is important to understand your beliefs about how people's problems develop and how change occurs when considering the whole person, which then directs you to the psychology paradigms that fit with your beliefs. In considering this, a critical aspect is how you believe you will facilitate change as a helping professional. For example, you may believe that problems develop because of an irrational thinking pattern and therefore that cognitive-behavioral therapy would be used to accomplish changes in problem behavior and to empower the client to be in control of his or her thought process

(Poczwardowski et al., 2004). Connecting your theoretical orientation to human behavior to your TOPE is imperative, as there must be consistency and congruency between the two.

A discussion involving the development of your theoretical orientation is always an interesting one to have because it is an experience very unique to the individual. However, in talking to my classmates about their writing process, I (EM) found it intriguing to know that most started developing their theoretical orientation by realizing how they viewed human behavior. They found that first developing their theoretical orientation to human behavior greatly informed their TOPE. This connection was made in thinking about how, as consultants, we believe that change is facilitated. This was also found to greatly influence the SPP interventions we would use. As well, developing a consulting style was informed from psychological theories and how one believes people's problems develop. In connecting your theoretical orientation of human behavior to your TOPE, keep in mind that athletes do not perform their sport in isolation from everyday life. It is important to remember the interpersonal relationships, academic life, and other life tasks and challenges acting upon the athlete that can ultimately influence an athlete's ability to perform in competition. In recognizing the athlete as a whole person, we believe that the value of developing a theoretical orientation to human behavior is made clear.

SPP Knowledge

In developing your TOPE, SPP knowledge is an integral part of knowing why you are delivering services to the client and how to go about doing so. A well thought-out theoretical orientation translates into a coherent delivery of sport psychology services (Poczwardowski et al., 2004). Thus, immersing yourself within the current SPP literature is an essential step not only for developing a well-grounded TOPE but also for gaining a broad understanding of the accumulated knowledge within the field thus far. Studying textbooks such as Cox (2011) and Williams and Krane (2014) is a time-consuming process; however, I (JF) found this to be a great step in familiarizing myself with the field as a novice practitioner.

Learning the scientific foundations of SPP in my (EM) first academic term allowed me to understand the history of sport psychology and its significant founders, organizations, and research—all of which were presented as a foundation to build onto my TOPE. I learned that although interventions, techniques, and methods are important, my attention needed to be first turned back to the importance of theoretical paradigms (Poczwardowski et al., 2004) in order to gain a better understanding of the mental and emotional processes necessary to facilitating performance excellence (Aoyagi & Poczwardowski, 2012). Through connecting my theoretical orientation of human behavior to my TOPE, I was able to connect psychological paradigms to SPP knowledge allowing for a consistent flow between the two.

Expert Approaches to Sport Psychology: Applied Theories of Performance Excellence (Aoyagi & Poczwardowski, 2012) greatly informed my writing, as it allowed me to benefit from the accumulated wisdom of great SPP practitioners. Reading this book was inspiring, as each chapter begins with an autobiographical sketch of the author. This allowed me to learn from their life stories and realize that even the greatest SPP practitioners felt confused and afraid at some point in their careers. It led me to remember that although I am a novice consultant with little experience, it was still important to make my TOPE personally relevant and meaningful by connecting it back to my own experiences, values, and beliefs. Through this book, I learned how exciting the exploration of theories of performance excellence can be, as theoretical paradigms can give greater structure and meaning to models, methods, and techniques (Aoyagi & Poczwardowski, 2012). This book allows for an expert display of SPP knowledge integrated into theories of performance excellence and gives the novice consultant the opportunity to enjoy the genius of some of the greatest minds in sport psychology, whether we agree with them or not.

As the large theoretical concepts begin to fall into place in your TOPE, you are then confronted with a plethora of SPP models, techniques, and interventions to choose from. I found creating a glossary of terms (another course assignment) that supported and informed my TOPE to be very helpful in organizing the concepts and selecting those that are most relevant and impactful. This way, although not directly mentioned in your TOPE, you have a way of organizing and better understanding the SPP models, techniques, and interventions that support and enact your TOPE. Connecting learned SPP skills to your theoretical orientation and ultimately to consulting allows for the novice consultant to realize that consulting is much more than just mental skills training (Aoyagi, 2013). Applied sport psychology is interdisciplinary in nature and requires the consultant to have both extensive educational and applied experiences. The ability to translate these complex theories, principles, mechanisms, and concepts into your work and into easily rendered information for the client is essential to delivering sport psychology services effectively (Poczwardowski & Sherman, 2011; see also Chapter 2).

Incorporate Interdisciplinary Knowledge

While one of the focus areas within the field of SPP is mental training, the process of achieving performance excellence requires a multidisciplinary effort. A performer's psychological skills do not exist in a vacuum; they are strongly influenced by biological, neurological, physiological, and environmental factors (Portenga, Aoyagi, Balague, Cohen, & Harmison, 2011). Therefore, it is important for you not only to have a well-developed understanding of the psychological effects of performance but to also see the mental side of performance as just a piece within a plethora of factors that influence performance. In other words, a good practitioner has an immense depth of knowledge within the SPP domain but also has an outstanding breadth of knowledge among other factors that contribute to high achievement (Sheth & Sobel, 2002).

For you to successfully incorporate interdisciplinary knowledge into your TOPE, it is highly recommended to initially develop a strong understanding of Dynamic Systems Theory (DST [Thelen, 2005]). DST posits that all events in an environment (i.e., system) are interrelated, and any actions will not just influence one specific thing but alter the entire environment (Bale, 1995). These systems are not just external events in the environment but also internal operations that impact human functioning (Thelen, 2005). This theoretical model has been used extensively in family therapy to help families understand how specific actions influence an entire family's functioning (Smith-Acuna, 2010), and also in helping athletes acquire strength and physical skills (Davids, Araujo, & Shuttleworth, 2005; Torrents & Balague, 2006). Among a multitude of examples, DST can help us understand how to facilitate team and organizational dynamics, integrate psychological and physical skills training, and understand the role of a consultant within an organization (Poczwardowski et al., 2004).

With DST knowledge, you can effectively integrate new interdisciplinary knowledge by seeing how mental skills fit into the complexities of a performing human and the complicated systemic environment that performance provides. As recurring evidence has indicated strong systemic connections between physical states, mental performance, and skill learning (Ericsson, 2006; Vickers & Williams, 2007; Wilson, Smith, & Holmes, 2007), developing a knowledge of motor learning principles can be highly effective in understanding the mind–body connection and the integration of mental and physical skills as impacted by the dynamic environment (Schmidt & Lee, 2013). With this knowledge, a consultant can understand why specific SPP interventions are useful and how to effectively integrate these interventions into a performer's daily routines.

Accordingly, the process of becoming a skilled SPP practitioner is not just a science but also an art (Poczwardowski et al., 2004). Therefore, incorporating interdisciplinary knowledge that fosters your ability to provide the best services for your clients is essential. Consulting practice knowledge helps to develop an interpersonal style that allows you to effectively communicate and collaborate with clients (Brown, Pryzwansky, & Schulte, 2010; Sheth & Sobel, 2002). Business practice development helps you gain entry with organizations, build clientele, and efficiently communicate what sport psychology services provide (Taylor, 2008). Interprofessional collaboration trains you to work as a team within a system of professionals in other disciplines (Interprofessional Education Collaborative, 2011). Often, you will be a member of a complex support system for performers involving trainers, doctors, academic support, coaches, and other staff. Therefore, knowing how to effectively communicate and work in a collaborative environment is essential for providing the best services to clientele.

Continuing Education and Service Delivery

Theory to Practice

Once you integrate knowledge and personal experience into an organized theoretical orientation, the next step is to practice conceptualizing and delivering interventions through this theoretical lens. Developing a TOPE will do no good if efforts are not made to implement it in practice. Acting from a theoretical orientation may not be the natural inclination for novice practitioners. Students may tend to focus on rigidly implementing specific interventions instead of trying to understand the client as a whole person and then acting (Tod et al., 2009). Thus, it may take a concerted effort on the part of students and supervisors to help develop the skill of conceptualizing from a theoretical lens. However, a well-developed theoretical orientation is one that has been continuously adapted and adjusted through experience. An individual can read a thousand books on how to dribble a basketball, but the person will never develop the skill unless that person actually practices dribbling for long periods of time. Learning service delivery for SPP practitioners is similar, in that you must gain experience delivering SPP services in order to develop into an advanced provider of performance excellence.

As a beginning SPP consultant, I (CD) felt a significant tension between developing a complex and sophisticated understanding of high performance mental behavior and how to present these ideas in a simple and coherent way to clients. As I reflected on the personal times I experienced peak performance, and on relevant literature on the topic, my TOPE became emphasized on the ability to "quiet" the mind and be in the present moment. As Gervais (2015) states, "Stringing together moments of being fully present allow us to touch our potential"—my applied work became focused on training performers to achieve this state. While there are many different empirical frameworks explaining in complexity why the present moment is an adaptive performance state (Hayes, 2004; Jackson & Csikszentmihalyi, 1999), in my work with teams and individuals I did not need to fully explain the theoretical underpinnings of a quiet mind. If I were to teach athletes to be in the moment and quiet their minds, teaching the process in an overly complex way would do the opposite and potentially have a detrimental effect on their performance. However, as I continued to struggle with the tension between deep knowing and providing tangible interventions, I realized that the more I knew, the more effectively I could teach these important concepts in the simplest way.

The train of thoughts described above shows that a well-rounded TOPE serves two purposes. One is to allow the consultant to very effectively observe and understand why an athlete is performing to or below the athlete's potential. Theoretical paradigms aid this process because they allow you to make sense of large amounts of information or to make hypotheses about clients' behavior based on limited information. Second, a TOPE also helps consultants develop a hierarchy of importance to their intervention plans and helps them make decisions about which interventions would be most helpful with a particular client (Aoyagi, 2013). However, you may find that your TOPE does not adequately explain what is occurring within clients or is not helping you make sense of the information that the client is providing. Difficulty in conceptualizing with your theory could be a sign of two different problems: lack of practice in conceptualizing or need for improvement in your TOPE. It may be difficult to discern between the two issues in the beginning because you may have additional areas for growth. However, engaging in self-reflective practice and consulting with your supervisor can help to distinguish between the two possible concerns.

Self-Reflective Practice

During the process of developing your TOPE and initial applied experiences, self-reflection and introspection are critical. Poczwardowski and Sherman's (2011) Revised Sport Psychology Service Delivery heuristic (SPSD-R) indicated that reflection and self-improvement are essential for an expert practitioner. This led the authors to consider education, training, and professional experience as the foundation to the SPSD-R. In the same manner that consultants strive to have their clients constantly seeking improvement, SPP practitioners should exhibit the same characteristics of continual growth and learning. In other words, the process of developing a TOPE may never end and is constantly evolving as a result of growth and adjustments from new empirical knowledge and continued professional experience. It is important to avoid looking at the model of theoretical orientation development as a linear process, but rather as an ongoing loop of continued learning through scholarly knowledge and personal experience.

In order for clients to receive competent, ethical practice, the process of self-reflection for young practitioners should be done with the supervision of a professional SPP consultant. Through supervision, the supervisees can process their experiences with the clients and help form a conceptualization of the clients' needs. Supervision can play a large part in helping you learn how to utilize your TOPE when working with clients (see Chapter 5 for more on supervision). It is a common and easy trap to jump into interventions prior to developing a full understanding of the client and formulating specific reasons guided by your TOPE for selecting interventions. However, your supervisor can help guide the discussion when speaking about clients from intervention to conceptualization. This will aid in developing your skill in practicing from the framework of your TOPE (Aoyagi, 2013). For example, supervisors can help you answer questions like how do you understand the client's behavior? How did the intervention you chose connect to your TOPE? What is the science underlying your belief that this particular course of action will lead to desirable change for the client? Although this may seem challenging or intimidating, growth will occur with a supervisor who appropriately questions and supports your approach and your methods to ensure you do not intervene too early or without a working hypothesis based upon your TOPE (Tudor & Worrall, 2004; Waumsley, Hemmings, & Payne, 2010). As you gain more experience, the process of self-reflection can be more autonomous and should follow a model similar to Holt and Strean's (2001) four-step model of self-reflection for neophyte consultants.

Peer Support

Even with expert supervision, a consultant should always be seeking additional support through peers and mentors. Creating a trusted group of colleagues is immensely beneficial to the development of your TOPE. When we (JF & CD) were initially creating our orientations, meeting with others in our cohort and discussing our ideas, possible interventions, and our beliefs about performance was one of the most helpful methods for learning. These relationships often last a lifetime, as Henschen (2014, October) emphasized the importance of learning from colleagues throughout his outstanding career in SPP. With peers, you may be able to speak more candidly and openly about your ideas in ways you may be unable or uncomfortable to do with a supervisor or mentor (for a more complete discussion, see Chapter 6, "Layers of Oversight"). This may help foster authentic ideas and beliefs about your orientation through critical reflection and open feedback with peers. Oftentimes, you may be able to learn more from dialoguing with close, trusted peers that share a similar excitement for knowledge as you do. Not only have we tried to maintain contact and support with fellow classmates throughout the years, but also we have learned from peers at other schools and specialties at conferences and workshops. These relationships provide you with an outside lens on SPP and help you think in ways that you have not considered before from close peers and professors.

Mentor Guidance

On the other hand, social comparison (as opposed to support) may impair individual TOPE development. A message that was reiterated throughout our course of study is that we are not our mentors. Mentors have a wealth of knowledge and experience from which students can learn. However, this does not mean that students should adopt their mentors' beliefs and orientations without first critically evaluating how the mentors' beliefs fit with the student's theoretical framework and individual style. As discussed in the model above, personal experiences and beliefs form the foundation of a TOPE. If these foundational beliefs differ from those around you, it would not make sense to try to adopt the same approach. Every consultant is unique; therefore, the blend of personal philosophy, theoretical paradigm(s), models, methods, and interventions that form your TOPE will become your professional fingerprint.

That being said, speaking with mentors can be very beneficial for providing guidance, perspective, and emotional support. From a perspective standpoint, it can be tempting to view our mentors as an unlimited fount of knowledge; however, they were once in exactly the same position as us. Additionally, having a trusting relationship with mentors who can provide constructive feedback can help you fine-tune your thought process and your practice. Receiving honest feedback about your TOPE can provide a better platform for improving it than if a mentor did not provide any constructive feedback. Novice students should be mindful that mentors do not expect students to have the "perfect TOPE." Indeed, mentors will understand better than students that there is no perfect TOPE. Rather than perfection, mentors expect students to give their TOPE the time, thought, and energy to develop it deserves based on experiences and on training.

Growth Mindset

Developing a TOPE is not an easy undertaking, particularly when done early in training. Feelings of discouragement, being unprepared, being overwhelmed, or vulnerability can be common. Thus, one of the first characteristics that we would encourage you to cultivate (if not already present) is a growth mindset (see Dweck, 2007). Inherent in the growth mindset is the belief that, while people differ in natural aptitudes or talents, everyone can change and grow through learning and experiences. Dweck's research on mindsets is applicable to the TOPE development process. Some students may feel that their TOPE is a direct reflection of their intelligence or of their ability to succeed in the field of SPP (i.e., fixed mindset). This feeling may be heightened if the TOPE is completed for a course project or is otherwise being evaluated in some capacity. I (JF) certainly caught myself comparing my own theory with others' theories in my cohort or worrying about what professors might think about my ideas when initially undergoing the theory development process. However, I felt freer and more comfortable within the process when I came to the realization that comparing myself or focusing on what others were doing was missing the point of the exercise. Developing a TOPE from a fixed mindset makes the true intention of undertaking this exercise a challenge because your TOPE is ultimately more about your clients than yourself. It is a tool for guiding clients to their best possible performance and their best possible selves, not an extension of the creator's intellectual capabilities.

A second application of growth mindset to the theory development process is openness to change within your theory. As a beginning consultant, I (JF) found myself leaning toward specific ideas that, theoretically, seemed very meaningful to me. However, I found that these ideas did not fit with my style of consulting or with my personal strengths when I actually attempted to integrate them into my practice. My (JF) TOPE has evolved and changed significantly since its initial draft. Thus, our biggest piece of advice regarding developing your TOPE is remaining open to changing views. It is important to "practice what we preach" as SPP practitioners in the TOPE development process and focus on the consistent pursuit of excellence. This ensures that your TOPE will grow and develop with you instead of becoming stagnant or ineffectual. We also believe that this will help maintain your self-compassion throughout the process. It is easy to become frustrated with your current stage of development or with not feeling like you have the "right" answer. Approaching from a growth mindset allows you to continuously push yourself and your capabilities while maintaining a healthy perspective.

Overall, expecting to have the perfect, or even a very effective, TOPE as a novice SPP practitioner is unrealistic. Practitioners may find that they still need to edit their TOPE even after years of work. Dr. Ken Ravizza is a perfect example of lifetime professional development. He focused on achieving flow in his consulting for more than 25 years before deciding it was overrated. Instead, he chose to shift focus to teaching athletes how to compensate and adjust, to be comfortable being uncomfortable, and to make the best of bad situations (Ravizza, 2012). Thus, it may be idealistic to believe that you will ever have certainty in the answers you seek. Keeping in mind your stage of training in addition to the wealth of knowledge that you have accumulated up until this point is important in maintaining your self-compassion.

Pragmatic Advice From a Professional Perspective

In addition to the wonderful and personal experiences, support, and advice shared thus far in the chapter from fellow students, here are a few brief observations from my (MA) experience supervising and mentoring students through the development of their TOPEs. In what a supervisor might identify as a parallel process, just as I advise students to be open to the ever-evolving nature of a TOPE, I have evolved my approach to teaching and supporting students in developing their TOPEs. As a result, while the essence of what I described in an earlier publication (Aoyagi, 2013) remains intact, there have been some meaningful changes.

The biggest shifts have been requiring students to incorporate a theoretical orientation to human behavior into their TOPE, and changing the nomenclature from "theory of performance excellence" to TOPE (theoretical orientation to performance excellence). The first shift was to address the paramount understanding that athletes (and performers in general) are people first, and therefore in order to understand the person and influence performance excellence one must have a theoretical understanding for human behavior. This is where the theoretical paradigms from general psychology that I have previously critiqued as being inappropriate for understanding performance excellence (Aoyagi, 2013; Aoyagi et al., 2012) are wholly appropriate. The shift in nomenclature was to more appropriately recognize that students are drawing upon the existing knowledgebase to formulate their TOPE, as opposed to generating new theory as the term "[my] theory of performance excellence" implied.

One of the most common questions from students is how elaborate and inclusive their TOPE should be. I address this as a balance between internal validity (i.e., trying to have the best, most complete explanation of performance excellence) and external validity (i.e., utility of the TOPE with clients in the real world). Given the multidimensional and individualistic nature of performance excellence, it is impossible that there will ever be a complete explanation, yet it is tempting to include many or all of the variables you have learned are related to performance excellence. This would result in a more predictive theoretical orientation that would have essentially no value in the real world because it would be too convoluted and complex to provide guidance on what is most important and where to start. The analogy here is a coach who tries to correct multiple technique problems at once, which results in no learning (or even regression) for the athlete being coached. Therefore, I recommend students include a maximum of five core components in their TOPE. Less is probably better, but in the beginning it may be challenging for students to reduce it further as they do not yet have the experience to know what components will end up being preeminent for them. Clearly, five (or fewer) components are not going to explain all dimensions of performance excellence, but they will allow for students to begin to filter the information they learn from clients through these core components to better understand the client and plan interventions.

Implicit within this pragmatic approach to TOPE development are two concepts worth making explicit. The first is that developing a TOPE is an iterative process wherein you will be regularly and consistently revisiting your TOPE and revising it based upon new understandings facilitated by professors in the classroom, supervisors and peers from your applied experiences, and most importantly your experiences implementing the TOPE with clients and the feedback you gain (from clients, supervisors, and self-reflection). Second, although your TOPE is meant to help you hypothesize and conceptualize clients (i.e., to predict what might be going on with the client and what might be helpful), it is also fine and effective to reverse-engineer your TOPE. In other words, rather than learning theory and then trying to apply it to clients, you can (and should) review recordings (audio, video) of your work and look for patterns and themes that typify your work with clients. Then, you can contextualize the work you have been doing within the scientific literature. For example, you may have been drawn to a cognitive-behavioral understanding of human behavior in the classroom, but in practice you notice you are more comfortable taking a Humanistic approach.

Finally, the most common characteristic I have identified among students who successfully navigate the process of developing a TOPE is a willingness to be vulnerable. An effective TOPE requires the courage to self-reflect and (re)examine one's core values and beliefs, often in the presence of peers and professors in an evaluatory position. It benefits from taking calculated (in collaboration with your supervisor) risks with clients and the openness to honestly self-evaluate and be evaluated by your supervisor and others. Refining your TOPE means talking about the good, the bad, and the ugly with your supervisor and compassionately accepting that you will not be able to be effective with all clients. The students that embrace this sort of vulnerability inevitably end up with stronger, more effective TOPEs and greater confidence and comfort with clients.

Conclusion

As highlighted in the model, we consider the process of developing a TOPE to be cyclical in nature in the sense that there may never be a true end point where you can consider your TOPE finished. This is because the field of sport and performance psychology and other fields are constantly changing. Thus, continued evaluation of and familiarity with the literature is imperative in ensuring you are up to date with the latest developments in the field. You may never be truly done acquiring theoretical SPP or interdisciplinary knowledge. Furthermore, continued education and service delivery will undoubtedly affect your own personal experiences and beliefs about human performance. Experience in working with performers and seeing what truly works with clients could either strengthen or significantly change your own thoughts and knowledge.

Limitations and Future Directions

One of the most significant limitations regarding the development and utilization of your TOPE is a lack of empirical validation. As discussed in the beginning of the chapter, there has been minimal focus on theoretical paradigms specific to the performance context (Aoyagi, 2013). This is not to say that professionals are not utilizing frameworks or philosophies when intervening with clients; however, many of these TOPEs are not found within the literature. Therefore, researchers have been unable to empirically assess the validity of various practitioners' theoretical paradigms. The first step in advancing, then, is by producing theories of performance excellence and articulating them within the SPP literature. This process of introducing implicit theoretical paradigms into the literature has already begun (see Aoyagi, 2013; Aoyagi & Poczwardowski, 2012), and the field can only benefit with the inclusion of other perspectives and other voices. Inclusion of these paradigms in the literature would also provide guidance for SPP students seeking to develop their own orientations.

Once theoretical paradigms are available for scientific scrutiny, the next step is for research professionals in the field to empirically test SPP theoretical paradigms. The use of unsubstantiated or pseudoscientific techniques can negatively impact clients either directly or indirectly (e.g., monetary cost, time). Additionally, the use of unsubstantiated techniques can decrease the credibility or influence of the field (Lilienfeld, Lynn, & Lohr, 2015). Thus, this testing would serve two purposes: to validate the field of SPP and to ensure that clients are given the best possible care. Much research has been conducted in SPP at the intervention level; however, little has been conducted for concepts at higher levels of abstraction. Researching and validating theories of performance excellence would provide empirical support for the field to other professions and to the public. The second, and perhaps most important, reason for empirically validating theories of performance excellence is to ensure that clients receive the most ethical and quality care possible.

Another significant limitation surrounding the development of one's personal theoretical orientation is the importance of quality education and access to competent supervision. Aoyagi et al. (2012) highlight the importance of obtaining competent supervision and the desire for more opportunities for students to be supervised by individuals with CC-AASP credentials (Certified Consultant, Association for Applied Sport Psychology). As this chapter has emphasized self-reflective practice with the help of a supervisor, we understand that finding opportunities to deeply engage in this practice may be limited by the ability to obtain a supervisor. As students, we were very lucky to have the ability not only to have competent supervisors during our master's program but to develop mentorship relationships with other CC-AASP professionals outside of our educational program. This involved working in counseling and eating disorder centers that specialized in sport psychology, and spending countless hours in conversations with professionals. The topics focused on not just sport psychology interventions but professional development topics including self-care and career planning. It has been shown that the student–supervisor relationship has been considered the single most important factor for the effectiveness of supervision (Kilminster & Jolly, 2000), and these types of individual relationships with mentors have stretched far beyond the academic realm and significantly contributed to early successes in consulting.

In conclusion, we want to emphasize that the process of developing a TOPE is not an easy and straightforward task. The initial excitement of consolidating knowledge can easily be derailed by difficult consulting sessions and early opportunities that may be perceived as failures by beginning consultants. However, the process of developing an orientation is very similar to the developmental trajectory of an athlete; there are times when it feels easy and understandable, but you will have frustrating setbacks and plateaus. Practice what we preach: in the same way that we strive to provide a safe and mastery-oriented climate for athletes, do the same thing for yourself. This happens by continuing to enjoy the process of learning and realizing that mastery is a journey, not a destination. Throughout your educational and professional journey, create support from professors and peers, seek outside sources of support, and try to learn from as many unique areas of knowledge as possible. If you are able to follow these guidelines, you may find that creating a TOPE is as satisfying as helping our clients reach their highest potential.

References

Aoyagi, M. W. (2013). Teaching theories of performance excellence to sport & performance psychology consultants-in-training. *Journal of Sport Psychology in Action, 4*, 139–151.

Aoyagi, M. W., & Poczwardowski, A. (Eds.). (2012). *Expert approaches to sport psychology: Applied theories of performance excellence*. Morgantown, WV: Fitness Information Technology.

Aoyagi, M. W., Portenga, S. T., Poczwardowski, A., Cohen, A. B., & Statler, T. (2012). Reflections and directions: The profession of sport psychology past, present, and future. *Professional Psychology: Research and Practice, 43*(1), 23–28.

Bale, L. S. (1995). Gregory Bateson, cybernetics, and the social/behavioral sciences. *Cybernetics & Human Knowing, 3*, 27–45.

Brown, D., Pryzwansky, W. B., & Schulte, A. C. (2010). *Psychological consultation and collaboration: Introduction to theory and practice*. London: Pearson.

Christensen, D. A., & Aoyagi, M. W. (2014). Lessons learned consulting at Olympic Trials: Swimming through pains. *Sport Psychologist, 28*(3), 281–289.

Covey, S. (1989). *The 7 habits of highly effective people*. New York, NY: Simon & Schuster.

Cox, R. H. (2011). *Sport psychology: Concepts and applications* (7th ed.). New York, NY: McGraw-Hill.

Davids, K., Araujo, D., & Shuttleworth, R. (2005). Applications of dynamical systems theory to football. *Science and Football, 5*, 537–550.

Dweck, C. S. (2007). *Mindset: The new psychology of success*. New York: Ballantine Books.

Ericsson, K. A. (2006). *The Cambridge handbook of expertise and expert performance*. Cambridge: Cambridge University Press.

Gervais, M. (2015, August 1). *Finding mastery intro* [Finding Mastery]. Retrieved from http://findingmastery.net/welcome-to-finding-mastery/

Hayes, S. C. (2004). Acceptance and commit therapy, relational frame theory, and the third wave of behavioral and cognitive therapies. *Behavior Therapy, 35,* 639–665.

Henriksen, K., & Diment, G. (2011). Professional philosophy: Inside the delivery of sport psychology service at Team Denmark. *Sport Science Review, 20*(1–2), 5–21.

Henschen, K. (2014, October). Lessons learned from a career in sport psychology. Lecture presented at the annual conference of the Association for Applied Sport Psychology, Las Vegas, NV.

Holt, N. L., & Strean, W. B. (2001). Reflecting on initiating sport psychology consulting: A self-narrative of neophyte practice. *The Sport Psychologist, 15,* 188–204.

Interprofessional Education Collaborative. (2011). *Core competencies for interprofessional collaborative practice.* Washington, DC: Interprofessional Education Collaborative.

Jackson, S. A., & Csikszentmihalyi, M. (1999). *Flow in sports: The keys to optimal experiences and performances.* Champaign, IL: Human Kinetics.

Lilienfeld, S. O., Lynn, S. J., & Lohr, J. M. (2015). *Science and pseudoscience in clinical psychology* (2nd ed.). New York, NY: The Guilford Press.

Kilminster, S. M., & Jolly, B. C. (2000). Effective supervision in clinical practice settings: A literature review. *Medical Education, 34,* 827–840. doi: 10.1046/j.1365-2923.2000.00758.x.

Newburg, D., Kimiecik, J., Durand-Bush, N., & Doell, K. (2002). The role of resonance in performance excellence and life engagement. *Journal of Applied Sport Psychology, 14*(4), 249–267.

Poczwardowski, A., & Sherman, C. P. (2011). Revisions to the sport psychology service delivery (SPSD) heuristic: Explorations with experienced consultants. *The Sport Psychologist, 25,* 511–531.

Poczwardowski, A., Sherman, C. P., & Ravizza, K. (2004). Professional philosophy in the sport psychology service delivery: Building on theory and practice. *The Sport Psychologist, 18,* 445–463.

Portenga, S. T., Aoyagi, M. W., Balague, G., Cohen, A., & Harmison, B. (2011). *Defining the practice of sport and performance psychology.* Retrieved from http://www.apa47.org/pdfs/Defining%20the%20practice%20of%20sport%20and%20performance%20psychology-Final.pdf

Practice Committee, Division 47, Exercise and Sport Psychology, American Psychological Association. (2011). *Defining the practice of SPP.* Retrieved from http://www.apa47.org/pdfs/Defining%20the%20practice%20of%20sport%20and%20performance%20psychology-Final.pdf

Prochaska, J. O., & Norcross, J. C. (2010). *Systems of psychotherapy: A transtheoretical analysis* (7th ed.). Belmont, CA: Brooks/Cole.

Ravizza, K. (2012). Dr. Ken Ravizza. In M. W. Aoyagi & A. Poczwardowski (Eds.), *Expert approaches to sport psychology* (pp. 201–215). Morgantown, WV: Fitness Information Technology.

Ryan, R. M., & Deci, E. L. (2000). Self-determination theory and the facilitation of intrinsic motivation, social development, and well-being. *American Psychologist, 55*(1), 68–78.

Schmidt, R., & Lee, T. (2013). *Motor learning and performance: From principles to application.* Champaign, IL: Human Kinetics.

Sheth, J. N., & Sobel, A. (2002). *Clients for life: Evolving from an expert-for-hire to an extraordinary advisor.* Detroit: Free Press.

Smith-Acuna, S. (2010). *Systems theory in action: Applications to individual, couple, and family therapy.* Hoboken, NJ: Wiley.

Stambulova, N., & Johnson, U. (2010). Novice consultants' experiences: Lessons learned by applied sport psychology students. *Psychology of Sport and Exercise, 11*(4), 295–303.

Taylor, J. (2008). Prepare to succeed: Private consulting in applied sport psychology. *Journal of Clinical Sport Psychology, 2,* 160–177.

Thelen, E. (2005). Dynamic systems theory and the complexity of change. *Psychoanalytic Dialogues, 15*(2), 255–283.

Tod, D., Andersen, M. B., & Marchant, D. B. (2009). A longitudinal examination of neophyte applied sport psychologists' professional development. *Journal of Applied Sport Psychology, 21*(Supp. 1), 1–16.

Torrents, C., & Balague, N. (2006). Dynamic systems theory and sports training. *Education, Physical Training, Sport, 1*(60), 72–83.

Tudor, K., & Worrall, M. (2004). Issues, questions, dilemmas and domains in supervision. In K. Tudor & M. Worral (Eds.), *Freedom to practise: Person-centred approaches to supervision* (pp. 79–96). Llangarron: PCCS Books.

Vickers, J. N., & Williams, A. M. (2007). Performing under pressure: The effects of physiological arousal, cognitive anxiety, and gaze control in biathalon. *Journal of Motor Behavior, 39*(5), 381–394.

Waumsley, J. A., Hemmings, B., & Payne, S. M. (2010). Work-life balance, role conflict and the UK sport psychology consultant. *Sport Psychologist, 24*(2), 245–262.

Williams, J. W., & Krane, V. (2014). *Applied sport psychology: Personal growth to peak performance* (7th ed.). New York, NY: McGraw-Hill.

Wilson, M., Smith, N. C., & Holmes, P. S. (2007). The role of effort in influencing the effect of anxiety on performance: Testing the conflicting predictions of processing efficiency theory and the conscious processing hypothesis. *British Journal of Psychology, 98*, 411–428.

2 From Science to Practice

The Hows of Translating Classroom Lessons to Field Experiences and Applications

Trevor A. Cote, Julie Vieselmeyer, and Artur Poczwardowski

During applied sport psychology training, student-consultants become immersed in a multidisciplinary field concerned with how clients' perspectives regarding their sport influence the pursuit for achieving athletic potential. Student-consultants then guide clients to acquire and apply mental skills essential for successful performance. The purpose of training for the practice of sport psychology becomes twofold: (a) to gain expertise in the theoretical underpinnings of sport psychology and, (b) while abiding by professional and ethical standards, to translate scientific knowledge into practical application to effectively implement interventions. The student-consultant's ability to translate theoretical concepts into a relevant and tailored approach will have a direct impact on the client's commitment to using mental skills and, consequently, will determine positive outcomes. During graduate training, there can be heavy emphasis (rightfully so) on learning a myriad of theoretical concepts. Additionally, knowing how to execute that knowledge by using language and illustrations that an athlete-client will understand is just as important. This chapter offers guidance and insight for student-consultants on how to take the science and theoretical knowledge from the classroom setting and translate this information into accessible and context-relevant consulting practices and mental skills that the athlete can successfully utilize for performance enhancement. For example, the student-consultant's own use of experience and transformative language is a key element of the intervention that propels the athlete's mental skill acquisition, practice, application, and refinement.

Student-consultants often have a wealth of information from their own sport or coaching experiences, yet their personality and athletic background would not be adequate to successfully engage with a client; thus, science and theory are a necessary foundation for optimal client work (e.g., Tammen, 2000; Tod, 2007). The student-consultant may draw from literature in psychotherapy, counseling, sport science, and sport psychology or choose an integrative approach by forming their own theory of optimal performance that then guides case conceptualization, goals, and methods of intervention (Aoyagi & Poczwardowski, 2011; see also Chapter 1). For example, a client may present with catastrophizing thoughts (e.g., "I'm never going to play again or be as good as I was!") regarding their return to sport from a season-ending injury. The student-consultant would be able to conceptualize the client's concerns through a cognitive-behavioral (CBT) lens because there is clear evidence of the client engaging in a common thinking trap or irrational belief (i.e., catastrophizing thoughts). Then work with the client could implement CBT-specific skills such as self-monitoring of automatic thoughts and cognitive restructuring to challenge the thinking trap and develop a rational and healthy response to the thoughts. As illustrated, the theoretical orientation drives the type and scope of interventions with the client, in which the student-consultant will aim to work in a collaborative manner to help clients develop a mental toolbox of skills (e.g., relaxation, self-talk, imagery, mental routines, etc.) that match the client's ability (i.e., physical and psychological). For clarity of our presentation, the fundamental skills of interest in this chapter will center on concentration, attention, and focus. Additionally, developmentally appropriate self-doubts and anxieties are part of the growing and learning curve for student-consultants and need to be factored into one's individual style of service delivery, addressed in supervision, and resolved, also using the tools of our own trade (Christensen & Aoyagi, 2014). (Please see other chapters for a discussion of these relevant issues.)

One of the pragmatic aspects of sport psychology is that clients will recognize the mental component to performance and most will have an intuitive sense of the skills and mental climate that help them perform their best. In contrast, this can present some challenges when the process of how to cultivate these skills and mindset may be less transparent, especially when the athletes' sport skills are seemingly much more proficient relative to mental components. Selecting language and illustrations that are familiar to the athlete-clients (e.g., words such as *dedication, effort, commitment,* and *determination*—simple demonstrations of mind–body connections) will increase their motivation to practice mental skills in a similar manner to rehearsing physical skills. Beyond the initial "elevator pitch" regarding what mental skills are and why they are important, student-consultants must use developmentally appropriate language and demonstrations that have the potential to resonate with the client and, furthermore, provide sport-specific examples to engage the client in the joint process of working together.

The consultative model as a collaborative process begins by discussing the athlete-client's strengths and weaknesses or perhaps completing a performance profile (i.e., an assessment in which athletes identify characteristics and psychological skills essential to a successful performance and then rate themselves on these characteristics; the profile serves as means of measurement, communication between the athlete and support staff, a roadmap for interventions, and monitoring progress [Weinberg & Williams, 2010]). Psychometric tests can also be used if students are trained to administer these tests. When (ideally) deepened and corroborated by observations (in practice and competition), the athlete-client and student-consultant should agree on goals that are clearly rooted in the definition of the problem (or case formulation), from which the student-consultant can propose a mental skills training program. During the initial stages of case formulation, establishing a positive working alliance and rapport with the client is key to a strong foundation for effective interventions (Silva, Metzler, & Lerner, 2011).

As student-consultants may rely on certain mental skills for a particular performance profile and facilitate a rigid approach to the agreed-upon intervention, a fundamental lesson is that the selection and the use of a mental skill is more successful with a client-centered approach and with flexibility. For example, Tod, Andersen, and Marchant (2009) found that student sport psychology consultants in training adopted a more flexible delivery with their clients over the course of the two-year training experience. In the qualitative study, the student-consultants reported putting more emphasis on listening to the client's needs rather than precisely following a protocol for a mental skill. Therefore, the consultant should fit the theory to the client and not the client to the theory. There is certainly more than one approach to accomplish the same outcome when working with a client, which is most often the approach and skills that best fit with the athlete-client's values, goals, characteristics, and environment (Brown, Pryzwansky, & Schulte, 2006). For the purposes of this chapter, the theory-to-practice examples that follow will center on the use of several mental skills to achieve *concentration* as an essential component of optimal performance. To set the foundation, various theories of concentration will briefly be defined and described as presented in a classroom context, and we will correspondingly show how such concepts informed the student-consultant's interventions.

Theory to Practice Example: Concentration

Concentration (or focus or attention [terms that are used interchangeably in this chapter]) is a common trait (ability, skill) desired by athletes, coaches, and sport psychology consultants seeking focus and exceptional performance (e.g., Jackson & Csikszentmihalyi, 1999; Orlick & Partington, 1988; Ravizza, 2012). If a client identifies concentration as an area for improvement or recalls struggles with focus, then working to reframe catastrophic thoughts, developing the ability to mentally let go of mistakes, identifying predominant attentional style and how to shift attention to fit the situation (Nideffer, 1976), or learning to concentrate on the task relevant cues could all potentially be the content of the intervention (Orlick & Partington, 1988; Weinberg & Gould, 2011). Because the purpose of the chapter is not conceptualization of the client's issues and concerns (a critical step in planning and designing sound interventions [Poczwardowski, Sherman, & Henschen, 1998]), we assume that the roots of concentration problems, their correlates, or both are addressed in a parallel and iterative (revisited) fashion. Further, a number of theories consider using a range of mental skills in isolation or in tandem to achieve desired focus for the athlete's competitive demands (see Aoyagi & Poczwardowski, 2012). Thus, while understanding these complexities, for the clarity of our narration, we will focus predominantly on self-talk as a skill that can be utilized with athlete-clients to assist them in attention management. First, we review theoretical constructs that link self-talk with attention. Second, we will describe in detail the process of translation of the theoretical content into language and experiences that are accessible to the client as follows: (a) student-consultant in the classroom, (b) personalizing the mental skill, (c) from self-knowledge to mental skill interventions, (d) from a dry (office) session to athlete practice and competition, (e) client's evaluation of the skill, and (f) reflection.

Theory and Supporting Theoretical Constructs

Self-talk may be one skill used to cultivate the client's desired type of focus. When inner dialogue (self-talk) becomes highly negative and the client is stuck in that deleterious perspective, optimal level of performance focus is affected. Therefore, the student-consultant may conceptualize the athlete's performance from a cognitive-behavioral approach, which suggests that understanding the relationship between thoughts, emotions, and behavior is key to selecting strategies and solving current challenges. Within the cognitive-behavioral tradition, Rational Emotive Behavior Therapy (REBT [Ellis, 1973}) indicates that core beliefs are the cause of maladaptive patterns of thinking, feeling, and behaving, and thus challenging these beliefs and adopting a more flexible approach is essential for achieving desired outcomes. Furthermore, REBT suggests that self-talk represents core beliefs, which is a worthy topic for client development. Applied to sport psychology, the A-B-C Model of Self-Talk (Ellis, 1973) posits that self-talk affects performance in the following way: (A) an activating event (e.g., missing an important shot in a basketball game) (B) leads to beliefs as evidenced by self-talk (e.g., "I'm so stupid—we'll never win" versus "The game isn't over yet—do your best") and (C) culminates in a consequence (e.g., hopelessness, anger, muscle tension versus optimism, motivated, relaxed [Perry & Marsh, 2000]). In other words, as Vygotsky's (1986) verbal self-regulation theory indicates, using self-talk can shift the object of attention, thus altering concentration. By changing thoughts that we give attention to, feelings are modified, which resultantly affects behavior (Hardy, Hall, & Hardy, 2005). Self-talk can be used in this manner to create an optimal mindset and regulate emotion and intensity/arousal (Johnson, Hrycaiko, Johnson, & Halas, 2004). For example, Ravizza's Rs of emotion management (i.e., recognize, release, regroup, refocus, ready, respond [Ravizza,

2012; Vernacchia, 2003]) utilize the skill of centering and self-talk (including cues words) to move beyond the mistake, attend to the present moment, and respond to the next play with trust and confidence.

Conroy and Metzler (2004) identified the following three types of self-talk that can be used in sport: positive, negative, and instructional. The goal in using self-talk is to help clients develop a method for focusing on task-relevant cues. Accordingly, self-talk content may vary by situational requirements and cultural differences but above all must be realistic and relevant. Emphasizing that self-talk is a skill and that strategic use of cue words or affirmations can be a great tool for concentrating on the task-relevant cues, rather than allowing self-talk to become a distractor, will serve to motivate and build confidence as the athlete-client practices and masters this skill (Miller & Donohue, 2003).

Translation

Prior to implementing the specific mental skill with the athlete, the student-consultant needs to have sound knowledge of the theoretical framework (i.e., specific theory/theories and additional theoretical constructs [if applicable]) and to think through the ways of translating this knowledge to practice. With seemingly unlimited access and resources to sport psychology literature and research, how can one learn to translate the knowledge into applicable conversations, illustrations, and practices with the client? Role-playing activities provide an invaluable practice for student-consultants to develop, evolve, and gain confidence in their ability to implement a mental skill (Aoyagi, 2013; McEwan & Tod, 2015; Silva et al., 2011). Not only does role-playing present another opportunity for feedback from a professor or peer, but it also strengthens the understanding of the skill (Aoyagi, 2013). While student-consultants will acquire the knowledge and theoretical understanding of their field of study, one of the true measures of "doing sport psychology" can be found in the *stickiness* of interventions. The evidence of successful interventions transpires when clients are able to deliberately and consistently utilize mental skills in practice and competition, regardless of setting and conditions, and, further, demonstrate an internalization of skills. As previewed earlier, this chapter will discuss six distinct stages that students-in-training can anticipate as they learn to translate classroom knowledge to field experiences and applications in the process of becoming a sport psychology professional. Anecdotes from a variety of individual athletes using self-talk to develop the skill of concentration will illustrate both effective and ineffective attempts to translate science to practice.

Delivery to Practice: Theories of Concentration

The first two authors will share their experiences in learning how to translate theories of concentration to practice as student-consultants with the third author having served as one of their supervisors in a three-quarter practicum sequence. As you follow the six stages in which language and illustrations develop from origination (in the classroom) to application (utilized by the athlete-client in competition), the examples must be read in context. Each stage provides a clear objective, and the examples provided by the first two authors can be used as a resource guide for how to make theoretical components of sport and performance psychology germane to our athlete-clients.

Student-Consultant in the Classroom

New sport psychology students are filled with enthusiasm and are eager to consume course material and scientific literature. Because motivation is high, timing is ideal for consultants in training to move from the role of observer to a role of a practitioner that seeks to apply theoretical concepts with clients. Student-consultants should begin by attempting to explain theory and related constructs in their own words. This suggests that the student-consultant create time to practice explaining out loud the theoretical concepts of sport and performance psychology learned in class. Absorbing the information is one task, but translating the knowledge into your own words is another. Next, the students will want to apply these principles to themselves and, subsequently, use concepts to explain and predict their own future behavior or performance. By conceptualizing their own performance in terms of scientific principles, theories will become more relevant, personalized, and more authentically articulated. Similarly, student-consultants may then seek to apply theory to other athletes they know or those in the media in a variety of sports to further understand the reach and extent to which theoretical concepts may fit a person, group, or situation. As the student-consultant applies theory frequently, the utility and practicality of a particular theory to conceptualize client behaviors and inform interventions in practice and competition settings will become exceedingly clearer. Concluding this stage of development, student-consultants should begin to build a working theory of performance excellence (see Chapter 1) that will provide additional guidance (to complement the formal sport psychology theories) for conceptualizing performance principles as applied to individual, team, and organizational behavior.

Personalizing the Mental Skill

At this stage of development, the student-consultants will want to embark on a journey to develop consulting skills and to master mental skills in their own area of sport performance. Becoming an effective sport psychology consultant is a twofold process that involves multiple approaches to developing the requisite skills. First off, consultants may consider role-playing with other developing student-consultants to gain useful feedback regarding their delivery style and the efficacy of their teaching of mental skills. Second, consultants who invest in knowing more about themselves by applying mental skills to their own performance endeavors and developing reflective practice will have greater psychological awareness, firsthand experience, increased credibility with clients, as well as enhanced self-efficacy in facilitating the athlete-client's skill development. Student-consultants will, moreover, be able to comprehend the practical challenges of implementing mental skills, which is critical in assuming a nonjudgmental and empathic mindset while assisting their athlete-clients. Subsequently, consultants will learn how to flexibly apply sport psychology principles and the importance of tailoring interventions to individual needs and learning styles. Student-consultants may imagine themselves in the role of client and consider designing their own mental skills training plan to better understand obstacles regarding adherence to such a training plan, the interplay between practicing physical and mental skills, and the progress curve associated with mental skills training. Likewise, in the same manner that a consultant may suggest a homework assignment or promote reflection to a client, the student-consultants may choose to use a training journal or self-talk log to develop their own reflective practice of both the development of consulting skills and the use of mental skills in their own sport performance.

Here is a brief illustration of how I (JV) was able to translate theories of concentration and self-talk strategies into tools for performing my best. An experienced marathoner, I was training to set a new personal record. In an endurance sport like distance running, physical and mental fatigue always becomes a factor that affects concentration. I knew that along with my physical training, utilizing mental skills consistently would increase my chance of success. First of all, I began with a self-talk log to bring greater awareness to my thoughts and internal dialogue (Burton & Raedeke, 2008). When fatigue and pain set in, my self-talk quickly became negative and filled with doubt, and, consequently, my motivation and effort diminished; when I felt good, self-talk was very positive. Second, I began to note the words and phrases I used when I ran well in hard practices and shorter races, and then began to decisively use the same self-talk when running became challenging.

While in some sports, positive self-talk may be the most useful, in a sport like running, it is inevitable that, at some point, the runner will not feel good and using positive self-talk may be unrealistic. Therefore, I focused on instructional self-talk (Conroy & Metzler, 2004). Finally, after "trying on" several phrases and words, I selected the word "commit," as it held deep meaning for me. Conceptualizing my performance using cognitive-behavioral theories, I selected the self-intervention A-B-C Model of Self-Talk (Ellis, 1973), and, in running, it functioned in such a way: (A) an activating event (e.g., pacing is off, fatigue, stomach cramps) (B) lead to beliefs as evidenced by self-talk (e.g., "I'm not going to achieve my goals—I might as well quit now" versus "Commit!! You've worked so hard for this, you are prepared, and you want to give your best today") and (C) resulted in a consequence (e.g., eyes focused, running tall and focused on form, increased determination and purpose). Over time, the simple cue word "commit" became tied to other mental skills in a more comprehensive mental routine. For example, this word was used along with imagery practice and in competition simulations, and over time the physical and mental response to hearing and saying "commit" automatically triggered an ideal race mindset associated with concentration. Furthermore, this word has become so meaningful to me that it transferred to other situations—for instance, to my coaching and consulting with athlete-clients, when fatigue or distractions can interfere with achieving objectives (Thelwell, Weston, Greenlees, & Hutchings, 2008).

At the conclusion of this stage of service delivery training, student-consultants' internalization of mental skills will be equivalent to automaticity of physical skills, where execution requires little cognitive effort or attention and skills have become part of the student-consultant's attributes. At this time, the student-consultant can easily converse about mental skills in a self-referenced manner. The student-consultant also comprehends the foundational concepts such that the skills can be applied to numerous situations, and the transfer of skills to new situations occurs efficiently. Intimate knowledge and proficiency in using mental skills leads to a further increase in the student-consultants' competence for their work with athlete-clients and boosts confidence surrounding effective service delivery.

From Self-Knowledge to Mental Skill Interventions

At this stage of development, student-consultants will want to have a refined, concise elevator pitch for how they conceptualize sport psychology, to understand the process of change, and to have a theory of performance excellence that will guide case conceptualization and intervention planning for individual athletes and teams. The first step to doing applied work is to immerse one's self in the team culture or world of the individual athlete. By taking time for observation, in the problem definition phase, a focus on learning and understanding the athlete-clients in their context will relieve pressure and the need to offer a "quick fix." There is a need and a value to being an active listener, before providing advice and mental skills; the student-consultant must begin to understand performance through the eyes of the athlete-client. As the student-consultant's language in the athlete-client's area of performance develops, so too does rapport. Highly effective consultants provide concrete and client-specific examples when executing an intervention (Hardy, Jones, & Gould, 1996). A sport psychology student may benefit from viewing developing consulting skills as a parallel process to athletes' developing mental skills. In essence, the student-consultant is seeking to become an expert on the client and the client's sport, whereas the client is seeking to become an expert in mental skills. Such an approach will go a long way in creating a collaborative relationship. Furthermore, the ability to understand the performance demands of the clients' sports and to interpret their experience using sport-specific language, illustrations, and metaphors will establish a common ground for work together and augment the working alliance.

The following anecdote illustrates how the use of an athlete's sport, in terms of language and metaphor, was the catalyst for making changes in the athlete's self-talk and, subsequently, concentration. A female collegiate rower was struggling with motivation and performance. When intensity during training or in a race was out of her comfort zone or when unpredictable events happened, the athlete's negative thoughts became so overwhelming that she would often give up. While the rower continued to attend sessions week after week, she reported that using cue words and affirmations was just was not working. Further discussion indicated she was not using self-talk deliberately and consistently due to her lack of buy-in about the power of self-talk and its role in performance. One day when discussing all the things that could go wrong in a regatta (rowing race), she mentioned that the most detrimental event would be "catching a crab" (i.e., when one is unable to release one's oar from the water and the blade acts as a brake that can completely stop the boat in motion, knock the air out of the rower, eject the rower from the boat, or even cause the boat to capsize). We talked about how catching a crab takes the boat off course and gets in the way of achieving one's goals. When this happens, the rower's sense of urgency and importance in having strategies to get out of this detrimental situation as quickly as possible and to get back on course is key. I (JV) pondered aloud, "I wonder if your negative self-talk acts as a 'mental crab,' when your thoughts take you off course and away from your goals." Immediately, the rower jumped on this idea with the realization that her negative self-talk was inhibiting her success. By using the language of her sport, the message and associated image was enough for the rower to invest in developing self-talk and mental strategies to aid her performance. Using both Nideffer's Attentional Styles (1976) and strategies to reframe catastrophic thoughts (Gauron, 1984; Hanton & Jones, 1999), we selected a few meaningful words and go-to phrases to redirect the rower's attention to task-relevant cues and prevent her thoughts and feelings from interfering with her performance. From this point on, the athlete was deliberate and successful in her mental practice; consequently, her testimonial, shared during a team meeting, increased buy-in from her teammates, and the athletes in the boat integrated their coxswain into a self-talk plan for races.

The student-consultant's understanding of concentration theories—and, closely related, how to guide self-talk practice to fit the context—was key to encouraging the athlete-client to integrate mental skills as part of her training. Second, the parallel process was key in this anecdote in which the student-consultant was devoted to learning about the athlete and the sport of crew and successfully demonstrated her expertise in sport psychology and, thus, successfully joined the client in a journey to help this athlete row her best.

Facilitating the Practice of the Mental Skill

In a controlled setting (one-on-one session), the student-consultant and client have successfully integrated (i.e., rehearsed) the new skill into the client's performance routine. A solid foundation has been built, but the ultimate *stickiness* of the skill (i.e., to be successfully used in the target context—competition) has yet to be solidified. In this stage of development, the student-consultant teaches the client how to adopt the mentality to consistently practice the new mental skill. It is the other variables that come into play in the actual target context (e.g., unexpected precompetition thoughts, inclement weather) where the athletes learn the most about their ability to implement the skills effectively and independently. Petitpas (2000) explained, "I want to ensure the athlete-clients are not only capable of demonstrating the desired behavior with me but they can also replicate the behavior in other situations" (p. 39). We strongly believe that the athlete's confidence and trust in the skill will only come from its consistent practice in real sport contexts (i.e., starting from the practice setting and ultimately used in the competition setting). The developmental process of the student-consultant learning how to effectively translate theory to practice shares a similar path of the athlete learning the new mental skills, both of which require deliberate practice (Owton, Bond, & Tod, 2014). The concept of practice is routine for athletes, but they are accustomed to the physical practice of the game. Again, it is the student-consultants' objective to smoothly guide the athlete-clients to include mental components into their already well-developed practice and competition routines.

How can the student-consultant drive home this idea without losing or frustrating the athlete-client with scientific jargon or it feeling like a burden of homework? The hope is that the athlete-client understands how important these skills and traits are for performing at one's best. When the athlete-clients report a concern that they do not have enough time for deliberate mental practice, the student-consultants can depend on the influence of language and examples to appeal to the athlete-clients. Clearly, matching language to the client's needs requires ongoing work and can continuously be shaped and reshaped depending on the context. "Unlike how we stick to certain models and theories, our language can change depending on the situation" (Poczwardowski, Sherman, & Ravizza, 2004, p. 456). One of the keys to influential language is the use of metaphors from the athlete's sport, by finding words and actions that are meaningful and specific to the client (Fifer, Henschen, Gould, & Ravizza, 2008).

Here is a brief display of how I (TC) was able to use appropriate language in a supportive way that facilitated the athlete-client's practice of the mental skills. A collegiate women's lacrosse athlete was having difficulty letting go and releasing the negative emotions from a mistake. The client described that she carried the weight of her mistakes throughout the game, which undoubtedly affected her concentration and performance. The theory driving the strategy was Ravizza's 4 Rs of emotion management, which was later adapted to just being labeled the "Rs" (recognize, release, regroup, refocus, ready, respond [Ravizza, 2012; Vernacchia, 2003]). We focused on centering, self-talk, and cue words, with the goal to stay in the present moment and move on to the next play with confidence. The client wrote the word "challenger" on her stick which symbolized *move on!*, *breathe*, and *challenge the next play with confidence!* During the controlled one-on-one sessions, the athlete-client was able to implement the skill successfully during multiple role-playing visualization scenarios. One of the techniques crucial for effectiveness of the mental skill was her ability to use a diaphragmatic breath to center herself for the next play. It was the cornerstone of the routine. The client knew the script and could perform well in sessions, but the skill was still not *sticky*. After a week of practice, the client reported that the utilization of the breath was ineffective, mainly because the client had minimal repetition and little interest in building a deliberate practice of breath awareness exercises. What was needed was the mental practice on and off the field, specifically around her ability to anchor herself through the breath awareness exercises. Successfully implementing the breathing skill in multiple settings would most likely build that coveted *stickiness* factor (Petitpas, 2000). My challenge was how to convey the importance of this mental practice and determine the best approach to fit the athlete's needs, expectations, and preferences.

In cognitive-behavioral strategies, homework is an instrumental component to the therapeutic process (Prochaska & Norcross, 2010), but many athletes may not like to hear that they are being assigned homework. Therefore, as I was listening to my client speak about her daily routines, she identified that going to the gym was an important activity for her physical and mental health on and off the field. The gym was a symbol of progress and positivity, so I utilized the comparison of engaging in the centering technique and breath awareness exercises as lifting weights for the mind, which I termed to the client as "mental repetitions for a more resilient mind." I taught the athlete that just like she hits the weights to physically prepare herself to succeed on the field, she will need to practice centering herself through the breath awareness exercises in various situations to successfully prepare herself to let go of mistakes, make the word "challenger" meaningful, and prepare her to perform at a higher level. Reassured by the support of my supervisor, for the next month, I sent emails, text messages, and in-person reminders asking her, "How was the gym today?" The focus and language was not the use of the term "homework" but a personalized question that signified progress and positivity. The athlete responded well to my approach, and, in one of our interactions, she reported that she had "gone to the gym today more than she has the entire month." The message of consistently engaging in the mental practice *stuck*! By using her interests, active lifestyle, and language, there were no more gaps between physical and mental practice. As follows, her ability to transition from the one-on-one sessions to her practice and competition was successful without ever feeling burdened by the task of formally assigned homework.

The implementation of the mental skill was effective in terms of frequency of practice, but effectiveness of progress was not fully experienced. The client reported that she had maintained the regimen during class, at practice, and in games, but she was still not consistently able to let go of her mistakes and move on to the next play especially during competition. In the next step, we will explore how guiding the athlete-client to assess and evaluate the effectiveness of using the mental skill is an essential part of the process.

Client's Evaluation of the Skill

In this stage of mental skills training, the athlete-client responds with internal and external feedback about the impact of the mental skill on performance to the student-consultant in a one-on-one session (in this example, it will continue to follow the athlete-client utilizing Ravizza's Rs of emotion management). Providing feedback to the student-consultant is an opportunity for the athlete-client to objectively evaluate and critique the skill, as well as make adjustments if necessary. As the student-consultant, it is important to be aware that the initial attempt to find the *sticky* language might not be completely successful; thus supervision may provide useful recommendations (please see Chapter 5, "Getting the Most From Supervision"). The following section will illustrate how I (TC), based on the client's feedback, was able to adapt my approach midway through our relationship to help the client evolve the mental skill into blossoming success.

The female lacrosse athlete came back for her scheduled session after a month of practicing the use of *challenger* as a cue to release and refocus. She reported that her ability to establish her breath as an anchor to refocus was successful, but the entire cycle of the mental skill was ineffective. She reported in session that during games when she was on the bench after a mistake, no matter how many times she completed the cycle starting with the visual cue on her stick, the mistakes constantly nagged and distracted her from the task-relevant cues of the present moment. Clearly, a different intervention altogether might be warranted here (perhaps the athlete might benefit from a mind–body intervention such as the relaxation response [Benson, 1975], which has been shown to decrease anxiety and increase self-awareness and self-regulation [Delmonte, 1985]), and yet one more attempt to see if there was still room for a better translation was granted an opportunity. It was during her explanation and process of taking me through her implementation of the skill where the solution appeared. The client put herself on the bench going through the *challenger* release–breath–refocus, when she said, "I just wish I had a door to slam shut on the bench!" That was the answer; my client needed something physical or tangible to manipulate to release the mistake. Through a collaborative effort, I guided the client to use her gloves and the strapping of the Velcro as the symbol of opening and closing the door. In her initial reaction, it looked as if a light bulb went off in her head. The new cycle started with opening the Velcro strap (obtaining self-awareness and self-control), closing the Velcro strap (move on! challenge the next play!), and breath (refocus for the next play, identify cues needed to execute the next play with conviction). In addition, "challenger" was written on her lacrosse gloves. With creativity, listening, and knowing the end-product of Ravizza's Rs, I was able to use self-talk, an image, an instantly accessible object, and a physical gesture that did not overwhelm the athlete in science and theory, while still demonstrating competency in the sport, how her mind works, and knowledge of a specific sport psychology tool (Fifer et al., 2008). With the athlete's commitment to practice, she went on to insert the new mental skill into her toolbox and was able to successfully move on from mistakes in order to be present for the next play. In the meantime, I continued the use my reminders of going to the "gym." This consistent maintenance of mental skill practice likely contributes to greater amounts of perceived performance excellence (Frey, Laguna, & Ravizza, 2003). Ultimately, it was the success she had in competition that solidified use of the mental skill.

The Reflection

The athlete has moved on, and so does the student-consultant, but the growth (professional and personal) from the collaborative relationship and experience continues to extend beyond the working relationship (see Chapter 8 for a full elaboration on reflective practice). Each relationship with a client creates a new opportunity to evolve your professional language, illustrations, and anecdotes that solidify the connection between theory and practice and may be used to assist future athlete-clients. For example, the phrase "going to the gym for mental reps" has been established as one of my go-to lines to convey the importance of the practice of mental skills. From the Ravizza Rs example, the athlete may not have been able to successfully implement the skill if it were not for several key strategies that are crucial to translating classroom material to fieldwork application.

In my (TC) reflection of integrating theory to practice with this particular athlete-client, I was able to record specific learned experiences. One, I gained a great amount of confidence taking on future athlete-clients. There was a sense of belief and trust in myself that I could be flexible and adapt to a client's presenting performance concerns. Two, it takes time to translate theory into practical skills for an athlete-client. Though I did not mention it in the example, in our very first session, my client was seeking tips to immediately impact her performance. Without completing a comprehensive performance profile, I blindly offered a technique without appropriate psychoeducation and integration of a theory. For example, I was in the middle of completing a research project on mindfulness meditation and gave my client a mindfulness audio recording to work on letting go of thoughts and returning to the breath. I felt pressure from my client and acted without optimal science to practice integration. Fortunately, I was aware of this rushed approached and was able to refocus my work to faithfully represent science to practice translation. Due to the fundamental nature of immediate feedback in sport, student-consultants need to be aware that the consultation process takes time; finding your unique language and adapting it to the language of your clients take time. Lastly, I learned I had a different style than my peers and that I needed to further solidify it through practice because there is no one way to execute a consulting relationship (Brown et al., 2006). The key was sticking to what was theoretically and ethically sound and unique to myself as a student-consultant.

Conclusion

The student-consultant's understanding of mental skills for optimal performance is a process of evolution that began with the consultant's own sport experience, developed through graduate training, and matured through understanding performance through the client's perspective. Thus, with accumulating experience and knowledge, the opportunity to educate and guide athlete-clients to reach their potential came to fruition. This chapter provided a glimpse of how a student-consultant can effectively translate experience and knowledge by using a collaborative, consultative method and, subsequently, tailoring mental skills interventions to enhance the athlete's performance. First, you must listen to the clients to find out how they best store new information. Second, immerse yourself into the clients' environments. By immersing yourself, you are able to identify the clients' colloquial language and use their words and lingo to translate the classroom material. Third, identify your philosophy (Poczwardowski et al., 2004) and confidently understand the performance concepts you are looking to teach, but be ready to be creative (Aoyagi, 2013; Fifer et al., 2008). Finally, be committed to expand your vocabulary and illustrations or analogies (pick one!) when the situation calls. Anyone can pick up a book and read the science and theories behind performance, but the art of the consulting process is influenced by the student-consultant's passion to continue to effectively bring to life the theories and principles in a way that is meaningful to the athlete-client. "Effective consultants have the ability to translate psychological principles and findings into concrete and practice terms that the athletes can understand" (Hardy et al., 1996, p. 292). The examples shared in this chapter illustrated the importance of using client-specific and sport-specific language for athlete-client interventions.

Here, we summarize some key take-away messages to guide a few steps in the readers' professional development:

- **Know the Theory and Be Confident.** Before stepping into a session, make sure you have practiced the delivery. Put your knowledge and skill to the test! One great way to expand your use of sport-specific language and examples is through the media. Find a real-life sport-specific situation and integrate the theory into the case. When the student-consultant demonstrates a consistent way of thinking and approach to performance, the athlete-client will feel even more confident in your ability to help and in mental skills training.
- **Reflect and Know Your Own Style.** The style and approach of the student-consultant is part of the intervention; therefore, identify your strengths, core values, and beliefs. It is vital to choose metaphors and language that fits the style and values of the student-consultant; otherwise, you risk sounding uncertain and anxious. Similarly, continue to grow along with your client; be flexible and adapt until you identify a consultative style and mental skill practice that resonates for both of you.
- **Immerse Yourself.** Most interventions need to be concrete, practical, sport-specific, and/or client-specific. The student-consultant must put in the time to listen and understand the sport from the client's perspective. Using the athlete-client's experiences, knowledge, sport language, and current use of mental skills provides a starting point for work together and will serve as a valuable tool in the future for translating theory to practice.
- **Be Creative and Collaborative.** When a planned intervention is unsuccessful, do not be afraid to use some imagination and be innovative as fitting to the situation.

Remembering that the consultative approach is collaborative and is essentially two experts coming together to produce optimal performance will relieve the pressure from having to provide an instantaneous solution. Much like physical skills, using mental skills is a process of trial and error that requires a tailored approach and fine-tuned adjustments to reach potential. Finally, sport psychology consultants at any stage of development should seek supervision for challenging cases to get another perspective on the athlete-client and related performance dilemma, and ongoing supervision of student-consultants is a most valuable resource.

- **Evolve.** When you have reached a stage in development where you feel a sense of mastery over theoretical concepts and confident about integrating performance principles into your client work, recall the idea of "consultant as a performer," as this concept holds true for students-in-training as well as those who reach expert status. We will always face new clients, in new sports with new challenges and demands requiring us to grow toward a more sophisticated integration of science and practice. Much like we expect our athlete-clients to mature and challenge their limits, we too, should act in a similar manner.

The journey of developing from student-in-training to novice and then to expert sport psychology consultant can be personally and professionally satisfying as you help athlete-clients achieve their dreams and goals. While science and theory are the cornerstones of our work from which we derive the tools that guide our interventions, it is the relationship with the athlete that drives successful client work, evidenced by clients achieving great performances as well as satisfaction in sport and life.

References

Aoyagi, M. W. (2013). Teaching theories of performance excellence to sport and performance psychology consultants-in-training. *Journal of Sport Psychology in Action*, 4(3), 139–151. doi: 10.1080/21520704.2013.792895

Aoyagi, M. W., & Poczwardowski, A. (2011). Models of sport psychology practice and delivery: A review. In S. D. Mellalieu & S. Hanton (Eds.), *Professional practice issues in sport psychology: Critical reviews* (pp. 5–30). London and New York: Routledge.

Aoyagi, M. W., & Poczwardowski, A. (Eds.). (2012). *Expert approaches to sport psychology: Applied theories of performance excellence*. Morgantown, WV: Fitness Information Technology.

Benson, H. (1975). *The relaxation response*. New York, NY: Avon Books.

Brown, D., Pryzwansky, W. B., & Schulte, A. C. (2006). *Psychological consultation and collaboration: Introduction to theory and practice* (6th ed.). Boston, MA: Pearson Education.

Burton, D., & Raedeke, T. (2008). *Sport psychology for coaches*. Champaign, IL: Human Kinetics.

Christensen, D. A., & Aoyagi, M. (2014). Lessons learned consulting at Olympic Trials: Swimming through growing pains. *The Sport Psychologist*, 28, 281–289.

Conroy, D. E., & Metzler, J. N. (2004). Patterns of self-talk associated with different forms of competitive anxiety. *Journal of Sport & Exercise Psychology*, 26, 69–89.

Delmonte, M. M. (1985). Meditation and anxiety reduction: A literature review. *Clinical Psychology Review*, 5(2), 91–102. doi: 10.1016/0272–7358(85)90016–9

Ellis, A. (1973). *Humanistic psychotherapy: The rational-emotive approach*. New York: Julian Press.

Fifer, A., Henschen, K., Gould, D., & Ravizza, K. (2008). What works when working with athletes. *The Sport Psychologist*, 22, 356–377.

Frey, M., Laguna, P., & Ravizza, K. (2003). Collegiate athletes' mental skill use and perceptions of success: An exploration of the practice and competition settings. *Journal of Applied Sport Psychology*, 15(2), 115–128. doi: 10.1080/10413200305392

Gauron, E. F. (1984). *Mental training for peak performance*. Lansing, NY: Sport Science Associates.

Hanton, S., & Jones, G. (1999). The effects of a multimodal intervention program on performers: II. Training the butterflies to fly in formation. *The Sport Psychologist, 13*, 22–41.

Hardy, J., Hall, C. R., & Hardy, L. (2005). Quantifying athlete self-talk. *Journal of Sports Sciences, 23*(9), 905–917. doi: 10.1080/02640410500130706

Hardy, L., Jones, G., & Gould, D. (1996). *Understanding psychological preparation for sport: Theory and practice of elite performers.* New York, NY: Wiley.

Jackson, S. A., & Csikszentmihalyi, M. (1999). *Flow in sports: The keys to optimal experiences and performances.* Champaign, IL: Human Kinetics.

Johnson, J. J., Hrycaiko, D. W., Johnson, G. V., & Halas, J. M. (2004). Self-talk and female youth soccer performance. *The Sport Psychologist, 18*, 44–59.

McEwan, H. E., & Tod, D. (2015). Learning experiences contributing to service-delivery competence in applied psychologists: Lessons for sport psychologists. *Journal of Applied Sport Psychology, 27*(1), 79–93. doi: 10.1080/10413200.2014.952460

Miller, A., & Donohue, B. (2003). The development and controlled evaluation of athletic mental preparation strategies in high school distance runners. *Journal of Applied Sport Psychology, 15*, 321–334. doi: 10.1080/714044200

Nideffer, R. M. (1976). *The inner athlete.* New York, NY: Thomas Crowell.

Orlick, T., & Partington, J. (1988). Mental links to excellence. *The Sport Psychologist, 2*, 105–130.

Owton, H., Bond, K., & Tod, D. (2014). "It's my dream to work with Olympic athletes": Neophyte sport psychologist' expectations and initial experiences regarding service delivery. *Journal of Applied Sport Psychology, 26*, 241–255. doi: 10.1080/10413200.2013.847509

Perry, C., & Marsh, H. W. (2000). Listening to self-talk, hearing self-concept. In M. B. Andersen (Ed.), *Doing sport psychology* (pp. 61–76). Champaign, IL: Human Kinetics.

Petitpas, A. J. (2000). Managing stress on and off the field: The littlefoot approach to learned resourcefulness. In M. B. Andersen (Ed.), *Doing sport psychology* (pp. 33–43). Champaign, IL: Human Kinetics.

Poczwardowski, A., Sherman, C., & Henschen, K. P. (1998). A sport psychology service delivery heuristic: Building on theory and practice. *The Sport Psychologist, 12*, 191–207.

Poczwardowski, P., Sherman, C. P., & Ravizza, K. (2004). Professional philosophy in the sport psychology service delivery: Building on theory and practice. *The Sport Psychologist, 18*, 445–463.

Prochaska, J. O., & Norcross, J. C. (2010). *Systems of psychotherapy: A transtheoretical analysis.* Belmont, CA: Brooks/Cole.

Ravizza, K. (2012). Dr. Ken Ravizza. In M. W. Aoyagi & A. Poczwardowski (Eds.), *Expert approaches to sport psychology: Applied theories of performance excellence* (pp. 201–215). Morgantown, WV: Fitness Information Technology.

Silva, J. M., Metzler, J. N., & Lerner, B. (2011). *Training professionals in the practice of sport psychology* (2nd ed.). Morgantown, WV: Fitness Information Technology.

Tammen, V. V. (2000). First internship experience—Or, what I did on Holiday. In M. B. Andersen (Ed.), *Doing sport psychology* (pp. 181–192). Champaign, IL: Human Kinetics.

Thelwell, R. C., Weston, N., Greenlees, I. A., & Hutchings, N. V. (2008). A qualitative exploration of psychological skills use in coaches. *The Sport Psychologist, 22*, 38–53.

Tod, D. (2007). The long and winding road: Professional development in sport psychology. *The Sport Psychologist, 21*, 94–108.

Tod, D., Andersen, M. A., & Marchant, D. B. (2009). A longitudinal examination of neophyte applied sport psychologists' development. *Journal of Applied Sport Psychology, 21*, 1–16.

Vernacchia, R. A. (2003). *Inner strength: The mental dynamics of athletic performance.* Palo Alto, CA: Warde Publishers.

Vygotsky, L. (1986). *Thought and language.* Cambridge, MA: The MIT Press.

Weinberg, R. S., & Gould, D. (2011). *Foundations of sport and exercise psychology* (5th ed.). Champaign, IL: Human Kinetics.

Weinberg, R. S., & Williams, J. M. (2010). Integrating and implementing a psychological skills training program. In J. M. Williams (Ed.), *Applied sport psychology: Personal growth to peak performance* (pp. 361–391). New York, NY: McGraw-Hill.

3 Recognizing, Understanding, and Resolving Ethical Issues

Leigh A. Bryant*, Megan M. Byrd*,
Jack C. Watson II, and Edward F. Etzel

This chapter is intended to inform students and young professionals of the many ethical issues and dilemmas they may face throughout their graduate training and early professional experiences. Additionally, the chapter discusses ethical decision-making so that when problems do arise, individuals feel equipped to deal with them ethically, efficiently, and thoroughly. The authors of this chapter have organized the content into the following seven sections: (1) Ethics Training, (2) Competency, (3) Confidentiality and Privacy, (4) Boundaries, (5) Technology, (6) Social Media, and (7) Self-Regulation and Self-Care. Each section will provide an overview of the topic and discuss how it is relevant to ethical decision-making. Following these seven sections, the authors have provided a "Case Example," which incorporates and highlights several ethical issues and dilemmas discussed throughout the chapter. Finally, a chapter summary and recommendations for graduate students and young professionals will be offered.

Ethics Training

Ethics training is imperative for all sport psychology consultants, but it is especially salient for trainees and students entering sport psychology consultation opportunities. Unfortunately, the focus on ethical dilemmas causes many students and professionals to overlook the fact that ethical standards and principles exist not only to uphold the minimum standards of the profession (i.e., remedial ethics) but also as a way to help practitioners do good work for the benefit of their clients, and over time reach their fullest potential (i.e., positive or virtue ethics [Knapp & VandeCreek, 2006]). According to Watson, Zizzi, and Etzel (2006), 64 percent of sport psychology graduate programs required professional ethics as part of graduate training. Methods of teaching ethics commonly included case studies, lectures and discussions in seminars, formal classes, and information integrated within other coursework. For example, at the authors' institution, graduate students are required to take an ethics course within the sport and exercise psychology program as part of the graduate curriculum. Additionally, students who are currently consulting with an athletic team are required to attend a biweekly group supervision class as well as a weekly individual supervision meeting that often include discussions of ethical practice.

Supervision is a cornerstone of learning and understanding ethics. As a supplement to coursework in this area, supervision provides the opportunity to engage in meaningful dialogue about the application of ethical standards and principles to specific situations that the consultant may encounter. Supervision can take many forms throughout one's training; the trainee may participate in individual, group, and meta-supervision (see Chapters 5 and 6).

---

*These authors are coauthors and are listed in alphabetical order.

These various forms of supervision allow the trainee to work with the supervisor, peers, and colleagues, which is often necessary in order to move "beyond codes and textbooks" to develop a "careful ethical awareness leading to prudent judgment and action" (Etzel, 2014, p. 8).

Competence

As Taylor (1994) has discussed, the issue of perceived competence—which is inherently tied to one's education, training, and experience—is largely "left to the professional" (p. 189). This lack of clarity on specifics and therefore dependence on general guidelines can be confusing for graduate students and young professionals who are looking to accurately present themselves to clients and appropriately align themselves with the professional practice of sport psychology. The American Psychological Association (APA) has endorsed a proficiency in sport psychology (APA Division 47, 2015), encouraging professionals to self-assess their skills and knowledge related to working with athletes.

Some practitioners assert that the client population is the main determinant of competence (Silva, 1989), while others maintain that it is the practitioner's skills (Gardner, 1991) that should be the focus (Taylor, 1994). Based on our interpretation of the APA (2010) and Association for Applied Sport Psychology (AASP [2015b]) Ethics Codes, it is our judgment that striking a balance between these two approaches may help students to clarify their own areas of competence and subsequently communicate their limitations and boundaries of practice to clients and supervisors. By identifying what populations they feel prepared to work with, students can identify areas where continuing education and/or referrals are necessary in order to avoid both ethical and legal consequences.

Titling

Once students begin their graduate programs or prepare to undertake their first consulting assignment, it is important to determine how to introduce, describe, and market oneself and one's services appropriately and ethically. What a student or novice consultant calls him- or herself reflects back on the field of sport psychology and represents the mission of the profession. Depending on state laws, licensing boards, and certain title use exceptions (e.g., working in state or federal government settings), students and young professionals may or may not be able to call themselves "sport psychologists" or use the word "psychology" anywhere in their title (Taylor, 1994). For that reason, other common titles for students with degrees in sport psychology include "mental coach," "mental trainer," and "performance enhancement consultant." In order to practice ethically, students and young professionals should review the ethics codes from the Association for Applied Sport Psychology (AASP), American Psychological Association (APA), American Counseling Association (ACA), as well as any other appropriate ethics codes for titling guidelines. Additionally, state licensure boards can help to determine whether the use of "psychology" or "psychologist" is appropriate and ethical.

Credentialing

Currently (at the time of publication), there is no established national or international model for training and credentialing in sport psychology, although some countries have established pathways to a particular legally protected title related to the practice of sport psychology (e.g., British Psychological Society, 2015). Training and credentialing are issues that have been discussed by many people in the field for decades. Despite the absence of one set of guidelines for training and credentialing, AASP endorses a certification process at the standard and provisional levels (AASP, 2015a). To achieve the standard level, one must have a doctoral degree (which includes the completion of specified courses) and complete 400 total hours of mentored experience in preparation and delivery of sport psychology and performance enhancement services. At the provisional level, one must have a master's degree (which includes the completion of specified courses) and complete 700 total hours of mentored experience in preparation and delivery of sport psychology and performance enhancement services. This certification is awarded through an application process to become a certified consultant, called the Certified Consultant, AASP, or "CC-AASP."

The CC-AASP indicates to other students, professionals, and the general public that a consultant has met a variety of course requirements and completed a certain number of applied hours with athletes, exercisers, and/or teams and groups. Training and credentialing will undoubtedly continue to be a topic of discussion within the field. It is the ethical obligation of students and professionals to remain up to date with recommended titles and training practices in their states and provinces in order to represent themselves in an accurate, responsible manner.

Confidentiality and Privacy

A clear understanding of confidentiality and privacy is the foundation of a trusting, productive consultation. Confidentiality refers to a practitioner's ethical (and often legal) obligation to protect information about work that he/she does with clients. While confidentiality is often discussed in tandem with privacy, the two terms are not synonymous. Privacy refers to a person's legal right to control what, when, and how much information about him/her may be shared with an outside party. A client's legal right to privacy is protected under the Fourth, Fifth, and Fifteenth Amendments of the United States Constitution (Koocher & Keith-Spiegel, 2008).

An example of these two terms working simultaneously often comes up in university settings, where the graduate student is serving as the primary consultant and the faculty member is serving as the student's supervisor. As part of the confidentiality agreement, a college athlete needs to be informed of your status as a student-trainee being supervised by a faculty member. Both student-trainee and supervisor should adhere to the client's right to privacy; however, because the supervisor is legally responsible for the trainee's decisions and actions (Fisher & Oransky, 2008), client notes and case details must be discussed with the supervisor, and therefore confidentiality is not fully upheld between the student-trainee and the client.

There are several limits to confidentiality beyond those that naturally occur due to the student–supervisor relationship. Consultants have an ethical obligation to break confidentiality in multiple instances, including cases where dangerousness, duty to warn and/or protect, and abuse or neglect arise. For example, if an athlete discloses that their parent is physically abusing a younger sibling, this information needs to be reported to the proper authorities. It should also be noted that confidentiality laws vary between states; therefore, students and practitioners must be aware of the legal ramifications and guidelines in the states in which they are consulting.

Consent and Assent

The distinction between confidentiality and privacy also presents itself when working with minors (i.e., those under the age of 18). In most cases, it is understood that there are benefits to maintaining a degree of confidentiality with a client who is a minor. This can help with rapport building and openness to services (Blom, Visek, & Harris, 2014). A client who is a minor does not, however, have the right to privacy that an adult client would have, given that persons under the age of 18 (or an age determined by state law) are not legally able to give consent (only assent). The client's parents or legal guardians must give consent on behalf of the child. Additionally, parents have the right to know what goes on in consultation sessions. It is up to the consultant, in collaboration with the parents and client, to determine how much information to share with parents. Our recommendation, based on our training, is to clarify the client's rights and to spend time reviewing the limitations to both confidentiality and privacy in accordance with the client's age, ability to give assent, the presenting concern, and other factors that are relevant to the specific case.

Third Parties

This chapter focuses on the processes of identifying and resolving ethical issues, and one of the most important things that students and young professionals can do at the start of any new consultation is to clearly delineate their role with the athlete and to whom, if anyone, information can be shared. Especially in scholastic and collegiate settings, it is critical to determine whether a coach, athletic trainer, or other staff member should be aware of sport psychology consultations with particular athletes. If athletes are mandated to seek consultation, then attendance records and basic overviews of session topics should suffice, given the provision of voluntary written permission on the part of the client. Clarifying the role of third parties when the consultant and client first meet can prevent ethical dilemmas later on in the consultation. This will also ensure that relationships between consultant and athlete, and consultant and coach, are mutually exclusive. The consultant should avoid blurring personal and/or professional boundaries so as to remain helpful to all parties involved.

This clarification is also helpful when determining the appropriateness of sharing materials—such as workbooks, handouts, or case notes—with persons outside of the consultation. For instance, third parties such as coaches who have referred clients or who are interested in the progress of the clients may request to see materials that an athlete is working on in a particular session. Further, supervisors and peers in a group supervision setting may ask a consultant to share specific handouts or techniques used with an athlete. Obtaining consent from the athlete and/or parent (if athlete is a minor) about sharing materials is a very important part of upholding confidentiality and informing clients of their rights.

Boundaries

It is an ethical necessity that sport psychology consultants maintain appropriate boundaries with clients. Boundary behaviors have been defined as "behaviors or activities that mark the limits or parameters of appropriate, good, and ethical practice, including both structural (e.g., roles, time, place-space) and process (e.g., gifts, language, self-disclosure, physical contact, interactional patterns) dimensions" (Lamb & Catanzaro, 1998, p. 498).

Due to the nature of sport psychology consulting, boundary behaviors may need more consideration than in a typical office-based counseling setting. Specifically, boundaries regarding time and space needed for sport psychology practice are not always congruent with the views of traditional therapy (Andersen, Van Raalte, & Brewer, 2001). For example, a therapist who eats lunch with a client may not be seen as practicing ethically, given the boundaries established in traditional counseling settings. However, if a sport psychology consultant travels with a team, he or she is very likely to find him- or herself sitting down to a meal with one or more athletes or coaches. This behavior may not be viewed as ethically questionable, since the consultant is traveling as a member of the training staff.

Boundary behaviors in consulting with collegiate athletes are also complicated by the National College Athletic Association (NCAA) rules and regulations that guide what are deemed appropriate and inappropriate benefits to be received by athletes. One such example of a boundary behavior that is further restricted via the NCAA is giving rides to student-athletes (NCAA, 2015). Consider the following example, which illustrates the intersection of personal and professional ethics and morals with NCAA rules:

> *After attending an evening practice, an athlete asks if you [consultant] could talk briefly about a performance issue that has been nagging him. You agree and the two of you meet inside the practice facility while the coach is in his office. Once the impromptu session has ended, you walk outside the facility with the athlete to pouring rain and darkness. All of his teammates have left, and because he is a freshman, he does not have a car on campus. The shuttle to campus is no longer running. He tries calling a teammate to return to pick him up, but to no avail. The athlete remarks that the walk back to his dorm in this weather is going "to suck" and that he dislikes walking in the dark. As the consultant, you are aware of the NCAA regulations regarding offering rides. Is it ethical to offer to give the athlete a ride back to his dorm?*

The above case study illustrates a boundary-crossing behavior that a sport psychology consultant may be faced with while working with a college athlete. Giving a ride to a client is not a traditional counselor–client interaction; however, giving a ride in the above situation could be helpful and potentially constructive. Boundary crossings are a deviation from a traditional client interaction, but they do not necessarily cause harm and may in fact be helpful and constructive (as opposed to boundary violations, which do cause harm to the client [Gutheil & Gabbard, 1998]). Correspondingly, as members of AASP (or other professional organizations), we have a responsibility to uphold ethical guidelines. AASP Ethical Principle E (Concern for Others' Welfare) states, "AASP members seek to contribute to the welfare of those with whom they interact professionally. When conflicts occur among AASP members' obligations or concerns, they attempt to resolve those conflicts and to perform those roles in a responsible fashion that avoids or minimizes harm" (AASP, 2015b). Herein lies the ethical dilemma of this perceived boundary-crossing behavior, as not offering a ride could cause potential harm to the client but could also be conceived as unethical and a violation of NCAA rules and regulations. A student's first instinct should be to consult with a supervisor or Certified Consultant. However, in the event that a supervisor is not available, students must make a decision that thoughtfully considers the potential ethical repercussions.

Multiple Roles

Consulting is complex, often involving multiple roles, vague boundaries, and substantial commitments of time (Andersen et al., 2001). As people increase their training and competencies, and work with a broader range of clients, the potential for multiple roles increases (Jones, Evans, & Mullen, 2007). Multiple roles are not necessarily "bad." Instead of avoiding multiple relationships, by maintaining boundaries, consultants can have consistent ethical practice while still being an effective consultant (Moleski & Kiselica, 2005).

A common multiple role for students is having student-athletes you consult with in classes that you teach. Some issues that arise with this multiple role are grading, favoritism, using more casual language, and subconscious biases (Watson & Clement, 2008; Watson, Clement, Harris, Leffingwell, & Hurst, 2006). Consider the following case example:

> *You have been working with a collegiate rowing team for two years and also have a graduate teaching assistantship in your department. You have two rowers in your Introductory Sport Psychology class. While attending practice, one of the rowers in your class asks you to clarify the homework assignment that's due tomorrow. She says she was going to e-mail you, but since you are at practice, could you just talk now?*

This example illustrates a common ethical dilemma caused by having multiple roles. Without banning athletes from your course, which would likely be unethical, this role is not one that can be easily avoided. One option would be to ask students to take another section of the course, if possible. Another option is to allow the student to take the course and to discuss with athletes that the relationship in the consulting realm will be different than the one in the classroom. For instance, if an athlete wants to talk about something happening within the team during class time, you can tell the athlete that you would be happy to discuss that after class, during practice, or during an appointment.

Another multiple role that you may be faced with while consulting is being asked to perform roles or take on responsibilities outside of consulting. For example, while traveling with a team, you may be asked to hold gear or drive a van of athletes from the airport to the meet. When making these decisions to take on multiple roles, refer to the AASP code of ethics regarding multiple relationships (AASP, 2015b). Standard 9a states, "AASP members must always be sensitive to the potential harmful if unintended effects of social or other nonprofessional contacts on their work and on those persons with whom they deal. Such multiple relationships might impair the AASP member's objectivity or might harm or exploit the other party" (AASP, 2015b). So long as engaging in multiple roles does not clearly cross ethical boundaries and create harm, engaging in certain acts may build rapport with the team and coaches. Communicating your role and professional boundaries is important to establish what your role on the team is and to prevent possible unethical situations from arising.

Another common multiple role is that of coach and consultant. While it may be appropriate for a coach to incorporate psychoeducation about mental skills to enhance the team's performance (Burke & Johnson, 1992), acting in both roles has the potential to blur relationships and roles (King & Churchill, 2008). However, while it may appear to be beneficial cost-wise for one professional with appropriate qualifications to fulfill two complementary roles (e.g., coach and consultant), it could have important ramifications for the athletes who are being served. They may not feel comfortable talking about performance issues with a person who is also on the coaching staff. Not only would this multiple role be a potential NCAA violation regarding number of coaches on staff and coachable hours, but it presents an ethical dilemma within the relationship. As sport psychology consultants, we have to stay within our competency and within our role on the team.

When you find yourself in a multiple role, the best course of action may be to look for ways to avoid the relationship, such as asking athletes to take a different course, finding another consultant to work with the athlete, only working with the athlete in group sessions, or changing courses with another graduate student. When these relationships are not avoidable, communication with the athlete about the potential risks, roles, and expectations for both of you in these relationships is essential. This conversation should happen as soon as the consultant is made aware of the relationship, so that it is delivered proactively as opposed to being done as damage control in the event that a problem should arise. Also, consultants should inform athletes about the potential hazards associated with the multiple roles and the reasons these hazards may occur. According to Watson and Clement (2008), the primary goals of this communication should be to (1) educate the client about multiple-role relationships and ethical guidelines, (2) create open lines of communication for further discussions, and (3) develop a strategy for dealing with any future problems that may occur as a result of this relationship.

Consulting in Nontraditional Settings

Sport psychology professionals may work in a variety of settings, including gymnasiums, locker rooms, practice fields, pool decks, and lunch rooms. Because of this variety, it is less a question of avoiding these situations than knowing how to handle yourself when they emerge (Brown & Cogan, 2006). Even walking with an athlete after practice, or sitting with an athlete during competition, could potentially become an impromptu consulting session. These moments provide a unique opportunity to consult with athletes in a comfortable setting and when they are in the sport environment. However, they can also be potentially unethical since confidentiality and anonymity cannot be guaranteed. Both client and consultant need to discuss these situations to the satisfaction of the client in advance.

Travel With Clients

Being invited to travel with a team is a great opportunity for a consultant that can result in increased rapport and comfort as well as an opportunity to learn about the nuances of the sport and team culture. When traveling with the team, you may have to decide where to sit on the bus or plane if your seat is not assigned to you. Would it be better to sit with the coaches or with the athletes? Another ethical dilemma may arise regarding what is acceptable and not acceptable to talk about. If you sit next to an athlete that you have consulted with in individual sessions, the athlete may want to use that time to talk about a performance issue. If you sit with the coaches, athletes may make an assumption that you are talking about them, or they may see you as a member of the coaching staff instead of your role as sport psychology consultant. If the travel includes an overnight stay, our recommendation would be to room with an athletic trainer or another support staff member as opposed to a member of the coaching staff or team. This preserves your role clarity and minimizes the risk of blurred boundaries.

Another circumstance is being invited to a team dinner or to a dinner with the coaches. Brown and Cogan (2006) suggested that it may not always be necessary to refuse to participate in these events, especially since such invitations are well-intended. However, as sport psychology consultants, we must always be cognizant of the social setting and make good professional and personal decisions when out in public. This also gives the consultant an opportunity to role-model appropriate professional boundaries for the athletes.

Overall, consulting in nontraditional settings can be challenging. The first responsibility is to remind athletes and coaches that you are not in a private, confidential setting and so other team members may be listening or able to hear what is being discussed. The maintenance of professional and personal boundaries allows us to uphold ethics to do no harm to clients while offering athletes sport psychology services as requested and needed.

Small-World Effect

Over time, consulting in a small town often leads to running into current and former athletes and coaches in the community—for example, while shopping for groceries or going out to dinner. The authors of this chapter have termed these encounters as the "small-world" effect. For example:

> *While standing in line to be seated at a local restaurant, an athlete I had recently had an individual session with entered with nonteammate peers. We made eye contact and then uncomfortably stood in the lobby. The athlete did not initiate contact with me, and so I took that as a cue to not initiate contact with him. Additionally, I did not want to have to explain how I knew the athlete or force him to explain to his peers how he knew me. Luckily, soon after his arrival, my table was ready, and I did not run across him for the remainder of the evening.*

The example illustrates a situation that a consultant would likely encounter, especially in a smaller town. One way to prevent potentially uncomfortable situations is to address that these run-ins may arise and discuss how you will handle the situation. By having these discussions, both you and the client know what to expect and how to act when it occurs. This is particularly important if you are living and consulting in a small community where the number of restaurants and entertainment venues are limited. Additionally, seeing an athlete or coach in public is a gentle reminder that practitioners should always be aware of how they are presenting themselves in public settings.

It should be noted that there is not a set formula for handling these situations. An encounter outside of the consulting environment may not go exactly as planned; therefore, we recommend that you process and debrief this with your client and supervisor. There are two benefits to the debriefing process with the client. The first is to remind and reinforce the athlete's rights to confidentiality and privacy. The second benefit is that, indirectly, this conversation may increase rapport between you and the client. If the clients know that you honor and respect their confidentiality and privacy, this may increase the therapeutic alliance.

Transference and Countertransference

In order to maintain boundaries with clients in sessions, a consultant must be aware of transference and countertransference with athletes, coaches, and teams. Transference has been defined as "the repetition, or rather new edition, of wishes, defenses, conflicts, and object-relations (e.g., parent–child) experienced within the therapeutic relationship" (Stevens & Andersen, 2007, p. 259). Transferential reactions may arise at any time and with any client throughout one's career, whether it is in the first or last session that you ever facilitate. One example of transference could be the client's projection of issues with a parent or partner onto the sport psychology consultant. Researchers have suggested that female consultants may be seen as fulfilling the role of mother, sister, or girlfriend (Yambor & Connelly, 1991); the nurturance or attention provided in a session may correspond to that provided by or expected from another loved one. Thus, it is imperative that the consultant establishes professional boundaries at the start of any consultation and periodically reflects on the client's word choice, body language, and patterns of behavior that may indicate an inappropriate or incongruent relationship that the client is subconsciously seeking to establish in session. For students who are just starting to see clients, it is recommended that you talk about issues of transference with your supervisor(s) and any peers who may have had these kinds of experiences while consulting.

Countertransference has been defined as one's "unconscious and conscious reactions to a client's transference" (Little & Harwood, 2010, p. 304). Countertransference can encumber the relationship that you build with each client, as well as complicate (ethically and conceptually) any consultation. Examples of countertransference may include the consultant placing the client in the role of a parent, teacher, teammate, coach, love interest, or sibling. While countertransference can be difficult to identify, we recommend that students and young professionals write thorough case notes and then review those notes with a supervisor. By reviewing notes with an objective third party, such as your supervisor, you may become more aware of whether you are using the consulting time to deal with your own personal issues rather than the client's presenting concerns.

Attraction and Repulsion

A rather common issue that can relate to transference and/or countertransference is that of attraction between the consultant and client. The definition of attraction is very broad, and may include subtopics such as romantic/sexual attraction, emotional attraction, or aesthetic attraction. For the purposes of this chapter, we will selectively focus on sexual attraction and the role that it may play in a given consultation. Many, if not all, of the athletes with whom consultants will work are part of an athletic population that is often physically fit and high achieving; as a result, consultants may find members of this population to be sexually attractive (Stevens & Andersen, 2007). Likewise, many sport psychology consultants may engage in self-care behaviors that include healthy eating and exercise and may therefore be perceived by their athletic clients as attractive. It is important to be aware of sexual attraction due to the fact that any sexual intentions or behaviors that occur in a consulting relationship are likely to have professional, ethical, and/or legal consequences if not handled appropriately.

Our suggestion to students and young professionals is to be aware of the vulnerabilities that exist in a consulting session. Ask yourself—what needs are being met by our consulting relationship? Little and Harwood (2010) have identified that the feelings of being needed and/or looked after may be two scripts that are played out in a consulting session. Similarly, consider whether the use of physical touch could increase feelings of vulnerability in either party. Therefore, the consultant must have a clear reason for physical touch that works in the interest of the client and does not cross professional boundaries. Asking the client if he or she is comfortable with physical touch can alert both of you to the unique nature of your professional relationship; this conversation can help to clarify the intention behind a behavior, as a hug or other physical gesture could be interpreted by the athlete as a sexual advance (Little & Harwood, 2010).

It is critical for consultants to be aware of and have policies in place for anticipated scenarios with clients of both the same and opposite sex. According to Little and Harwood (2010), "boundaries in sport psychology are often less rigid, more complex, and often more difficult to maintain than those in traditional clinical psychology or counseling" (p. 303). Because of the complexity of the consulting relationship, consultants should communicate their boundaries clearly with each athlete at the start of a new consultation, or at the start of each season if the athlete is a returning client. When the unexpected boundary issue does arise, the consultant is encouraged to take the necessary time to process any intention or behavior with the client as deemed appropriate and subsequently take the case to a supervisor.

Students and professionals must adhere to professional standards and ethics regarding sexual relations with former and current clients. According to AASP Ethical Standard 9c, "AASP members do not engage in sexual relationships with students, supervisees, and clients over whom the AASP member has evaluative, direct, or indirect authority, because such relationships are so likely to impair judgment or be exploitative" (AASP, 2015b). Regardless of what ethical code or guidelines you follow, keep in mind that as a helping professional, there is always the risk of doing harm when you enter a relationship outside the professional scope of practice.

In addition to issues surrounding attractiveness on a friendly or romantic/sexual level, repulsion must be considered. It is possible that you as the consultant will be repulsed—or have a strong dislike—for a particular client over the course of your training and career. These feelings of dislike may come from a high degree of dissimilarity between you and the client (Speight & Vera, 1997), a specific personal characteristic (e.g., race or ethnicity), or a behavior that is reported to you (e.g., the athlete bullies others, engages in deviant sexual behavior). While it is acceptable to enjoy sessions with some clients more than others, it is not generally acceptable for you to approach sessions with hostility, disgust, or detachment; doing so would likely promote an unwelcoming environment, which could lead to issues with rapport, transference/countertransference, and nonmaleficence.

It is the authors' recommendations that consultants be aware of their verbal and nonverbal behaviors while in session, as each athlete (depending on personal and situational factors) may interpret these behaviors differently. Additionally, consultants should delineate their professional boundaries to each client up front to avoid possible confusion about the nature of the consulting relationship later on. Third, consultants are encouraged to discuss the role of physical touch with their supervisors to determine its therapeutic relevance with each client. Finally, it is critical that consultants look "inward" at the reasons behind their feelings of wanting to be helpful, appreciated, liked, or loved by their clients, and to seek appropriate counsel on these needs, wants, or desires throughout their graduate training and professional development. The ethics regarding engaging in a sexual or romantic relationship with a client are clear and nonnegotiable; however, the ethics regarding romantic relationships and friendships with coaches and other support staff such as athletic trainers are not as clearly defined. In the same way that a consultant may feel a sexual attraction to an athlete, attraction could form with a coach, especially one of similar age. A platonic friendship with a coach or other staff member appears to fall within the boundaries of acceptable behaviors as a professional. However, when the coach, or athletic trainer, is clearly not the client, would a romantic relationship be ethical?

Even though there is no direct ethical standard or principle related to relationships with coaches and support staff, it is our recommendation that romantic relationships be avoided while actively consulting with a team. A romantic relationship with a coach could impact one's ability to maintain boundaries and impact athletes' willingness to seek your services, knowing that you are involved with their coach. Furthermore, in their case study, Lubker and Andersen (2014) stated that dating a coach could potentially damage your reputation, the coach's reputation, and the perception of the field of sport psychology.

Consultants must be cognizant of the potential for boundary issues to arise given the nature of sport psychology consulting. It is the consultant's responsibility to utilize sound ethical decision-making and supervision in order to address issues such as multiple roles, travel with teams, transference and countertransference, and attraction and repulsion.

Technology

With the ever-evolving state of technology, discussing the possible consequences of electronic communication is becoming imperative. Phone calls, text messages, and emails are often more convenient than meeting in person and often expected by Millennial clients. However, these types of communication often pose risks to ethical practice in general, and confidentiality more specifically. At the start of any new consultation, as part of informed consent, it is suggested that the consultant and client discuss the role that phone calls, texts, emails, and other online communication (e.g., Skype, FaceTime) may play in the consultation. A written waiver is one way that clients can indicate that they have been made aware of and understand the potential threats to confidentiality related to the use of technology for communication and consultation. It is also recommended that consultants who engage in email communication with clients put a "disclosure" note at the bottom of their automatic signature that contains a warning that a recipient cannot guarantee client confidentiality or privacy.

Just as electronic communication cannot be considered fully confidential, saving and sending case notes electronically can present ethical dilemmas for the consultant. Case notes are essential, as they provide documentation of each session with a client, and are useful during supervision sessions. However, the method by which these case notes are shared should be thoroughly considered. For example, is it ethical to email your case notes to your supervisor on a university server? If so, do you encrypt these emails? How about the "name" of your documents; do you use client initials, pseudonyms, or de-identify your clients? These questions are essential to discuss with your supervisor at the outset of your work together. Additionally, it is suggested that you make the contents of an email clear by including some descriptor in the subject line. This way, a supervisor will know if it is intended for their eyes only. An example in which this subject line suggestion may come into play is if you were to accidentally send an email to the wrong person or persons. If you are lucky, the recipient(s) may not open your attachment but rather notify you that you have sent your case note to the wrong person.

Social Media

Social media is a convenient and popular mode of communication, particularly for adolescents and young adults. Social media sites such as Facebook, Instagram, and Twitter have connected sport psychology consultants and students to invaluable networking connections and provide a wealth of information on sports and athletes. For example, using Twitter to build a professional reputation and create impact by regularly tweeting about sport psychology topics or issues can boost the field (Cha, Haddadi, Benevenuto, & Gummadi, 2010). Another benefit of following social media pages of the team you work with are access to information in real time, such as live scores when you are not traveling with the team. Also, it can provide a way to communicate with the team, such as sending reminders about recovery techniques.

While this technology has many benefits, it can also lead to ethical boundaries being crossed or violated, and its use is an ongoing debate in the field. Some of these ethical considerations and boundaries to discuss are confidentiality and accessibility (Cotterill & Symes, 2004). Social media communication is public information that *lasts forever*. It is not a confidential means of communication or interactions. Some ethical considerations to explore when choosing to use social media sites are having a personal or business account, following athlete and/or team accounts, and accepting athletes', coaches', or parents' friend requests.

We recommend creating a business email account to maintain boundaries. By refraining from posting personal information, information that could be seen as controversial, and information unrelated to sport psychology consulting, students and young professionals can establish and hopefully maintain more clear boundaries with their online presence and uphold professional identity. When you post from your social media account, you are representing your school and organization. With this increased personal exposure comes an added responsibility of professionally appropriate tweeting on Twitter or posting on Facebook. Furthermore, from either a business or personal account, your social media activity is not private, so thinking about your own intentions and career aspirations is an important consideration when deciding to "tweet or not to tweet." Some professionals in the field have outlined a strict policy of not following athletes, coaches, or parents on social media sites and include that policy in their contracts and informed consent documents. Developing a similar policy would avoid ethical dilemmas and decisions each time you are sent a request.

With regard to following athletes and teams on social media, following the team page rather than the individual athlete would likely be the most prudent option. You can reap the benefits of using social media such as score updates and team news that would not directly expose you as the consultant associated with that particular team. By following individual athletes, other athletes may surmise that you are working individually with that person and jeopardize confidentiality. Even if no risky boundary behaviors are present, it may not be worth the chance that one could occur or that an athlete's trust or confidentiality is lost.

If coaches, parents, or athletes send "friend" requests, it may be helpful to explore the motives for these requests before deciding to accept. If the motive is for personal reasons, it may not be in the best interest of both parties to be connected. This may blur the boundaries of the professional relationship. There are likely no potential benefits to the client and some potential risks. However, if the motive is professional in nature, connecting on social media may be worth exploring. For instance, if you post videos or links to sport psychology information, it would be a benefit for your client. Additionally, the social media connection may be used to develop future networking opportunities. Ultimately, in order to be effective, a consultant should be self-aware so that boundary behaviors, in person or online, are thoughtfully addressed.

Self-Regulation and Self-Care

One of the main tenets of the AASP (2015b) and APA (2010) Ethics Codes is nonmaleficence—i.e., "do no harm." In addition to proper training and supervision, students and young professionals must be aware of their own self-care habits and how these may influence the consulting relationship (Barnett, Baker, Elman, & Schoener, 2007). Consultant self-regulation—where a consultant periodically reflects on his/her mental and physical health, support system, and general well-being—is very important. Healthy patterns related to sleep, hygiene, diet, and exercise patterns can be facilitative to the sport psychology consulting relationship. Johnson et al. (2008) discuss the concept of *psychological fitness*, defined as the "emotional or mental stability of a professional that is most relevant to one's capacity to practice safely and effectively" (p. 590).

As students and young professionals, we will likely increase the chance of doing good work and decrease the chances of unintentionally doing harm when we look out for our own health and choose to be fully present with each client, as opposed to dealing with internal struggles and feeling preoccupied. Failure to self-reflect and self-regulate can lead to consultant impairment. Impairment has been broadly defined as "encompassing diminished professional functioning attributable to personal distress, burnout, and /or substance abuse and . . . unethical and incompetent professional behavior" (Forrest, Elman, Gizara, & Vacha-Haase, 1999, pp. 631–632). According to the ACA Ethics Code C.2.g. (2014), impaired consultants should "limit, suspend, or terminate" their work until impairment has ceased.

Supervisors can be useful in assessing student well-being, as many ethical codes across the helping professions discuss the supervisor's role as a gatekeeper for the profession (e.g., ACA Ethics Code F.6, 2014). Should a student or young professional be deemed unfit to see clients, supervisors can provide recommendations for medical or psychological assistance, and, in some cases, additional training and coursework.

Case Example: Ethical Decision-Making in Action

The following paragraph presents the case of "Jane." The authors of this chapter sought to incorporate several potential ethical issues into this case so that readers may exercise their ethical knowledge and judgment in identifying and processing potential outcomes:

> *Jane is a 20-year-old female tennis player in her junior year of college. She's currently ranked at number five in singles and number three in doubles in her university's conference. Jane feels that she can be ranked higher if given the opportunity and is very dedicated to the team. She is sensitive, emotional, and cries easily (i.e., when she is both happy and sad). During practices and matches, she displays verbalized, negative self-talk, which leads to her not performing at her best. The negativity is contagious, as it upsets her teammates, and no one seems to be able to calm Jane down. Her coach is supportive of Jane overall, but is really tired of her behavior, specifically when it affects the team climate. At the end of the season, Jane considered retiring instead of playing for her senior year. Her coach sensed that Jane needed to talk to someone outside of the team and referred her to you. During the intake, Jane reveals to you that she has not talked to her coach about retiring or any other plans for her senior year; however, when you review informed consent, she says that she is comfortable with you telling the coach that she met with you. She cries from the start of the session and rather consistently for the next 50 minutes that you are with her. Because of her inconsolable crying, it is difficult to make sense of Jane's story and presenting concerns. You are frustrated and at a loss to be helpful to her. Nevertheless, at the end of the session, Jane indicates that she wants to come back next week. Jane left the session and went straight to practice. Less than 30 minutes go by, and you receive a call from her coach, who asks you: "What the heck is going on with Jane?"*

In order to identify, explore, and resolve the potential ethical issues in this case, we will use the eight-step ethical decision-making model described by Corey, Haynes, Moulton, and Muratori (2010) in their textbook of clinical supervision in helping professions:

Step 1: Identify the Ethical Problem or Dilemma

In this case, we have identified three possible ethical dilemmas. First, there is the dilemma of whether to respond to the coach's inquiry about what is going on with Jane. Second, there is an issue of the competence of the consultant. Third, the consultant's frustration may be interfering with the consultation.

Step 2: Identify Potential Issues Involved

Potential issues involved in Jane's case are informed consent, confidentiality, competency, countertransference, client safety, and multiple roles. Keep in mind that these are potential issues, so there may be more or fewer depending on how the case is conceptualized.

Step 3: Review Ethical Codes and Guidelines

For this case, we are using the AASP Ethics Code (2015b) to guide our decision-making process. The following principles and standards are applicable to this case: Competence (Principle A), Multiple Roles (Standard 9), Boundaries (Standard 2), Informed Consent (Standard 17), Confidentiality (Standard 18), Referrals (Standard 12), and Do No Harm (Standard 6).

Step 4: Know Applicable Laws and Regulations

The consultant needs to be aware of NCAA regulations regarding mandated sessions and benefits to athletes. Additionally, the consultant must be aware of state laws regarding licensure and competency (e.g., not being a psychologist, diagnosing Jane).

Step 5: Obtain Consultation

The consultant should meet with the supervisor to discuss the case and explore the consultant's feelings of frustration. Also, during this supervision session, the consultant should determine the best course of action.

Step 6: Brainstorm Possible and Probable Courses of Action

First, to address the coach's inquiry, the options include the following: (a) Tell coach about Jane's attendance, as Jane provided informed consent to do so. However, the consultant should not disclose the details of Jane's case with the coach. (b) If Jane had not provided consent to disclose her attendance, then the consultant would not be able to discuss this case. Second, to address the issue of Jane's case falling outside of the consultant's competency, he/she must take into consideration his/her training and experiences in conjunction with consulting with a supervisor. If the supervisor and consultant determine that Jane's case is outside of the consultant's competency, then a referral should be made. Third, to address the issue of the consultant's frustration with Jane's case, the options include the following: (a) discuss the possibility of countertransference with the supervisor, (b) address the consultant's self-care, and (c) address the consultant's source of frustration (e.g., consultant self-doubt, Jane's crying).

Step 7: Enumerate the Consequences of Various Decisions

If the consultant chooses not to tell the coach anything about Jane's case, then it is possible that the coach will (a) become angry with the consultant, (b) hold it against Jane, or (c) stop making referrals to the consultant. If the consultant does disclose details of Jane's case, then it is possible that the coach will continue to ask for more information and that Jane could feel that her confidentiality has been compromised. If the consultant chooses to continue to work with Jane (i.e., the case is within his/her competency), then the consequences may include (a) continuing to be frustrated with Jane and jeopardize rapport and (b) having to continue to explore feelings of frustration with the consultation during supervision. If the consultant chooses to continue to work with Jane, and it is not in his/her competency, the probable consequences include (a) doing more harm than good for Jane and (b) continuing to be frustrated. If the consultant refers Jane to a third-party because it is outside of his/her competency, then it is possible that Jane becomes distressed or feels abandoned and/or that Jane chooses to no longer seek help.

Step 8: Decide on the Best Course of Action

A prudent course of action in Jane's case, based on all of the information gathered would be as follows:

1. Educate the coach about confidentiality as it applies to Jane's case.
2. Inform the coach that Jane is attending sport psychology consultations, but the content of those sessions is confidential.

3. Consult with the supervisor to discuss the case and explore frustrations related to Jane's session.
4. Based on previous training and current supervision, determine the consultant's level of competency to work with this client or if a referral is needed. If a referral or clinical treatment is deemed necessary, proceed to steps 5 and 6.
5. Meet with Jane to explain the referral process and that sport psychology consulting can still be an option for her tennis-related concerns if she so chooses.
6. Lastly, recommend that in order for sport psychology consulting to be most effective, she should simultaneously see someone for personal counseling.

Concluding Thoughts

The benefits of serving as a sport psychology consultant can be numerous and fulfilling. However, as evidenced in the previous pages, consultants are likely to encounter many ethical dilemmas. The purpose of this chapter was to help students and young professionals to better identify and conceptualize scenarios in which a professional and/or personal risk is involved. A discussion of the foregoing topics will help advance your understanding and application of ethical concepts in your training and practice. Additionally, while "sticky situations" may be challenging, it is our hope that you will find ethics to be both practical and useful, due to the important role they will play in your consulting endeavors.

References

American Counseling Association. (2014). *2014 ACA code of ethics*. Retrieved from http://www. counseling.org/resources/aca-code-of-ethics.pdf

American Psychological Association. (2010). *Ethical principles of psychologists and code of conduct*. Retrieved from http://www.apa.org/ethics/code/index.aspx

American Psychological Association, Division 47: Exercise and Sport Psychology. (2015). *APA sport psychology proficiency*. Retrieved from http://www.apadivisions.org/division-47/about/sport-proficiency/index.aspx

Andersen, M. B., Van Raalte, J. L., & Brewer, B. W. (2001). Sport psychology service delivery: Staying ethical while keeping loose. *Professional Psychology: Research and Practice*, 32(1), 12–18.

Association for Applied Sport Psychology. (2015a). *Become a certified consultant*. Retrieved from http://www.appliedsportpsych.org/certified-consultants/become-a-certified-consultant

Association for Applied Sport Psychology. (2015b). *Ethics code: AASP ethical principles and standards*. Retrieved from http://www.appliedsportpsych.org/about/ethics/ethics-code

Barnett, J. E., Baker, E. K., Elman, N. S., & Schoener, G. R. (2007). In pursuit of wellness: The self-care imperative. *Professional Psychology: Research and Practice*, 38(6), 603–612.

Blom, L. C., Visek, A. J., & Harris, B. S. (2014). Ethical issues in youth sport consulting. In E. F. Etzel & J. C. Watson (Eds.), *Ethical issues in sport, exercise, and performance psychology* (pp. 25–32). Morgantown, WV: Fitness Information Technology.

British Psychological Society. (2015). *Sport and exercise psychology*. Retrieved from http://www.bps.org.uk

Brown, J. L., & Cogan, K. D. (2006). Ethical clinical practice and sport psychology: When two worlds collide. *Ethics & Behavior*, 16(1), 15–23.

Burke, K. L., & Johnson, J. J. (1992). The sport psychologist-coach dual role position: A rebuttal to Ellickson and Brown (1990). *Journal of Applied Sport Psychology*, 4, 51–55.

Cha, M., Haddadi, H., Benevenuto, F., & Gummadi, K. (2010). Measuring user influence in Twitter: The million follower fallacy. In *International AAAI Conference on Weblogs and Social Media*. Retrieved from https://www.aaai.org/ocs/index.php/ICWSM/ICWSM10/paper/view/1538

Corey, G., Haynes, R., Moulton, P., & Muratori, M. (2010). *Clinical supervision in the helping professions: A practical guide* (2nd ed.). Alexandria, VA: American Counseling Association.

Cotterill, S. T., & Symes, R. (2004). Integrating social media and new technologies into your practice as a sport psychology consultant. *Sport & Exercise Psychology Review*, 10(1), 55–64.

Etzel, E. F. (2014). Some impressions on ethics in sport and exercise psychology. In E. F. Etzel & J. C. Watson (Eds.), *Ethical issues in sport, exercise, and performance psychology* (pp. 3–11). Morgantown, WV: Fitness Information Technology.

Fisher, C. B., & Oransky, M. (2008). Informed consent to psychotherapy: Protecting the dignity and respecting the autonomy of patients. *Journal of Clinical Psychology, 64*(5), 576–588.

Forrest, L., Elman, N., Gizara, S., & Vacha-Haase, T. (1999). Trainee impairment: A review of identification, remediation, dismissal, and legal issues. *The Counseling Psychologist, 27*(5), 627–686.

Gardner, F. L. (1991). Professionalization of sport psychology: A reply to Silva. *The Sport Psychologist, 5*, 55–60.

Gutheil, T. G., & Gabbard, G. O. (1998). Misuses and misunderstandings of boundary theory in clinical and regulatory settings. *American Journal of Psychiatry, 155*, 409–414.

Johnson, W. B., Forrest, L., Rodolfa, E., Elman, N. S., Robiner, W. N., & Schaffer, J. B. (2008). Addressing professional competence problems in trainees: Some ethical considerations. *Professional Psychology: Research and Practice, 39*(6), 589–599.

Jones, L., Evans, L., & Mullen, R. (2007). Multiple roles in applied setting: Trainee sport psychologist, coach, and researcher. *The Sport Psychologist, 21*, 210–226.

King, N. M. P., & Churchill, L. R. (2008). Clinical research and the physician-patient relationship: The dual roles of physician and researcher. In P. A. Singer & A. M. Viens (Eds.), *The Cambridge textbook of bioethics* (pp. 214–221). Cambridge: Cambridge University Press.

Knapp, S., & VandeCreek, L. (2006). *Practical ethics for psychologists: A positive approach*. Washington, DC: American Psychological Association.

Koocher, G. P., & Keith-Spiegel, P. (2008). *Ethics in psychology and the mental health professions: Standards and cases* (3rd ed.). Oxford, NY: Oxford University Press.

Lamb, D., & Catanzaro, S. (1998). Sexual and nonsexual boundary violations involving psychologists, clients, supervisees, and students: Implications for professional practice. *Professional Psychology: Research and Practice, 29*, 498–503.

Little, G., & Harwood, C. (2010). Enhancing our understanding of the potential violation of sexual boundaries in sport psychology consultancy. *Journal of Clinical Sport Psychology, 4*, 302–311.

Lubker, J. R., & Andersen, M. B. (2014). Ethical issues in supervision: Client welfare, practitioner development, and professional gatekeeping. In E. F. Etzel & J. C. Watson (Eds.), *Ethical issues in sport, exercise, and performance psychology* (pp. 151–162). Morgantown, WV: Fitness Information Technology.

Moleski, S. M., & Kiselica, M. S. (2005). Dual relationships: A continuum ranging from the destructive to the therapeutic. *Journal of Counseling & Development, 83*(1), 3–11.

National Collegiate Athletic Association. (2015). *NCAA Division I manual*. Indianapolis, IN: NCAA.

Silva, J. M. (1989). Toward the professionalization of sport psychology. *The Sport Psychologist, 3*, 265–273.

Speight, S. L., & Vera, E. M. (1997). Similarity and difference in multicultural counseling: Considering the attraction and repulsion hypotheses. *The Counseling Psychologist, 25*(2), 280–298.

Stevens, L. M., & Andersen, M. B. (2007). Transference and countertransference in sport psychology service delivery: Part I. A review of erotic attraction. *Journal of Applied Sport Psychology, 19*, 253–269.

Taylor, J. (1994). Examining the boundaries of sport science and psychology trained practitioners in applied sport psychology: Title usage and area of competence. *Journal of Applied Sport Psychology, 6*, 185–195.

Watson, J. C., & Clement, D. (2008). Ethical and practical issues related to multiple role relationships in sport psychology. *Athletic Insight, 10*(4). Retrieved from http://www.athleticinsight.com/Vol10Iss4/Multiple.htm

Watson, J. C., Clement, D., Harris, B., Leffingwell, T. R., & Hurst, J. (2006). Teacher-practitioner multiple-role issues in sport psychology. *Ethics & Behavior, 16*(1), 41–59.

Watson, J. C., Zizzi, S., & Etzel, E. F. (2006). Ethical training in sport psychology programs: Current training standards. *Ethics & Behavior, 16*, 5–14.

Yambor, J., & Connelly, D. (1991). Issues confronting female sport psychology consultants working with male student-athletes. *The Sport Psychologist, 5*, 304–312.

4 Being Comfortable With Being Uncomfortable

Expanding Your Competence Zone

Laura Reutlinger, Jeb Clay, Jessica Eichner, and Cindra Kamphoff

Starting out in a new field of practice is a daunting task for any sport psychology consultant in training. In the beginning stages of limited knowledge and limited experience, feelings of uncertainty and being uncomfortable are common occurrences. When a consultant in training does not embrace being uncomfortable, it can be detrimental to the client receiving services. Being unable to embrace uncomfortable moments can lead the consultant in training to experience discouragement and a lack of confidence, and can lead them to make an unclear decision about what the client needs in the moment.

A common goal for consultants in training in sport psychology is to cultivate competence in their zone of practice in order to best serve the client. Feeling uncomfortable while cultivating competence is normal and should be expected. However, a consultant in training who is able to be comfortable with being uncomfortable will be able to expand his or her competence zone more quickly and continue to grow throughout his or her professional career.

Three Factors That Allow You to Be Comfortable Being Uncomfortable

The key to becoming comfortable with the uncomfortable is to push beyond perceived barriers and limitations in order to increase competence as a consultant in training. We believe that the ability to consistently push past perceived barriers in order to increase competency as a consultant in training is contingent upon three factors:

1. Cultivating a growth mindset: embracing challenges and persisting in the face of setbacks and perceived limitations, as these situations are seen as opportunities for learning, development, and expanding competence zones.
2. Implementing deliberate practice: seeking activities and opportunities that specifically are designed to improve competence and the level of performance of a consultant.
3. Fostering a supervisory relationship with a mentor: gaining the assistance of a developed professional to help guide consultants in training through feedback and reflective practice.

Learning, practicing, and utilizing support from others are consistent themes that appear in the process of improving at anything in life, and the keys to improving consulting are no different. Throughout this chapter, we provide an explanation of the literature, examples of our own personal experiences, and practical implications to help guide consultants in training to work beyond perceived barriers and limitations. With the information provided, it is our hope that consultants in training will be more willing to embrace challenges, seek opportunities to grow in order to better serve their clients, and gain support from supervisors or mentors in order to expand their competence and learn to be comfortable being uncomfortable.

Factor 1: Cultivating a Growth Mindset

Carol Dweck is one of the world's leading researchers in the field of motivation with a focus on why people succeed and ways to foster success (Dweck, 2010). In her book, *Mindset: The new psychology of success*, Dweck (2006) coined the terms "fixed mindset" and "growth mindset" in order to help us understand the way in which individuals view challenges and develop motivation in the face of setbacks. Fixed mindset and growth mindset can be applied to gaining success in a number of areas throughout life, including education and professional development.

Growth-minded individuals embrace challenges and persist in the face of setbacks, as growth-minded individuals see these situations as opportunities for learning and development. When embracing a growth mindset, effort is viewed as necessary for achievement in order to keep stretching beyond perceived limits. According to Dweck (2006), effort is what ignites ability and promotes growth over time. A growth-minded consultant in training seeks out new learning opportunities and takes on challenges in order to stretch his or her knowledge and ability. A growth-minded consultant would see talent as a trait to build on and develop, not a trait that is simply on display (Dweck, 2009). From a consulting perspective, there is always room for improvement, and consultants in training should always be looking for opportunities to reach beyond the level of which they thought they were capable. Growth-minded consultants in training learn from criticism and find inspiration in the success of others because they are able to learn from the ideas and experiences of others. For example, when an individual meeting with a client does not go smoothly, a consultant in training should seek feedback from a peer or a mentor. Listening to objective feedback about the situation can help the consultant recognize areas for improvement. Reflection on received feedback and development of a plan for improvement will help expand competence for future sessions. Consistent evaluation of work and striving to make improvements will allow consultants in training to embrace a growth mindset and take on challenges with determination to be the best consultants they can be.

Fixed-minded individuals tend to avoid challenges and quit in the face of setbacks because they perceive failure as a sign that they are incapable. Effort is seen as pointless and threatening because ability and talent are viewed as traits that should come natural and easy. A fixed-minded individual likely would ignore critical feedback because the feedback questions his or her ability, and the success of others is viewed as threatening to his or her status at the top of the rank (Dweck, 2006). Consultants in training with a fixed mindset will not be able to effectively enhance their knowledge or ability because they may not seek opportunities outside their comfort zone. Fixed-minded consultants in training may not utilize peers as resources for feedback because their peers are seen as the competition rather than guiding forces. Due to the factors listed previously, it is difficult for fixed-minded consultants in training to continue to grow and change as professionals. They likely will be uncomfortable with change and pushing themselves to expand their zone of competence. Fixed-minded consultants in training remain stagnant because they are unwilling to try new methods that challenge their competence. As the field of Applied Sport Psychology continues to develop, fixed-minded consultants will get left behind, as they refuse to follow the changing trend of development within the field.

In the educational setting, a growth mindset has been shown to improve academic performance of students at all levels. Yeager and Dweck (2012), for example, examined the effects of implicit theories on students' academic and social resilience. The differences between entity theory (or fixed mindset) and incremental theory (or growth mindset) demonstrated a significant influence of mindset on academic success. Results of Yeager and Dweck's study showed that mindsets are malleable, and a growth mindset will foster greater resiliency in the face of academic and social challenges. For example, examination of mindset perspective and grade point average (GPA) showed that students with an incremental theory perspective, or growth mindset, were able to improve their GPA about .23 points throughout the course of one academic year (Yeager & Dweck, 2012). This research is particularly applicable for consultants in training because it demonstrates the importance of learning from challenges and setbacks. Students who embraced challenge and used feedback to learn showed greater improvement over time than students who accepted failure as the end-all option (Yeager & Dweck, 2012). Consultants in training will experience setbacks and failure over the course of their training, but they will be able to show greater improvement over time by embracing a growth mindset throughout their professional career.

Yeager and Dweck suggested that training on mindsets in academic settings, rather than training on boosting one's self-esteem, would be more beneficial in helping students overcome challenges with effort and embracing new problem-solving skills. Overcoming challenges with a growth mindset will help consultants in training foster new problem-solving skills and develop new approaches for interpreting feedback from others to enhance their professional consulting skills. Embracing a growth mindset will allow a consultant to grow and expand with the field. A growth-minded consultant will see the changing field as an opportunity to stay current and provide the best experience for his or her clients.

A growth mindset has been found to (a) foster a healthier attitude toward practice and learning by embracing challenges, (b) foster a hunger for feedback, (c) lead to greater resiliency, and (d) significantly improve performance over time (Dweck, 2009). Leaders with a growth mindset can have a positive effect on their peers, leading their peers to greater success in sport and in life (Chase, 2010). Chase defined leadership as a behavioral process of influencing individuals and groups toward set goals or specific objectives, which significantly impacts the thoughts, behaviors, and feelings of other people. Based on this definition, a consultant in training is becoming a leader, as he or she would be leading clients on a journey toward performance enhancement. Research in leadership has suggested that the ability to lead can be learned and has also demonstrated that growth-minded leaders can have greater positive influence on their employees (Chase, 2010). These results implicate that a consultant in training can learn to be a leader. As consultants in training continue to grow as professionals, they can use their leadership skills to have a greater, more effective influence on their clients. Dweck (2006) suggested that a leader's fixed or growth view of his or her abilities to lead can greatly influence whether or not (s)he is an effective leader. A consultant with a growth mindset can pass the ability to learn with a growth mindset on to his or her clients by serving as a role model. Setting a good example for clients by embodying the principles of a growth mindset will in turn help clients develop a growth mindset for their own journey.

Jim Collins (2001) stated that the top, most influential executives inspire others to develop a growth mindset by demonstrating a growth mindset within themselves. A study of CEOs from some of the world's top companies revealed that CEOs with a growth mindset believe leadership is about growth, a passion to get better, and having gratitude toward others (Chase, 2010). Collins further suggested that most people have the potential to evolve into top executives under the right circumstances, meaning that consultants in training can transform themselves into effective consultants given the right environment. Effective environments for developing top consultants include self-reflection, conscious personal development, and involvement with a mentor or teacher (Collins, 2001). A growth-minded consultant in training will seek out a trusted supervisor or mentor to gain feedback. A growth-minded consultant in training will also set aside time for self-reflection in order to recognize areas for improvement and develop plans to make improvements. Taking time to deliberate on feedback from peers and personal feedback will allow a consultant in training to determine his or her own path to success.

Fluctuation between a fixed and growth mindset will occur within an individual over time. People have elements of both fixed mindset and growth mindset in different areas of their lives (Dweck, 2006). For example, a consultant in training may have a growth mindset working with a small group of athletes but a fixed mindset working with a large group. Adopting a growth mindset for multiple consulting styles and environments can help individuals work through challenging situations and the adversity that life presents. Maintaining a growth mindset is not an easy task; however, embracing a positive, growth mindset gives people the courage to work harder and go after their goals (Dweck, 2006). Adopting a growth mindset allows people to go from a "judge and be judged" framework to a "learn and help learn" framework (Dweck, 2006). Growth-minded consultants will be focused on learning and enhancing their own skills as professionals while helping clients to learn and enhance their skills as well, rather than being focused on acquiring the label of being a "good consultant." Adopting a growth mindset will allow consultants in training to embrace opportunities to learn, which promotes consistent growth and development as a professional.

My Experience in Consulting: Cultivating a Growth Mindset

My (LR) first experience with an individual client was particularly anxiety producing because it was uncharted territory for me. I was very nervous to be in an individual session with a client, dependent only on my own knowledge to lead the session. As a student still learning, I was unsure if I could help another person enhance his or her performance. As I talked to my peer about this anxiety, I realized it was natural and normal to be nervous, and embracing this discomfort was my only option.

I quickly realized that going into the session feeling underqualified and underprepared was not the way I wanted to start off my career as a sport psychology consultant. The nervousness I felt going into my first session scared me into a realization that feeling comfortable was completely up to me. This was the beginning of the growth mindset mentality for my consulting practice. I knew that I was going to need to use these interactions as learning opportunities to develop my consulting style. Peer feedback played an integral role in my development as a consultant. I sought advice from others in my graduate program to get their opinions and feedback. I was given feedback regarding ideas for workshop activities, concepts to cover during sessions, and ways in which to tweak my consulting style to be more effective. I interpreted their feedback in a manner that would be beneficial to my growth as a consultant. For example, when I received feedback from a peer who suggested I should present confidence in a less theoretical way at a workshop with a high school basketball team, I saw the feedback as a way to grow and develop my skills. I self-reflected on my sessions through mental and video playback. My self-reflections combined with peer feedback allowed me to adjust my consulting style in an approach that fit with my personality and my goals as a consultant.

Going into the second individual session, I cultivated a growth mindset. This perspective allowed me to see failure as feedback, and I was able to put on a confident face in front of my client. I would tell myself that I was the expert in the room, and I needed to speak with confidence and conviction. If I presented myself in this manner, as if I was 100 percent sure on all the material I was presenting, the client would not know that butterflies were circling in my stomach. I worked to embrace the butterflies. I left the second session feeling much better about my consulting abilities and knowledge within the field. Following my first individual consulting session, I made a commitment to myself to enhance my professional development in any way I could, reading material related to the field and seeking opportunities to gain experience. I wanted to make sure I was as prepared as I could be going into each interaction with a client, so I could help the client in the best way possible. Embracing a growth mindset has helped me develop as a consultant because I am able to see every opportunity as a chance to learn. The pressure to be perfect is minimized when I know that no matter how the session goes, I would be able to learn something from each experience. I looked at my career development as a lifelong learning process, rather than a race to get to a finite state at the top. Committing to enhancing my own confidence as a consultant has significantly helped my professional development over the last year. The feeling of being uncomfortable before workshops or sessions has never completely gone away, but I look at it as a sign that I am continuing to push myself beyond my comfort zone and enhance my competence. Nerves are part of embarking on something unknown. I do not know what my limit is or will be when it comes to consulting knowledge. If I am continuously pushing myself to be better, I do not think there is a limit because the field is always growing and changing. New knowledge is presented almost every day, and, if I am to continue to improve, I welcome the nerves as a sign of challenge and growth.

Practical Implications for Cultivating a Growth Mindset

Embracing a growth mindset will allow a consultant in training to continue to learn and develop as the profession continues to grow. Through self-reflection and supervision from a mentor, a consultant in training can be constantly monitoring his or her progress and make changes where needed in order to succeed. Developing as a consultant is a challenging time with many roadblocks and setbacks. Appreciating a growth mindset will help a consultant in training learn from these challenges and discover new ways of thinking and delivering his or her message to clients in a more efficient manner. Here are several ways you can develop a growth mindset:

- **Self-reflection.** Reflect on your experiences daily. Look for areas where you can improve, as well as areas where you are succeeding. Reflecting on your personal experiences will help to foster a growth mindset, allowing you to continue to develop as a professional. Recognizing areas where you need improvement leads to the next step of developing a plan to advance in these areas.
- **Seek out learning opportunities.** Pursuing learning opportunities will help you advance in the areas where you need improvement. Embracing a growth mindset means approaching challenges with a drive to learn and succeed. Taking on the challenge of increasing your knowledge of theories and practice will help to enhance your zone of competence, allowing you to be more comfortable in situations where you were not comfortable before. Potential learning opportunities may include personal development classes in subjects such as positive psychology or skills such as public speaking, reading new research studies and books, or observing other professionals in your area of interest.
- **Collaborate with a supervisor or mentor.** Work in partnership with a supervisor who will serve as your mentor as you grow in your professional career. A mentor will be able to provide you with direction and feedback regarding your consulting practice and business development. A mentor can also assist you with ethical dilemmas that are sure to occur throughout your interactions with clients.

- **Embrace feedback from peers.** Your peers are an excellent resource for collaborating for professional development. Embracing their feedback is an integral part of growing as a consultant. Reflecting on ideas presented with your peers can allow you to consciously make improvements to your consulting practice.
- **Overcome adversity with growth.** Challenges and adversity are anticipated elements of a consultant in training's experience. Knowing how to approach and overcome these challenges with a growth mindset will help you continue to advance in your professional practice. Seeing challenges as an opportunity to learn is a key feature to growth. Embrace self-reflection and peer feedback to develop a plan for overcoming adversity.
- **Practice what you preach.** Set a good example for your peers and your clients by practicing the same growth mindset that you are asking them to adopt. We cannot ask our clients to embrace a growth mindset if we are not willing to do so ourselves because clients will see through the hypocrisy. Practicing what you preach will allow you to learn from your own experiences and bring those lessons into your consulting practice, which will in turn be beneficial for building rapport with your clients.

Factor 2: Implementing Deliberate Practice

Ericsson, Krampe, and Tesch-Römer (1993) stated that achieving expert performance is a slow process that requires roughly 10 years or 10,000 hours of deliberate practice. Deliberate practice consists of taking part in activities that are designed specifically to increase performance. Deliberate practice involves two areas of growth: improving previously learned skills and extending the reach and range of these skills (Ericsson, Prietula, & Cokely, 2007). As a consultant in training, deliberate practice involves seeking out and taking part in opportunities in which there is an explicit goal of increasing competency. For example, if a consultant in training wants to improve working with a softball team, he or she must seek out opportunities to work with softball athletes. The consultant in training must put forth intentional effort in order to expand his or her competence zone, but there must also be careful examination and feedback from a mentor (Ericsson et al., 1993). Becoming an expert requires a mentor that is able to give constructive and even painful feedback (Ericsson et al., 2007).

Ericsson et al. (1993) defined deliberate practice as "a highly structured activity where the explicit goal of which is to improve performance" (p. 368). The researchers argued that this process is not inherently enjoyable, due to the goal of simply "improving" rather than generating external rewards such as money or social status. Being comfortable with the uncomfortable calls for consultants in training to be placed in situations that may test their ability to stay motivated, like working with an individual or team in which they have no previous knowledge. Gaining experience in new situations is important to increasing competence as they allow the individual to continuously grow and improve through deliberate practice. Examples of new situations could include working with a team by yourself for the first time, working with a sport that you have little or no experience participating in, or even working with a team of the opposite gender.

Being willing and ready to participate in any situation is crucial to deliberate practice as well as gaining competency. Being proactive in these situations will expand the range of skills the consultant in training has to offer. Since deliberate practice is not particularly enjoyable, the consultants in training must work to cultivate and maintain their intrinsic motivation for consulting. Self-determination theory, which discusses the continuum of motivation from extrinsic to intrinsic, has three basic tenets of motivational needs:

autonomy, relatedness, and competency. All of the three elements of self-determination theory are crucial for consultants in training when dealing with prolonged uncomfortable tasks; they are essential for functioning and optimal development (Deci & Ryan, 2011). Writing a specific goal of what area(s) the consultant would like to improve will increase the autonomy the consultant in training has while delivering services. Surrounding one-self with like-minded individuals that have similar life and career goals will increase the amount of relatedness an individual feels while being placed in uncomfortable situations. To increase competence, the consultant in training should search for multiple opportunities to teach the same skill; as Ericsson et al. (1993) stated, "Deliberate practice would allow for repeated experiences in which the individual can attend to the critical aspects of the situation and incrementally improve her or his performance in response to knowledge of results, feedback, or both from a teacher" (p. 368).

Experience is essential for becoming an expert or achieving mastery but is not the most significant piece of enhancing competence. Simply "doing" does not equate to deliberate practice. Consultants in training typically begin practice under the supervision of a mentor and gradually climb the ranks of competence. In the beginning of this process, experience or "doing" is necessary in order to understand the basics of the tasks required. A consultant in training can become more proficient by gaining more experience. However, the key to becoming an expert is to move beyond "the basics" by implementing continuous improvement and gaining feedback from a mentor. If the consultant in training continues to implement deliberate practice techniques, then mastery can be reached (Ericsson, 2006). These deliberate practice techniques would include setting a specific goal for each task, reflecting on feedback given, and creating new tasks designed for overcoming any weaknesses that may be apparent.

My Experience in Consulting With Deliberate Practice

In the fall of 2014, my (JC) second year as a sport psychology graduate student, I began working with my first female team. The structure of this relationship included weekly team workshops delivered by myself, several other graduate students, and my supervisor, as well as brief individual sessions. We did not start our individual sessions until we had delivered three team workshops, so I was familiar with all of the individuals on this team.

Going into the first week of individual sessions, I was a little nervous about what to expect while working with female athletes. I did my very best to be objective, to be open-minded, and to work to understand their perspective as I entered the room for my first session. I needed to be crisp, confident, and relaxed in order to provide the best services possible to each athlete throughout the evening of sessions.

On the first day of individual meetings, my first client, "A," walked into the room a few minutes late. She was apologetic about her tardiness and immediately started questioning what we were supposed to do in these individual meetings.

A: So, what are we supposed to do here? Tell you about everything that is bothering us?
JC: These sessions are meant for you to get more individualized work on your mental game. Is there something you would like to discuss at the moment?
A: Well, I'm just having a really tough time with my coach; I just don't think she cares about me at all.

Before I had any time to explain what, how, or why these individual sessions were supposed to work, I was thrust into a crucial conversation. I was able to facilitate this session in order to understand her current frustrations, as well as gain a background of her sport experiences. I knew this athlete would need a lot of guidance as we continued to work together.

I was able to understand the issues "A" was having with her coach. At times, she would be very receptive to our work, and other times she seemed to have no hope at all about her sport or resolving any of the issues she mentioned. She eventually opened up to me that she was debating quitting the team. I was very objective with her during these conversations, and we discussed both quitting and continuing with the team.

The relationship continued in this way for about half of the athletic season and then had a major turning point that stretched my competence zone. "A" came into the session looking a little more distraught than usual. As we started the session, she became more visibly upset and then began to speak very emotionally.

A: Well, something really bad happened to me this summer that I'm just really depressed about and I can't let go.

JC: Thanks for telling me this.

A: (Tears starting to form) It's just something that I hate thinking about and I just feel so bad about it.

JC: Is this something that you feel is affecting your daily life, and your performance?

A: I think so; I just can't stop thinking about that day last summer. I'm really trying everything I can to be happy, but it's just not working. I hate that I can't be happy anymore, no matter what I do. I hate who I am because of it.

JC: I can see that you're upset about this incident, and that it's hard for you to be open about it. So this is affecting you daily?

A: Yes, I'm just not happy no matter what I'm doing.

I approached this situation very cautiously and relied on my micro-skills of reflection of feeling, empathy, and paraphrasing when responding to my client. I felt competent in my ability to handle the interaction but was being pushed to the very depths of my ability in this moment. I knew that this athlete needed help that I could not deliver, and I had an ethical responsibility to take action. I responded with honesty, compassion, and a willingness to help her. We had an open discussion about her working with a university counselor and discussed a strategy for following through with this decision.

After this final session, I immediately contacted my supervisor and expressed my desire to refer this athlete to the University Counseling Center. We carefully went through the reasons for my concern and both agreed that this was the correct decision. My supervisor then made a phone call to this department, and we were able to set up a time for "A" to meet with a professional at the university.

Ericsson (2006) stated that deliberate practice calls for "specific tasks that are invented to overcome weaknesses, and performance is carefully monitored to provide cues for ways to improve it further" (p. 368). This experience consisted of deliberate practice because I was able to gain a wide variety of experiences, including the referral process. Specifically, I was able to sharpen my counseling skills, which allowed me to build a strong connection, or rapport, that was crucial for this athlete's well-being. The high level of rapport that was built with this individual enabled her to open up to me and finally receive the proper help that was necessary. Through service delivery and using feedback from a supervisor throughout the process, I was able to enhance my competence zone as a consultant by working with a female team as well as better understanding referral and how to build rapport with clients.

Practical Implications of Implementing Deliberate Practice

Implementing deliberate practice will allow a consultant in training to break past perceived barriers and expand competence during uncomfortable situations. Taking action and being proactive is essential to deliberate practice and expanding knowledge. Deliberate practice can be maintained by applying these tips during your journey:

- **Set goals for each team or individual session.** Set goals for each session, or when you deliver services. Deliberate practice states that a specific goal should be created for each task.
- **Seek explicit feedback related to your goals.** Show your mentor the goals that you have prior to your service delivery. This will allow them to give you direct feedback and measure your proficiency.
- **Gain ample experience working with groups and individuals.** Experience is essential for a consultant in training; remember that it takes 10,000 hours to become an expert. Ask an old high school or youth coach if you can deliver a team session for 30 minutes—every opportunity counts.
- **Listen to feedback, and learn from it.** When you are given feedback in regard to your service delivery, thoroughly digest this information and take action. Go back to the literature, or look into other literature that relates to this topic.
- **Reflect often.** A period of in-depth reflection should take place after service delivery. Create a worksheet that will help you analyze your performance and reflect at a deeper level.
- **Blog for reflection.** Blogging is a great way to document your thoughts about an incident or topic (while protecting confidentiality) and is a way to impact others. A personal blog site can increase competency because it will allow you to write about challenging topics in a nonacademic voice. This form of reflection will allow you to create new goals in the future when similar situations arise.
- **Read other consultants' materials.** Consultants in the field are continuously writing books meant for athletes and coaches. Reading these materials can give you new ideas and help you find your voice. This can help maintain intrinsic motivation as well as guide new goals that you can implement in your practice.
- **Mentor other sport psychology students.** Becoming a mentor to other students is a great way to increase your knowledge and ability to explain the services delivered. Taking on the task to become a peer mentor will allow you to increase your competency in all areas of the field.
- **Implement mental skills training into your life.** Understanding how to use the skills you teach athletes in your own life will drastically increase your competence. This will push you to gain a deeper understanding of what you teach to athletes and allow you to overcome any weaknesses you may see within a specific topic. A tenet of deliberate practice is to strengthen a weakness in your area of expertise.
- **Watch and learn from others.** Study other consultants, business leaders, speakers, or even coaches. Watch how they interact with others and consider what makes them successful. This will help you find your own philosophy and increase competency.
- **Gain related knowledge that is useful.** There are many different areas of study that can positively influence your work as a consultant. Understanding how to implement these teachings will influence your work in a more holistic way.
- **Expand the population you deliver services to.** Expanding your services by working with athletes of different sports, ages, races, genders, religions, sexual orientations,

and ability levels can allow you to increase your competency. Push yourself to work with populations that you have little to no background with. This diversification of clients will expand your competence zone and ability to connect with a variety of individuals.

- **Continue to work on other skills.** In order to increase your competency, set goals to improve upon other skills that influence your delivery. Public speaking, counseling, or even studying other sports that you have little knowledge of will increase your competence when delivering services.

Factor 3: Fostering a Supervisory Relationship With a Mentor

Practicing as a consultant in training in the field of sport psychology requires the application of theory to practice. Theory is primarily taught in the classroom, whereas the application of theory can be practiced with the exposure to teams, athletes, and coaches. Consultants in training generally benefit most from being "thrown into the field" to learn to apply theory to practice (Tonn & Harmison, 2004), and this process can certainly cause the consultant in training to feel uncomfortable! Finding out what works and what does not work when working with teams, athletes, and coaches as a consultant in training is a constant occurrence. This process can be very uncomfortable because consultants in training are working to understand their own style of service delivery, gain competency in the field, and project that competency to athletes and coaches.

The process of training as a consultant should not be done alone. A consultant in training will benefit most from these experiences through the guidance of a mentor, or through the process of mentoring or supervision. Supervision is the process of learning through reflective practice with the assistance of an experienced professional (Hutter, Olden-Veldman, & Oudejans, 2015). Additionally, reflective practice includes bringing self-awareness to one's development as a professional consultant (Stambulova & Johnson, 2010). Reflective practice could include recording experiences that you encountered during workshops or individual sessions or having open conversations with a peer mentor or with your designated supervisor. Supervision is an extremely important aspect of training because you are learning from and being trained by a professional in the field. Learning from your supervisor or peer mentor by asking questions about situations that they have experienced will benefit you when you experience a similar situation in the future (Andersen & Williams-Rice, 1996).

The goal of supervision is to develop competent and ethically sound consultants by allowing them to learn from the experiences of their supervisors or peer mentors (Hutter et al., 2015). Supervisors or peer mentors should be able to educate and provide guidance to consultants in training through their own training and personal experiences in the field. An effective supervisor or peer mentor should aid developing consultants by guiding them through their needs and helping them to overcome doubts or negative behaviors in order to best serve the athlete or client (Andersen & Williams-Rice, 1996). By guiding the consultant in training through doubts that he or she may experience, the supervisor or peer mentor has the opportunity to normalize reservations (and feelings of discomfort) of the consultant in training and reassure him or her that being afraid, nervous, or uncomfortable is part of the learning process.

Through the supervision process, there are many benefits that consultants in training can experience. A supervisor or peer mentor can help the consultant in training understand the best practices of consulting (e.g., how to speak effectively to an audience, how to engage the audience, practicing ethically, developing a consulting philosophy/style) as well as manage the situations that cause stress for the consultant in training (Hutter et al.,

2015). The direct supervisor may not always be able to attend every workshop; therefore, having a peer mentor as well may help provide more immediate feedback. Further, having consultants in training reflect on their experiences as practitioners allows the supervisor or peer mentor to guide them through the learning process, resulting in an improvement of self-awareness of the consultant in training (Hutter et al., 2015) and an acceptance of being comfortable with the uncomfortable. There is no course that can teach consultants in training everything they can expect from consulting. The key is for consultants in training to learn from their experiences and continue to improve. For more discussion on the process, models, and benefits of supervision, please see Chapter 5.

My Experience in Consulting With Fostering a Supervisory Relationship With a Mentor

I (JE) remember the first time I presented part of a workshop for a boys' basketball team. I had been going to plenty of workshops as an observer prior to when I actually presented, but I was still terrified to speak in front of a group of high school boys. Being a female consultant, I was worried that they would not pay attention to anything I had to say or take me seriously. During this particular workshop, I was given the opportunity to present an activity to the group. Leading up to the actual activity, I was so worried about what I was going to say, when I should say it, and how I should present myself in front of this basketball team. I was more confident in the fact that this was an activity that I had done myself prior to the workshop, but I was still uncomfortable because I had never explained it to anyone else, much less a group of high school boys. When the transition happened, letting me know that it was time for my activity, I took a deep breath and found a spark of confidence in the fact that this was already something that I had done before. Then there was a slight turn of events. There was one basketball player that did not have a partner, so I had to become his partner. Not only did I have to explain the activity to this group of boys, but I had to participate in the activity as well. This was something that I was definitely not prepared for, but, knowing that I knew the activity and the objective of the activity, I was confident in trying to relay the underlying message.

However, when I debriefed the activity, I had only one question that I asked the team before I panicked and let another graduate student take over. I botched the debrief, the most important part of an activity. I was so focused on the activity that I did not think ahead to the questions I wanted to ask during the debrief. After the workshop was done, I was looking for any kind of feedback I could get. The graduate students that were there told me not to worry about it and that I had done fine. This was not the type of feedback that I was looking for! Obviously, there was still a lot for me to learn to become comfortable in front of a team. As part of our graduate program, I was paired up with a second-year graduate student (a peer mentor that was assigned by our supervisor) whom I could talk to about these situations. As we sat down to talk, she gave me great advice to take into consideration. She told me to write down all the questions that I had wanted to ask after the workshop was over. This way, I could make reference to those questions for future workshops so I would not forget. Being able to talk to a fellow student in the program and get her feedback was extremely helpful for me as a consultant in training. It was reassuring to know that at one point, she was in the position that I was currently in. Being students under the same supervisor meant that the advice she was giving to me was probably advised to her. So, even though I was not speaking directly with my supervisor, the supervisor's experience was translated through my peer mentor. I was able to learn from that experience and take steps toward becoming a better consultant. I was comfortable approaching the second-year consultant that I was paired with to ask her questions. Knowing that she was also in my position made me feel better about asking those questions without being ridiculed. She was able to give me advice, free from judgment, and I was able to grow from the mistakes I had made. Having supervision from my professors and from a second-year graduate student in my program, I am able to ask questions and bounce ideas off them and receive the feedback I need. I found comfort in knowing that I can trust my cohorts and professors because they want me to succeed and do well. Knowing they believe in me relieves tension in approaching them for advice or asking them a question. In order to grow, you have to expand your competence zone by asking questions and seeking supervision.

Practical Implications for Fostering a Supervisory Relationship With a Mentor

The supervisor is not meant to hold the hands of the consultants in training throughout their training process. Instead, the supervisor should allow the consultants in training to experience challenging situations, knowing that there is a professional to aid them through their decision-making process. The process of supervision should help build independence as well as autonomy.

Here are several ways you can develop and properly utilize supervision:

- **Find a supervisor.** Supervision promotes both autonomy and independence as well as prevents the consultants in training from "doing harm" to their clients. Gaining a supervisor will allow you to openly address issues with him or her, thereby creating competence and problem-solving abilities. There are two types of supervision: direct and indirect. Direct supervision is when the supervisor is physically present and able to give you feedback immediately or when the supervisor watches a video of your work and provides feedback. Indirect supervision is when you are able to report to your supervisor after the fact and receive feedback. Supervision, or mentorship, is required to gain certification from the Association for Applied Sport Psychology (CC-AASP).
- **Engage in regular reflective practice with your supervisor.** As a consultant in training, reflecting on your own experiences with a supervisor will allow you to grow. This will allow you to gain an understanding of your own strengths and weaknesses and, with the help of a supervisor, work toward improvement. For example, if you were having trouble connecting with the athletes in a team session, you could reflect on your experiences and then discuss the situation with your supervisor. Your supervisor could then provide you with feedback for improvement.
- **Ask about specific topics within supervision.** This should include how to build rapport with clients, conduct an intake session, keep records of the sessions, and understand ethical considerations. The consultant in training could provide mock individual sessions that could take place with another graduate student, or your supervisor could watch a recording of your work with a client (with the client's permission).
- **Enroll in counseling course(s).** Taking several counseling courses will allow the consultant in training to gain experience with a "client" and gain experiences in the listening and reflection skills that are essential to be an effective consultant. In addition, consultants in training could use these counseling courses to practice self-reflection in order to increase their awareness while interacting with clients.
- **Gain a high professional self-efficacy (Tod, Andersen, & Marchant, 2011).** This type of self-efficacy occurs when the developing consultants view client interactions as nonthreatening. They start to implement coping strategies to deal with stressful

situations and learn how to handle stressful situations appropriately. Being able to handle situations like this allows developing consultants to build self-efficacy and competence in their ability to be effective consultants.

- **Establish a professional philosophy (Poczwardowski, Sherman, & Ravizza, 2004).** Creating and recording a professional philosophy will reinforce personal core beliefs and values and help guide your practice. Understanding your professional philosophy will allow you to consider how you consult, your role with the client, your goals as a consultant, and interventions to implement.
- **Try the key validation process (Skovholt & Ronnestad, 1992).** This process allows you to try different consulting styles and find what works best for you. In order to see what works and what does not work for you, you should try different consulting styles during workshops and individual sessions. If it does not feel good to you, then you should consider a different approach.
- **Practicing client-led sessions.** Practicing mock sessions will allow the consultant in training to learn how to ask questions and direct conversations in a way that facilitates the conversation rather than trying to actively problem solve or find a solution.
- **Use a metasupervision model.** Metasupervision is the supervision of supervision. Within a metasupervision model, the main supervisor oversees peer supervision in order to educate and further expand knowledge of being a consultant. This is an effective way for the consultant in training to ask previous consultants about their past experiences and helpful tips they have learned during their training. There could be multiple meetings where the consultant in training can ask questions and address concerns.

Get Comfortable Being Uncomfortable: A Professional's Perspective

In the last few years, my (CK) consulting practice has grown considerably. I attribute this growth to my ability to embrace being uncomfortable and move beyond my comfort zone on a daily basis. When we stay in our comfort zone, we do not grow. We play small and live small. We just "survive," settle for less, and are okay with being like everyone else. We let fear, doubt, regret, and insecurity get the best of us when we live and work in our comfort zone. For the first five years of my consulting practice, that is exactly what I did; I played small. I did not get out in the public with my message often. I wondered what people would think, questioned if I could work big, and wondered if I could reach my big dreams as a consultant. I delivered content and activities the way I thought that everyone else did in sport psychology.

Magic started happening a few years ago when I worked on a daily basis to get out of my comfort zone and embraced feeling uncomfortable. I realized that outside our comfort zone, we dream big, explore new things, and embrace the unknown. When we act in spite of the fear, we grow by leaps and bounds. I made a conscious decision to lean into the discomfort on a daily basis. Whenever I felt the pit in my stomach or had the thought that what I was doing was "too big," I said to myself, "You are on to something. Go for it!" To be clear, it was not always easy, but I did it anyway! I realized that fear and discomfort would always be there when trying new things and growing. You can let the fear freeze you, or you can "lean in" (Sandberg, 2013). You can let the fear overtake your body and mind by letting yourself question if you should take the risk and doubt your ability. Or you can "lean in" and take command of yourself and make the decision to do it. Just as we tell our athletes and performers we serve, we can train ourselves to lean in to the discomfort. We can do this by keeping the people that we serve as our focus, remembering our ambition to be better consultants, or focusing on what we or others will gain when we embrace the uncomfortable. Either we can grow through taking risks, or we can decide to be mediocre consultants. I choose to grow. What do you choose?

Potentially, my biggest growth experience of getting out of my comfort zone has been my work with college, high school, and NFL football players and teams. My work with football teams started several years ago and more recently has grown into an opportunity to work with an NFL team. While working with football teams, I stand out—I do not look like others in the room. I am a woman and usually the only woman in the room. My size also makes me stand out—I am short (around 5 feet 1 inch tall), whereas most of the athletes on the football teams are around 6 feet tall. I have studied and watched the game but did not grow up playing football. There are many times that these three factors (my gender, size, and playing experience) could have stopped me from working with football teams, making a difference, and helping them master the mental game. I would have stopped working in football if I let fear and anxiety take over my mind, emotions, and body. Instead, when I felt the uncomfortable feeling, I decided to lean in and continue pursuing my dream. Recently, I have made an entirely new mindset shift, and I have begun to see how being a woman can actually be an advantage in the football space. I have done this with the help of other women in sport psychology who work with male teams. They have taught me to see how my caring demeanor and approach as a woman brings value to the culture of football. This shift in my mindset has allowed me to embrace my authenticity and be more comfortable standing out.

Another incredible growth experience of getting out of my comfort zone happened in February 2015, when I was asked to dance in the competition Dancing with the Mankato Stars. The competition was similar to the popular NBC show *Dancing with the Stars* but performed locally to raise money for the American Red Cross. I was paired up with a partner who dances dubstep, a specific type of hip-hop danced to electronic music. I had the opportunity to introduce more than 3,000 people to the field of sport psychology, which I believe is part of my life's purpose—to advance the field of sport psychology. I wanted to master dubstep as best I could in five weeks and perform well on stage to show people that you could learn anything if you decided to and had enough desire and energy. Each time that I felt that pit in my stomach while I was learning and performing dubstep, I leaned in and worked to dance with passion and energy. As a result, we performed an incredible dubstep routine and earned a second-place finish. My practice grew 25 percent immediately after I performed dubstep in Dancing with the Mankato Stars because more people knew about my work and were introduced to the field.

In the last few years, I have pushed myself in other ways and embraced the uncomfortable, which has in turn grown my practice. I participated in a year-long public speaking training with the National Speakers Association and became a member of the organization. I started a podcast on iTunes, launched my first online course hosted on my personal website, and have weekly radio and TV spots. The first time I did all of these things (i.e., recorded my first podcast, launched my first course, and went on live TV), I felt uncomfortable and uncertain because I had never done it before; but I did it anyway! I provide these examples to illustrate that there are many ways to grow your influence and impact the world with your message and gifts. It is difficult to grow your influence, however, if you stay in your comfort zone.

As professionals, we need to continue to embrace the uncomfortable and move beyond our comfort zone. If we stay in our comfort zones, we become professionally stagnant, and the field of sport psychology will not grow like it could. When you feel the pit in your stomach, remember that you are on to something. You can decide to back off, or you can lean in and embrace being uncomfortable. To do this, keep in mind the bigger picture of the contribution and difference you can make, and keep in mind the people that you serve. When we all continue to embrace the uncomfortable, we help grow the field of sport psychology. Let's do it together!

Conclusion

The sport psychology consulting process can be exciting, enjoyable, and extremely fulfilling when things are going smoothly. As a consultant in training, things going smoothly and as planned is a rarity, which can produce many uncomfortable moments. Just as with any profession, learning is a never-ending process, filled with many ups and downs. The willingness to break through perceived barriers and maintain professional service delivery during uncomfortable moments is crucial in the field of sport psychology. In order to maintain professional service delivery, consultants in training must become comfortable being uncomfortable while expanding their zone of competence.

Throughout this chapter, three factors for increasing comfort and competence have been presented. Embracing a growth mindset during the training process is crucial for the development of effective professional practice. The goal of every consultant is to meet the needs of the client and teach him or her the tools to reach optimal enjoyment and peak performance within the athletic experience. In order to facilitate this experience for athletes, teams, and coaches, the consultants must be able to consistently regulate their own internal struggles. Implementing deliberate practice is one way a consultant in training can hone his or her consulting style in the most effective manner. Seeking out opportunities that challenge a consultant in training's competence zone is an effective way to gain experience and to gain opportunities for self-reflection. Fostering a supervisory relationship with a mentor is a beneficial means to access an objective opinion and source of advice regarding a consultant in training's development.

A consultant in training will experience moments of doubt and insecurity. In fact, seasoned professionals still experience cases of nerves. Being uncomfortable is a sign that a consultant is being pushed outside his or her competence zone. When a consultant is able to embrace being uncomfortable as an opportunity for growth, he or she will be able to expand his or her current zone of competence. Therefore, being uncomfortable should be a normal and expected part of consultants' experiences, as they are constantly trying to push themselves to be better than they were before. The three key factors discussed in this chapter (cultivating a growth mindset, implementing deliberate practice, and fostering a supervisory relationship with a mentor) will allow a consultant in training to embrace uncomfortable experiences and work to confidently deliver sport psychology services while expanding his or her competence zone.

References

Andersen, M. B., & Williams-Rice, B. T. (1996). Supervision in the education and training of sport psychology service providers. *The Sport Psychologist, 10*, 278–290.

Chase, M. A. (2010). Should coaches believe in innate ability? The importance of leadership mindset. *Quest, 62*, 296–307.

Collins, J. (2001). *Good to great: Why some companies make the leap and others don't.* New York: HarperCollins.

Deci, E. L., & Ryan, R. M. (2011). Self-determination theory. *Handbook of Theories of Social Psychology, 1*, 416–433.

Dweck, C. S. (2006). *Mindset: The new psychology of success.* New York: Random House.

Dweck, C. S. (2009). Mindsets: Developing talent through a growth mindset. *Olympic Coach, 21*(1), 4–7.

Dweck, C. S. (2010). *Mindset: About the author*. Retrieved from http://mindsetonline.com/aboutthe-author/index.html

Ericsson, K. A. (2006). The influence of experience and deliberate practice on the development of superior expert performance. In K. A. Ericsson, N. Charness, P. J. Feltovich, & R. R. Hoffman (Eds.), *The Cambridge handbook of expertise and expert performance* (pp. 683–703). New York, NY: Cambridge University Press.

Ericsson, K. A., Krampe, R. T., & Tesch-Römer, C. (1993). The role of deliberate practice in the acquisition of expert performance. *Psychological Review, 100*(3), 363–406.

Ericsson, K. A., Prietula, M. J., & Cokely, E. T. (2007). The making of an expert. *Harvard Business Review, 85*(7/8), 114–121.

Hutter, R. I., Olden-Veldman, T., & Oudejans, R. D. (2015). What trainee sport psychologists want to learn in supervision. *Psychology of Sport and Exercise, 16*, 101–109.

Poczwardowski, A., Sherman, C. P., & Ravizza, K. (2004). Professional philosophy in the sport psychology service delivery: Building on theory and practice. *The Sport Psychologist, 18*(4), 445–463.

Sandberg, S. (2013). *Lean in: Women, work, and the will to lead*. New York City: Knopf.

Skovholt, T. M., & Ronnestad, M. H. (1992). Themes in therapist and counselor development. *Journal of Counseling & Development, 70*, 505–515.

Stambulova, N., & Johnson, U. (2010). Novice consultants' experiences: Lessons learned by applied sport psychology students. *Psychology of Sport and Exercise, 11*, 295–303.

Tod, D., Andersen, M. B., & Marchant, D. B. (2011). Six years up: Applied sport psychologists surviving (and thriving) after graduation. *Journal of Applied Sport Psychology, 23*(1), 93–109.

Tonn, E., & Harmison, R. J. (2004). Thrown to the wolves: A student's account of her practicum experience. *Sport Psychologist, 18*(3), 324–340.

Yeager, S. Y., & Dweck, C. S. (2012). Mindsets that promote resilience: When students believe that personal characteristics can be developed. *Educational Psychologist, 47*(4), 302–314.

5 Getting the Most From Supervision

Lessons on Exploration, Communication, and Applications

*Annamari Maaranen-Hincks, Erika D. Van Dyke,
Shu Jiang, Adisa Haznadar, and Judy L. Van Raalte*

Supervision entails the familiar student role of being instructed and evaluated, and also the less familiar and potentially uncomfortable roles of being vulnerable, honest (with one's supervisor and oneself), reflective, and insightful. In short, the skills to succeed and gain the most as a supervisee are different than the skills developed in a traditional classroom. This chapter will provide students with an understanding of what these skills are and how to develop them. Specifically, models of supervision, responsibilities of supervisors and supervisees, supervisee challenges, and multicultural considerations in supervision are discussed.

Introduction

The Certification Review Committee of the Association for Applied Sport Psychology (AASP) uses the following definitions of supervision and mentorship:

> An intervention that is provided by a senior member of a profession to a junior member or members of that same profession. This relationship is evaluative, extends over time, and has the simultaneous purposes of enhancing the professional functioning of the junior member(s), monitoring the quality of professional services offered to the clients she, he, or they see(s), and serving as a gatekeeper for those who are to enter the particular profession.
>
> (Bernard & Goodyear, 2014, p. 9)

Ideally, supervision guides the trainee's self-exploration by aiding in identifying the trainee's strengths, weaknesses, and needs (Van Raalte & Andersen, 2000). Supervision in applied sport psychology is similar to other relatively long-term interpersonal relationships. In addition to the ideal outcomes of supervision relationships, such as personal and professional growth, self-knowledge, and understanding of the trainee, the relationship can also be burdened with conflicts, frustrations (Van Raalte & Andersen, 2000), and other challenges, discussed in this chapter.

Models of Supervision

In the graduate training of most helping professionals, extensive supervision is a vital part of the training process. For example, clinical psychologists are required to complete anywhere from 3,000 to 6,000 hours of supervised practice and internship training, depending on the state, as a part of licensure requirements (Association of State and Provincial Psychology Boards, n.d.). In sport psychology, AASP requires 400 hours of supervised experience for consultant certification, 100 of which need to be spent working with individuals or groups, but the content and processes of the required applied work are not clearly stated.

Competency-Based Model

Competency-based supervision (Falender & Shafranske, 2014) is a metatheoretical approach to supervision that can be implemented within a broad range of supervision models (Farber & Kaslow, 2010). In addition to the focus on ensuring client welfare by developing clinical competencies of the supervisee, competency-based supervision helps in organizing the supervisee's and supervisor's competencies (Falender & Shafranske, 2014). That is, the supervisor and supervisee collaborate in identifying the skills, attitudes, and knowledge that comprise each competency. The supervisor and supervisee together determine specific ways to enhance the learning of the supervisee and monitor and evaluate his/her development (Falender, 2014).

Many components have been discussed in the literature as being important to an effective supervision process, including multicultural and diversity competence, receiving and providing feedback, self-assessment, discussion of transference and countertransference, and a supervision contract (Falender, 2014; Falender & Shafranske, 2014). The supervisory alliance has been acknowledged as the essential and foundational component of clinical supervision (Falender, 2014; Falender & Shafranske, 2014), as the supervisory relationship has been shown to strongly correlate with supervisee satisfaction. The supervisory alliance is developed through collaboration between the supervisor and supervisee in regards to the developmental goals of the supervisee (Falender, 2014). Supervisee self-disclosure has also been shown to be correlated with supervisee satisfaction (Inman & Ladany, 2008).

Van Raalte and Andersen (2000) discussed five models of supervision that all share the common goal of developing competent sport psychology professionals: (a) behavioral models, (b) cognitive-behavioral models, (c) phenomenological models, (d) psychodynamic models, and (e) developmental models.

Behavioral Models

Behavioral models of supervision can be appealing, particularly to beginning sport psychology trainees, because they focus on supervisee skill development, such as guided imagery skills and relaxation induction, in a relatively straightforward and structured way. The supervisor's role is directive and instructional, with an emphasis on reinforcing desirable trainee behaviors and correcting less desirable or incorrect behaviors. Less emphasis is placed on the relationship between the supervisor and supervisee.

Cognitive-Behavioral Models

Cognitive-behavioral models of supervision parallel the process of sport psychology service delivery in that what happens between the sport psychologist and an athlete also occurs in supervision. For example, if the sport psychology trainee is considering introducing imagery skills in the work with athletes, the supervisor may instruct the supervisee to mentally rehearse the upcoming session with the athlete. Similarly, supervisors might challenge supervisee faulty thinking (e.g., I must be a perfect sport psychologist), just as the supervisee might challenge such thoughts of delivering perfect performance with the athletes they work with.

Phenomenological Models

Phenomenological models of supervision are based on the research and theory of humanistic and existential psychology and focus on creating a supportive environment in which supervisees can grow and develop at their own pace. In this approach, supervisors create a safe and nonthreatening environment by providing empathy and unconditional positive regard to the supervisee. In comparison to the behavioral and cognitive-behavioral models of supervision, this approach provides little structure and direction, and thus may be anxiety provoking for beginning supervisees.

Psychodynamic Models

Psychodynamic models of supervision are based on Freud's work and focus on the relationship between the supervisor and supervisee. The basic idea of this model is that the way the supervisee relates to and interacts with the supervisor is directly connected to the way the supervisee connects to and interacts with his/her athlete-clients. The supervisor's role in this approach is to help the supervisee gain awareness of what the supervisee brings to the relationship and to understand the dynamics of his/her interactions with athlete-clients, particularly as they relate to issues of transference and countertransference. Like phenomenological models of supervision, psychodynamic models of supervision are often challenging for beginner supervisees.

Developmental Models

Developmental models of supervision focus primarily on the evolution of the relationship between the supervisor and supervisee. The model includes four stages of growth that can be applied to all of the models described previously. In the first stage, beginner supervisees are often anxious and have low tolerance for ambiguity. Therefore, behavioral models of supervision might be used to provide structure, while still leaving room for autonomy and development. In the second stage, supervisees gain more independence from the supervisor as they begin to feel competent and start developing their personal approaches to service delivery. This might be an appropriate time to move to phenomenological models of supervision to support the development of supervisee autonomy. In the third stage, supervisees are nearly independent practitioners, and their relationship with their supervisors becomes collegial. In this stage, psychodynamic approaches to supervision may be particularly helpful as supervisees are ready for in-depth exploration of their relationships with athlete-clients. In the fourth and final stage, supervision has developed into a mutually beneficial relationship between peers. Ideally, collegial supervision continues throughout the professional lives of sport psychology service providers.

Responsibilities of Supervisors

Two broad competence areas for supervisors are outlined in the literature: (a) knowledge and skills to provide the type of services that one's supervisees are providing and (b) knowledge and skills in supervision itself (Barnett, 2010; Roth & Pilling, 2008). Therefore, to be a competent supervisor, specialized training in supervision should be obtained. Such training can guide supervisors in the development of a good working relationship with supervisees (Borders et al., 1991). Developing such a relationship takes time and effort. The supervisor must be present for the supervisee, be respectful and empathetic, listen attentively, and encourage the supervisee's expression of feelings and opinions, thus creating a safe, nonjudgmental, and supportive environment. Through the process of self-assessment and reflection, supervisors can become aware of their own strengths and limitations and commit to lifelong learning and professional growth (Bernard & Goodyear, 2014).

Although establishing a good, trusting, and mutually respectful working relationship is imperative in the supervision process, the responsibilities of supervisors do not end there. At the beginning of a new supervision relationship, a clear blueprint of the supervision relationship should be provided to the supervisee; the supervisee should be well informed about the processes and expectations of supervision (Knapp & VandeCreek, 2006). Supervisees should enter the supervisory experience knowing the conditions necessary for their success or advancement, including the personal and interpersonal competencies they will be required to demonstrate (Forrest, Elman, Gizara, & Vacha-Haase, 1999). Supervisees should also be informed about the type of supervision method that will be used, the time that will be allotted for supervision, the expectations and the theoretical orientation of the supervisor, and the type of documentation required for supervision (Cohen, 1979; McCarthy et al., 1995; Pope & Vasquez, 2011). One mechanism to accomplish this is the use of a supervision contract (e.g., Sutter, McPherson, & Geeseman, 2002). Another possibility is for the supervisor and supervisee to discuss these aspects of supervision and reach a verbal agreement about the process. When supervision is part of an academic class, supervision details may be spelled out in the course syllabus.

In order to ensure the well-being of the supervisees and their clients, supervisors must value the ethical principles of their profession by following the ethical guidelines and preparing their supervisees to do the same. The manner in which supervisors exercise their ethical responsibilities can have multiple effects, including those on the supervisory relationship, the supervisee, the client being served by the supervisee, and even the general public (Goodyear & Rodolfa, 2012). Supervisors should direct and encourage, but also monitor, those who enter the helping professions. Therefore, evaluation of the supervisee is one of the most important responsibilities of a supervisor, and at the same time the most challenging.

Student Experiences With Supervisor Responsibilities

Among the many important responsibilities that effective supervisors embody, I (EV) think the one that touched me most was my supervisor's ability to create a safe holding environment. Barnett and Molzon (2014) noted that for supervisees to truly benefit from supervision, "the supervisee must perceive the supervisory relationship to be sufficiently safe to be able to openly share thoughts, ideas, experiences, and feelings with the supervisor" (p. 1054). As a true novice in the field, I came in to supervision with reservations about being fully transparent in admitting mistakes and areas in which my understanding was not yet up to par. Within the safe space established by my supervisor, I came to feel more comfortable disclosing my thoughts, feelings, strengths, and weaknesses as they were, rather than how I thought they "should" be. As a result of my disclosure of the aspects of my work with athletes that were going well and the areas that could use improvement, my supervisor was better able to offer guidance and support so that I could learn and improve in my delivery of services to athletes.

Since the value of supervision rests largely on supervisee disclosure (Falender, 2014), and since my ability to candidly disclose rested largely on the safe holding environment created by my supervisor, over time I became increasingly aware of what a gift it was that my supervisor was so adept at her role. I was appreciative of the warmth, empathy, understanding, and genuine care that my supervisor conveyed relative to my development as a competent practitioner. These characteristics were ones I came to value, internalize, and emulate in the working alliance I developed with my athlete-clients. I now see more clearly that the empathic supervisory alliance established by my supervisor not only helped me to get the most out of supervision but also allowed me to experience firsthand the qualities that would help me to become an effective athletic counselor.

Reflecting on my own positive experiences working with my supervisor also made me consider how drastically different my time in supervision might have been had my supervisor not created a space in which learning was encouraged. Placing myself in the shoes of a supervisee who may be learning to cope with an intimidating supervisor has allowed me to more fully appreciate my supervision experience. Rather than feeling that my ability to work with athletes was contingent upon practicing my new role perfectly, I was instead guided by my supervisor to understand that making and learning from mistakes was part of my job as a supervisee and that being open and receptive to feedback was a key responsibility that would enable me to grow and become a more competent practitioner.

I remember a supervision experience early in my role as an athletic counselor when I nervously told my supervisor that I was uncertain about whether or not I addressed one of my athlete's presenting concerns appropriately in our session. I listened with great relief as my supervisor replied, "Would you be willing to bring your concern to supervision today so we can talk about it as a group? It could be a nice learning opportunity for everyone." In that moment, I felt supported by my supervisor and comforted by the notion that my potential mistake might serve a learning purpose not only for myself but for my peers as well. The way my supervisor reframed the mistake as a learning experience helped me to feel more comfortable bringing my concerns to supervision and more open to the feedback I would receive. Realizing the powerful impact a safe holding environment can have on supervisees—for better or worse—serves to highlight how important it is for supervisors to be mindful of the type of space they are creating for their consultants in training. Although this discussion does not change the fact that supervisees often do not have a choice when it comes to selecting a supervisor, it does provide perspective on how supervisor responsibilities can have a profound impact on the trainee's experience in supervision.

Responsibilities of Supervisees

Supervision is an important part of the training that an applied sport psychology consultant undergoes to become a competent, knowledgeable, and ethically sound practitioner (Van Raalte & Andersen, 2000). Hutter, Oldenhof-Veldman, and Oudejans (2015) defined learning in supervision as "learning on the basis of reflective practice with a supervisor," and they suggested that a primary intent of supervision should be to "develop self-directed learning by the supervisee" (p. 101). Through the process of supervision, the learning-practitioner comes to develop sophisticated approaches to managing the challenges of applied practice through a process of ethical decision-making (Barnett & Molzon, 2014). As outlined in the preceding section, supervisors play a vital role in shaping and guiding the ethical practice of supervisees; however, supervisees also have many responsibilities for ensuring the well-being of their athlete-clients and fostering a safe and effective space for supervision. The present section will focus on the responsibilities that supervisees have for contributing to an effective supervisory experience.

Development of supervisees into competent, emotionally aware, motivated, professional, autonomous, and ethical practitioners may occur as they establish their theoretical identities and awareness of, and respect for, individual and multicultural factors (Loganbill, Hardy, & Delworth, 1982). Van Raalte and Andersen (2000) noted eight specific responsibilities of supervisees in the supervision process:

- Prepare for supervision sessions.
- Keep up-to-date progress notes on individual athlete meetings and group presentations.

- Critically examine strengths and weaknesses as sport psychologists.
- Continually seek clarification of roles and expectations.
- Do not conceal any information about athlete sessions or group meetings from supervisors.
- Provide feedback to supervisors on the supervisory process.
- Maintain ethical responsibilities to athlete-clients.
- Seek to emulate a model of ethical and professional behavior in interactions with athletes and supervisors.

(p. 159)

Although additional supervisee responsibilities undoubtedly exist (e.g., responsibilities to athlete-clients and to peer supervisees), this list provides a helpful foundation of several key elements of the supervisee role. In the paragraphs that follow, several of the above responsibilities of supervisees will be discussed in further depth.

Preparing for supervision can include review of progress notes and previous sessions. This process is accomplished more easily if progress notes are kept up to date. Although paperwork can be challenging for busy trainees, learning how to manage this aspect of service delivery via supervision is a valuable skill.

Critically evaluating strengths and weaknesses as practitioners facilitates the development of self-awareness. Falender (2014) included metacompetence (i.e., knowing what we do not know, or being able to identify weaknesses and the skills that still need to be developed) as an important aspect of competence-based supervision practices. Engaging in self-reflection practices may provide helpful insight to trainees regarding both what they know and what they do not yet know. Holt and Strean (2001) provided a detailed account of the self-reflection process that a neophyte sport psychology consultant went through during his training. In their account, the trainee completed a narrative of self (i.e., a self-reflective writing technique) to explore his approach to sport psychology consultation with an athlete. As a result of his critical incident reflection and guidance from his supervisor, the trainee came away with increased self-awareness that allowed him to improve upon his service delivery. When supervisees know what they do not know, they may be more inclined to reach out for guidance to resolve ethical challenges and dilemmas. Supervisee unwillingness to undergo self-examination and reflection has been shown to be one of the issues contributing to poor supervision outcomes (Wilcoxon, Norem, & Magnuson, 2005). Critical evaluation of their competency as budding professionals thus seems to be a particularly noteworthy responsibility of supervisees.

Due to the fact that much of the supervision process is dependent on the content shared by supervisees regarding their interactions with teams and individual athletes, supervisee disclosure of strengths and weaknesses is a critical element of effective supervision (Falender, 2014). Transparency of consulting experiences in supervision allows for concerns and dilemmas that may have ethical implications to be addressed. In group supervision, sharing strengths and shortcomings provides the opportunity for vicarious learning related to the work of all trainees.

Participating in supervision may appear to be a one-way street with the supervisor providing direction to trainees. It is a responsibility of trainees, however, to provide feedback to the supervisor with regard to the supervision process. The challenges associated with providing such feedback in a manner that protects the supervision relationship can parallel the process in the trainee's sessions with athletes where feedback from the athlete is also appropriate. When the sharing of feedback between supervisors and supervisees is a mutual exchange, it helps to create an open supervisory alliance and to emphasize the value of ongoing professional growth. In addition, when the provision of feedback occurs in a two-way exchange, both supervisor and supervisee have the opportunity to clarify roles and expectations to maintain the integrity of the supervisory relationship.

If we refer back to the supervision processes outlined previously, we see that internalizing the supervisor may be an effective way to learn, and in turn demonstrate, ethical and professional behavior throughout applied work within supervision and counseling settings. Supervisors model a myriad of professional and ethical behaviors including those related to confidentiality, dual roles, professional boundaries, and competency. By emulating the professional behaviors of supervisors, trainee sport psychology consultants can become more competent and ethically sound practitioners in their own interactions with athletes and supervisors.

Although internalizing the best practices of a supervisor is valuable for developing competence, it is also important for supervisees to incorporate their own theory, philosophy, and style of counseling or consulting (see Chapter 1). This process may be encouraged in supervision. Van Raalte and Andersen (2000) noted that supervisors can help supervisees hone their theoretical orientations through open discussions in which both parties air their personal counseling or consulting styles. The supervisory relationship may thus serve as a helpful space in which supervisees can become competent practitioners by both emulating the supervisor and clarifying their own counseling philosophy and style. In this way, trainee sport psychology consultants may merge foundational aspects of the supervisor's professional practices with their own theoretical orientation to develop a personal style of counseling that resonates with the individual.

With regard to group supervision practices, internalizing the supervisor has important implications for peer interactions as well. Emulating effective supervisory practices may help supervisees become more thoughtful, respectful, and supportive peers in group supervision settings, and may help supervisees better understand appropriate and professional ways to offer both positive and constructive feedback to peers and supervisors. Although establishing a group supervision environment built on trust stems from the supervisor (Barnett & Molzon, 2014; Falender, 2014), such an environment must be upheld by all supervisees involved in order to facilitate open discussion and disclosure. When each individual takes responsibility for his/her part in perpetuating this type of supervision environment, there is a greater likelihood for honest sharing to become the precedent and for everyone to learn lessons from the insights and experiences each supervisee brings to the group.

Student Experiences With Supervisee Responsibilities

As a novice counselor entering the field, I (SJ) care about the quality of my work and being prepared for supervision. I usually review my case notes and other athlete files, consider my conceptualization of each case, and revisit the theoretical underpinnings of my approach before supervision meetings. Completing these tasks makes me feel prepared, deepens my understanding of the work, and can help build my confidence. Confidence is important because it is easy to be intimidated and feel vulnerable when talking about applied experiences, especially as a new trainee. I have realized, however, that being open with my supervisor has been the key to my professional development and that it is okay, and even necessary, to discuss my shortcomings and worries, as well as my strengths. For example, I was once requested by a coach to check athletes' performance on their midterms, which was neither my right nor my obligation. Feeling confused and upset about the situation, I turned to my peers and supervisor for guidance. We found out that all of the athletes on the team had signed a release that allowed the coach to review their grades. That said, if the athletes felt that their grades were important to address during an individual session, I was more than happy to hear their thoughts and feelings about them. However, the athletes could also choose not to share their grade information with me. Another dilemma I encountered in my applied work was related to my religion. I am a Buddhist, and certain behaviors that my athlete-clients discussed are forbidden in my religion, making the topics uncomfortable for me to discuss in a nonjudgmental manner. As I brought this issue up in supervision, my supervisor helped me to analyze the pros and cons of seeing athlete-clients from the same and different religions than mine and to construct a plan for how and when I should refer athlete-clients to someone else. Such experiences in supervision ensured that I was providing my athlete-clients effective and ethical services and boosted my confidence as an athletic counselor.

The group supervision setting has helped me to become more comfortable with receiving, processing, implementing, and providing feedback. Learning about the experiences of others near my level of training and finding myself able to consider the experiences of my peers and provide suggestions to them has greatly facilitated my self-exploration, awareness, and insight, all of which are crucial components of professional development. As with any new craft, developing as an applied sport psychology consultant is associated with learning how to navigate challenges that arise as a trainee in the field. In the following section, commonly encountered challenges among supervisees are discussed, and possible ways of managing those challenges are offered.

Supervisee Challenges

The applied sport psychology consultant in training has many things to learn before becoming a competent practitioner. Many of these learning moments can be satisfying to trainees as they become aware of their personal and professional growth in the field. Some of these learning moments, both those related to the trainee and those related to the supervision relationship, can be challenging, especially in the beginning. With regard to supervision, Baird (1999) suggested three main resistances that trainees may encounter: resistance to self-awareness, resistance to admitting ignorance, and resistance to change. Beyond these areas of resistance are additional challenges the learning professional may experience, such as sharing personal strengths, weaknesses, and conflicting values in the supervision relationship; learning to establish professional boundaries; engaging in self-care; and giving and receiving feedback. Each of these challenges is discussed in more detail later.

Sharing personal strengths and weaknesses with peers and supervisors can be a new experience for supervisees. Often, beginning applied sport psychology consultants are "overly worried about judgments of right or wrong or good and bad concerning their service delivery" (Andersen, Van Raalte, & Harris, 2000, p. 177). Such dichotomous thinking can make it feel intimidating for supervisees to honestly express successes and setbacks at first. As discussed earlier in the chapter, it is the responsibility of the supervisor to establish a nonjudgmental supervisory alliance built on trust (Falender, 2014); however, it is the responsibility of the supervisee to sustain the effective supervision space by disclosing openly in return. With this type of transparency in the supervisory alliance, supervisees can develop into more competent practitioners as they learn from the feedback provided relative to both their strengths and weaknesses.

In situations where the supervisor does not create a safe space for supervision or when conflicting values and beliefs between the supervisor and supervisee result in fundamental differences regarding the approach(es) thought to be most fitting for a given athlete-client, service delivery can be compromised (Pettifor, Sinclair, & Falender, 2014). Through self-reflection and open communication, both supervisors and supervisees may become more aware of their values and beliefs and how they influence their perspectives on supervision and practice. Mutual appreciation of differences in worldviews can help promote a supervisory alliance where each member feels respected (Pettifor et al., 2014). Differing cultural values in a supervision relationship will be discussed later in this chapter.

A strong desire to help athlete-clients is one reason why individuals may choose to enter into the field of sport and performance psychology (Andersen et al., 2000). The need to help others may pose a challenge to supervisees when they no longer feel needed by the athletes with whom they have come to establish satisfying and rewarding professional relationships. Part of the trainee's learning is to come to understand that in providing a beneficial support resource, the goal is to take oneself out of a job (Van Raalte & Andersen, 2000), thereby enhancing the athlete's independent functioning, rather than making the athlete-client dependent on the services provided (Barnett & Molzon, 2014). Just as supervisors foster the autonomy of the supervisee, so must the supervisee learn to foster the autonomy of the athlete-client.

One of the ethical responsibilities of applied sport psychology consultants throughout their work with athletes is to establish professional boundaries (Barnett & Molzon, 2014; Whelan, n.d.). For some, maintaining these boundaries can be challenging in practice, especially if the supervisee is working with athlete-clients in the institution they are attending and thus travel similar circles outside of the classroom. Neophyte trainees who may not yet be comfortable in their role as counselor may default instead to more familiar friend-like interactions with their athlete-clients (Van Raalte & Andersen, 2000). Although it may at times seem appealing for trainees to befriend their athletes, the importance of maintaining professional boundaries with athlete-clients is paramount when fostering an ethical working alliance. Outlining the nature of the working relationship between the trainee and the athlete through informed consent and open communication at the beginning of the relationship can help in establishing appropriate boundaries from the onset and can avoid potential role blurring between the supervisee and athlete-clients. Establishing appropriate boundaries is especially important in small-world college settings where one may encounter an athlete-client in counseling, classroom, athletic, and even social contexts.

Supervisees may encounter additional challenges as they strive to juggle multiple time commitments, including those of student and applied practitioner. Self-care has been described as "the need to take adequate care of ourselves on an ongoing basis to help prevent burnout and resultant problems with professional competence while promoting psychological wellness" (Barnett & Molzon, 2014, p. 1056). Given the many challenges and stresses that supervisees may experience as emerging mental health professionals, self-care is especially important (Barnett & Molzon, 2014). In order to continue providing beneficial support services to athlete-clients, supervisees must also take adequate care of themselves. Learning to find a balance among professional obligations, student responsibilities, and personal life can be challenging. When supervisors assess (Falender, 2014) and model (Barnett & Molzon, 2014) effective self-care strategies and address issues of self-care, burnout, and professional competence during supervision (Bernard & Goodyear, 2014), supervisees may discover ways of coping to seek balance in their lives as they embrace their new roles as applied sport psychology consultants.

Giving and receiving feedback is considered an essential element of the training involved to become a competent, knowledgeable, and ethical applied sport psychology consultant (Andersen, Van Raalte, & Brewer, 1994; Barnett & Molzon, 2014; Falender, 2014). Although some individuals find receiving feedback to be challenging (Wilcoxon et al., 2005), others find giving feedback to be of equal or greater challenge. Providing feedback to a supervisor, who holds greater authority and power in the supervisory alliance, may be a new, intimidating, and uncomfortable experience for supervisees. However, providing feedback to supervisors regarding the process of supervision is one of the responsibilities of supervisees (Van Raalte & Andersen, 2000). When supervisors actively convey their openness to receiving feedback, supervisees may come to view feedback as a way of strengthening the supervisory relationship (Barnett & Molzon, 2014), rather than as an intimidating experience.

In addition to providing feedback about the supervision process to supervisors, learning to provide feedback to peers is also a valuable skill. Feedback to peers is ideally provided in a manner that expresses support yet also conveys constructive information. Such feedback can begin with an open-ended question, such as, "*How is your applied work going?*" This lets the supervisee-peer know that his/her perceptions are important, which welcomes mutual sharing of thoughts and feelings. Giving feedback can also be approached through a *good, better, how* conversation—that is, a discussion of what is going well, what could go better, and what could or will be done to make improvements. When the feedback stems from a place of support and caring about each other's professional growth, as opposed to critique, the process may feel more natural and less intimidating to the pair involved.

Student Experiences With Supervisee Challenges

As a student, I (EV) like feeling competent in my learning and being perceived by peers and teachers as someone who understands what is expected of me in academic settings. Not knowing all of the answers in the beginning is a natural part of classroom learning, and so I am comfortable asking questions and seeking clarification to further my understanding of the concepts being presented. As a beginning athletic counselor and supervisee, however, I found "not knowing" to be quite challenging. My fieldwork involved doing athletic counseling before I felt fully competent in my new role. I found myself wondering if I was going about my applied work with athletes the "right" way. When it came to supervision, part of me was hesitant to let my supervisor and peers know that I really did not know what I was doing. At the same time, another part of me wanted them to know my reservations so that I could feel supported in the learning process. This challenge was greatly eased by the open and accepting space created by my supervisor and upheld by my supervisee-peers. I came to realize that we were all in the same boat and to value the shared exploration of ways that could help us grow in our new craft of service delivery to athletes.

In addition to our group supervision sessions, my cohort and I were also responsible for weekly fieldwork updates in an online discussion forum. The forum was for us to post confidential descriptions of our most recent athletic counseling experiences with teams and individuals as well as for asking questions of the group. Posting weekly questions to the forum was greatly beneficial as it made having questions a natural part of our professional development as applied practitioners, leaving us feeling that not having all the answers was normal. In addition to posting weekly questions, we were also responsible for responding to several of the questions posed by our peers. The process of answering the questions of my peers helped me to realize that I, in fact, had developed competence in areas of our field and was able to share my strengths with the group in a manner through which we could all benefit.

In keeping with my desire to feel competent in my work with athletes, I was also fearful of making a mistake that might hinder the relationships I was beginning to develop with my supervisor and athlete-clients. When every part of my fieldwork seemed like a novel experience, I worried that it was only a matter of time before I would take a misstep that would change how my supervisor and peers viewed the integrity of my applied work. Some part of me held the belief that to be good at "doing" sport psychology meant to be free of mistakes that might tarnish my competency. However, through my time in supervision, I have come to understand that mistakes are an inevitable, even valuable, part of learning and becoming a more effective athletic counselor.

The importance of making and learning from mistakes during professional development has been supported within existing supervision literature (Andersen et al., 2000), and several common mistakes observed among graduate students have been noted, including the following:

> (a) filling a group psycho-educational presentation with too much information; (b) missing important information an athlete is trying to communicate; (c) miscommunicating athlete concerns to the coach; (d) not establishing clearly who the client is; (e) blurring professional boundaries; (f) making minor confidentiality blunders (e.g., telling another sport psychology graduate student "I am working with Joe X"); (g) entering into areas beyond one's competence (often in a well-meaning attempt to "help" the athlete); and (h) attempting to do too much for athletes, unwittingly fostering athlete dependency.
>
> (p. 137)

In my graduate fieldwork experience, two of the common mistake areas listed previously—blurring professional boundaries and making minor confidentiality blunders—were particularly challenging as I served as a coach, teacher, and sport psychology trainee in a small college environment. On occasion, athletes with whom I worked in a team setting turned up in one of my classes, which presented a dual-role conflict. Part of my learning curve as a student was realizing that often resolving issues of this sort may not occur through clearly delineated black-and-white solutions. Through group supervision discussions, we came to the conclusion that as long as I did not simultaneously teach and offer individual counseling services to athletes, which would be a clear dual-role conflict, perhaps an informed decision could be made by talking with the athletes about their comfort with the situation. It is entirely possible that athletes might feel comfortable having me as both a teacher and an athletic counselor for team programming, and may even welcome seeing a familiar caring adult in class. In such cases, the athletes might decide to stay in my classes and participate in team programming that I cofacilitate with my peers. On the other hand, athletes might feel uncomfortable with the different hats I would need to wear in each context—grading as an instructor and purely supporting as a counselor/consultant. In this case, athletes might choose to drop my class and enroll in an alternative class. This challenging situation helped me to realize the value of supervision for navigating these gray areas and for guiding service delivery that would be in the best interest of the student-athlete. By speaking with athletes about the potential for blurred professional boundaries, I was able to move forward in a manner that was sensitive to individual experiences while still doing fieldwork in a "small world."

Another part of my fieldwork responsibility involved observing the athletes with whom I worked in their daily practice setting. "Hanging out" in practice helped me to learn more about the sport, see team dynamics play out in real time, check in with coaches, show my personal investment, and provide support. I remember one occasion when I was observing tennis athletes, and members of the soccer team (with whom I also worked) walked by and called out, "Hi!" . . . "Do you work with them too?" . . . "You like us best right?!" In the moment, I was unsure of how to respond and simply mentioned with a smile something about not being partial to any one team. Although their tone was light and in a sense demonstrated the rapport we had established in our working relationship, I was immediately concerned about this confidentiality blunder. This moment struck me as just one of the challenges of practicing sport psychology/athletic counseling in a small college community.

Upon self-reflection, I was not entirely content with my response and thought it would be a good idea to bring this interaction to supervision for discussion. When I shared my concerns with my supervisor and supervisee peers, we were able to discuss potential implications of the situation. We decided that although this interaction was probably not ideal, it was also not likely to be harmful to the athletes involved. Often athletes talk to each other, even those from different sports teams, and may be aware that students of our program often work with multiple teams. This group discussion was comforting and helped me become more aware of the challenges inherent to these types of open observation settings in our field. My immediate concerns about the incident were assuaged through our group discussion in supervision; thus, I was glad I shared my fieldwork challenge so that I could receive support and suggestions on how to improve for the future. Personal anecdotes such as these help to illustrate the fact that mistakes do happen during the learning process, and it is the willingness to learn and be receptive to feedback that allows the supervisee to grow and become a more competent practitioner.

Multicultural Considerations in Supervision

Supervisees and supervisors can come from different cultures and have diverse worldviews (Duan & Roehlke, 2001; Pettifor et al., 2014). International graduate students have been conceptualized as being in a "double liminal"—that is, they are navigating their roles between the host culture and home as well as between student and professional (Park-Saltzman, Wada, & Mogami, 2012, p. 896). Developing a positive relationship with their supervisors can help international students—and other students with differing beliefs, values, and worldviews from the mainstream American culture—to effectively navigate through the professional transition they are sharing with their peers and also the cultural transitions they are going through (Park-Saltzman et al., 2012).

According to Pettifor et al. (2014), a successful multicultural supervision relationship should be based on a respectful collaboration, in which expectations are clearly defined and the cultural differences and conflicts that stem from differing worldviews of the supervisor and supervisee are addressed (Duan & Roehlke, 2001). When the multicultural dimensions of the supervisory relationship are not addressed, difficulties may ensue in the supervision process. For example, mentoring without deliberate attention to cultural differences and issues may result in assimilating the mentee into the dominant culture, which can be disadvantageous and even harmful to mentees whose worldview, beliefs, and values can be different from the mainstream American culture (Park-Saltzman et al., 2012).

Pettifor et al. (2014) outlined several examples of possible issues in multicultural supervision. One of the most prevalent issues stems from the power difference between the supervisor and supervisee (Pettifor et al., 2014). Supervisees may feel uncomfortable introducing the topics of culture, ethics, and globalization, due to their subordinate position and a desire to maintain interpersonal harmony in the supervision relationship (Park-Saltzman et al., 2012). Discussion of racial, ethnic, and cultural issues in supervision is an important aspect of supervision that can be overlooked. Although more than 93 percent of supervisors of cultural minority interns report having addressed their lack of experience in cross-racial supervision and the cultural difference between them, only 50 percent of racial minority interns report having received such acknowledgement (Duan & Roehlke, 2001).

When considering multicultural issues related to supervision, a broad understanding of individual and group differences is valuable. Research indicated that compared to Caucasian trainees, African American trainees expect their supervisors to be less empathetic and respectful (Vander Kolk, 1974). In Asian cultures, failing to fulfill one's role and social expectations and responsibilities results in losing face (Triandis, 2001), which in turn can lead to feelings of embarrassment and shame (Yeh & Huang, 1996). In order to avoid losing face, Asian supervisees may be hypercritical of their work, withhold their opinions in supervision, or be overly receptive of the advice and feedback of the supervisor (Park-Saltzman et al., 2012). Developing as a professional in a culturally sensitive supervision relationship can help Asian trainees to reframe their differences as signs of strength as opposed to deficits or weaknesses. Minority supervisees in general have been shown to put a greater importance on the perceived liking of their Caucasian supervisors (Cook & Helms, 1988).

Although creating a positive learning environment is primarily the responsibility of the supervisor, the supervisee can also take an active role in creating such an environment and being open to exploring multicultural issues (Park-Saltzman et al., 2012). Duan and Roehlke (2001) proposed three ways the supervisee can take a more active role in eliciting the supervisor's respect, liking, interest, and valuing, all characteristics shown to be particularly important for cultural and racial minority supervisees (Cook & Helms, 1988): (a) engage in self-disclosing, as it has been shown to play an important role in a supervisor's satisfaction with the supervision relationship; (b) be open and committed to learning, which has been shown to be a highly desirable quality from the supervisor's perspective; and (c) have an open and committed mindset as it may in turn facilitate the supervisor's effort in creating an equally satisfying multicultural supervisory experience. Being aware of and discussing multicultural issues is important for everyone, even if trainees and supervisors were to be from the majority culture, because the athlete-clients and/or coaches the trainee works with might be from another culture.

Student Experiences in Multicultural Supervision

My (AH) interest in sport psychology led me from my home country of Bosnia to master's degree programs in Greece and Germany, where I had my first experience with multicultural applied sport psychology supervision. One might even say that this supervision was "multi-multicultural." That is, the athlete-clients were Greek, the trainee was Bosnian, and the supervisors were Greek. To further the multicultural complexity of the situation, the Greek supervisors had trained in the United States and United Kingdom and differed in their approaches to teaching, training, and supervision from a hands-on experiential approach to a more academically centered problem-solving perspective. Besides the differences, both supervisors had one thing in common: a willingness to facilitate my learning process and help me overcome challenges.

At the start of my applied work, I was excited to begin working with athletes but also somewhat uncomfortable. Although I had learned about sport psychology services, I still felt that I was starting the practicum experience without knowing exactly what I was doing. As I began my applied work, I also began supervision. In supervision, I was expected to discuss what went well in my sessions but also to reveal my shortcomings, weaknesses, and challenges, and to consider how I could improve. Sharing successes was comfortable and positive, but talking publicly about my shortcomings was more challenging. The challenge was magnified by my culture; in Bosnia, students have the role of "learner," and they are expected to soak in knowledge and to accept the wisdom passed on to them. Therefore, if I looked at my supervision experience from my cultural lens, acknowledging my shortcomings would have indicated that I had failed to be a good learner.

In order to get the most out of my applied sport psychology and supervision experiences in a multicultural environment, I needed to adjust to the environment, university system, and people. People in Greece appeared to me to be more "laid-back" than in my home country; they were eager to help others, genuinely interested in other people, and appreciative of life. The most difficult thing for me to adjust to, however, was the academic culture, in which critical thinking was encouraged, expected, and embraced. Due to my differing cultural background, this "questioning mindset" was a challenge for me because I felt that I would be disrespectful if I questioned my professors and their ideas. I remember sitting in the first few classes without asking any questions or making any comments because I was worried about how I would come across and concerned that I might ask a stupid question. Looking back, I could imagine that my teachers and supervisors might have perceived my respect and an eagerness to learn as lack of preparation or disinterest.

I was lucky that my supervisors were comfortable with multicultural issues and understood that asking for help might not be something that is a natural part of everyone's culture. I was relieved when my supervisors reached out to me and acknowledged my hesitancy to make comments and ask questions. By reaching out to me when I was struggling and welcoming my input on what was going on, my supervisors opened the door for us to explore cultural and other issues. As I grew more comfortable in the Greek culture and the Greek university culture, I became accustomed to asking for help and taking an active role in my learning so that my supervisors did not always have to take that first step. I remember with satisfaction and pride when I asked my male supervisor for advice on how to approach a Greek athlete who favored a traditional male role and was uncomfortable with asking for help and working with a female sport psychology consultant.

This positive environment, however, did not develop overnight, but rather over time with many bumps along the way. I remember a situation in class when one of my supervisors described a class assignment, noting that every student was expected to meet the same requirements. Although the expectations and goals were clear, they were also somewhat overwhelming for me because I did not have a strong research background, and I felt that I was behind some of my peers in the program. I tried to keep up by working very hard because I did not want those differences to be noticed. In retrospect, the same situation could have been handled differently if all the parties involved kept the cultural perspective in mind. For example, it would have been helpful for the professor to address or consider the differences among students on a variety of issues, such as language level, educational background, general and specific interests, and majors. Also, as a student supervisee, I could have brought the different burdens that the same assignment had for students into the teacher's awareness.

Overall, my experience of studying in a different country and culture and working with multicultural supervisors helped me to become who I am today. Initially, as a trainee, I was afraid to ask questions, but I have learned that it is okay, and often expected, not to know everything. I have learned that I can reach out for help, and that equally exposing my shortcomings and strengths is an essential part of the learning and growing process. Through my own experiences, I have realized that a multitude of challenges related to multicultural supervision exist, but the benefits in trainee skill development and service delivery make the struggle to address multicultural issues in supervision worthwhile.

Summary

Supervision is an important aspect of the learning process for trainee sport psychologists. As such, both supervisors and supervisees have many responsibilities for ensuring the well-being of athlete-clients and for maintaining an open supervisory relationship that facilitates the professional growth of the trainee. The supervision process may follow different models of supervision, such as competency-based (Falender & Shafranske, 2014), behavioral, cognitive-behavioral, phenomenological, psychodynamic, and developmental models (Van Raalte & Andersen, 2000). Regardless of the preferred model of supervision, supervisors should not only have knowledge and skills to provide the types of services their supervisees are providing, but they should also obtain specialized training in supervision itself. Such training can guide supervisors in creating a nonjudgmental supervisory environment that is based on respect, trust, and support. The supervisors are also responsible for communicating a clear blueprint of the supervisory relationship to the supervisee, including the responsibilities of the supervisee and what type of supervision will be provided, as well as following and modeling ethical guidelines of their profession.

Supervisees also have many responsibilities in the supervision process. Several of the noteworthy supervisee responsibilities that were discussed in this chapter included preparing for supervision sessions, keeping current progress notes, critically examining strengths and weaknesses as trainee sport psychologists, being open and honest about applied work with supervisors, providing feedback to supervisors, and behaving ethically and professionally during interactions with athletes and supervisors (Van Raalte & Andersen, 2000). Given the many responsibilities and new roles of supervisees, it is not surprising that engaging in supervision comes with challenges. Several challenges that supervisees often encounter were discussed in this chapter, including openly disclosing personal strengths and weaknesses in supervision, maintaining professional boundaries, managing conflicting values between supervisor and supervisee, giving and receiving feedback, and learning to find a balance among professional obligations, student responsibilities, and personal life.

Finally, as supervisees and supervisors come from different cultures and have diverse worldviews, discussion about multicultural considerations in the supervision process is important. In order to create a positive supervisory relationship, expectations should be clearly defined and the differences in culture and worldviews between supervisors and supervisees should be addressed (Duan & Roehlke, 2001). If such differences are not addressed, many difficulties in the supervisory relationship may emerge, including assimilating supervisees into the dominant culture, supervisees' hesitation to introduce cultural topics in supervision, supervisees being hypercritical of their work, and supervisees withholding their opinions and other important information from supervisors (Park-Saltzman et al., 2012). The supervisees can take an active role in creating a positive supervision relationship by engaging in self-disclosing, being open and committed to learning, and having an open and committed mindset (Duan & Roehlke, 2001). To provide the readers with a deeper understanding of how to get the most out of supervision, student experiences in supervision were shared throughout the chapter.

References

Andersen, M. B., Van Raalte, J. L., & Brewer, B. W. (1994). Assessing the skills of sport psychology supervisors. *The Sport Psychologist, 8*, 238–247.

Andersen, M. B., Van Raalte, J. L., & Brewer, B. W. (2000). When sport psychology consultants and graduate students are impaired: Ethical and legal issues in training and supervision. *Journal of Applied Sport Psychology, 12*, 134–150.

Andersen, M. B., Van Raalte, J. L., & Harris, G. (2000). Supervision II: A case study. In M. B. Andersen (Ed.), *Doing sport psychology* (pp. 167–179). Champaign, IL: Human Kinetics.

Association of State and Provincial Psychology Boards. (n.d.). *Handbook of licensing and certification requirements*. Retrieved from http://www.asppb.org/HandbookPublic/handbookreview.aspx

Baird, B. N. (1999). *The internship, practicum, and field placement handbook: A guide for the helping professions* (2nd ed.). Upper Saddle River, NJ: Prentice Hall.

Barnett, J. E. (2010). *Ask the ethicist: Supervisors need competence too!* Retrieved from http://www.divisionofpsychotherapy.org/ask-the-ethicist-supervision/

Barnett, J. E., & Molzon, C. H. (2014). Clinical supervision of psychotherapy: Essential ethics issues for supervisors and supervisees. *Journal of Clinical Psychology, 70*(11), 1051–1061. doi:10.1002/jclp.22126

Bernard, J. M., & Goodyear, R. K. (2014). *Fundamentals of clinical supervision*. Upper Saddle River, NJ: Pearson.

Borders, L. D., Bernard, J. M., Dye, H. A., Fong, M. L., Henderson, P., & Nance, D. W. (1991). Curriculum guide for training counseling supervisors: Rationale, development, and implementation. *Counselor Education and Supervision, 31*, 232–237.

Cohen, R. J. (1979). *Malpractice: A guide for mental health professionals.* New York, NY: Free Press.

Cook, D., & Helms, J. E. (1988). Visible racial/ethnic group supervisees' satisfaction with cross-cultural supervision as predicted by relationship characteristics. *Journal of Counseling Psychology, 35*, 268–274.

Duan, C., & Roehlke, H. (2001). A descriptive "snapshot" of cross-racial supervision in University Counseling Center internships. *Journal of Multicultural Counseling and Development, 29*, 131–146.

Falender, C., & Shafranske, E. (2014). Clinical supervision: The state of the art. *Journal of Clinical Psychology, 70*(11), 1030–1041.

Falender, C. A. (2014). Clinical supervision in a competency-based era. *South African Journal of Psychology, 44*, 6–17.

Farber, E. W., & Kaslow, N. J. (2010). Introduction to the special section: The role of supervision in ensuring the development of psychotherapy competencies across diverse theoretical perspectives. *Psychotherapy: Theory, Research, Practice, Training, 47*(1), 1–2. doi:10.1037/a0018850

Forrest, L., Elman, N., Gizara, S., & Vacha-Haase, T. (1999). Trainee impairment: A review of identification, remediation, dismissal, and legal issues. *Counseling Psychologist, 27*(5), 627–686.

Goodyear, R. K., & Rodolfa, E. (2012). Negotiating the complex ethical terrain of clinical supervision. In L. D. Knapp, S. J. Gottlieb, M. C. Handelsman, & M. M. VandeCreek (Eds.), *APA handbook of ethics in psychology, Vol. 2: Practice, teaching, and research* (pp. 261–267). Washington, DC: American Psychological Association.

Holt, N. L., & Strean, W. B. (2001). Reflecting on initiating sport psychology consultation: A self-narrative of neophyte practice. *The Sport Psychologist, 15*, 188–204.

Hutter, R. I., Oldenhof-Veldman, T., & Oudejans, R. D. (2015). What trainee sport psychologists want to learn in supervision. *Psychology of Sport and Exercise, 16*, 101–109.

Inman, A. G., & Ladany, N. (2008). Research: The state of the field. In A. K. Hess, K. D. Hess, & T. H. Hess (Eds.), *Psychotherapy supervision: Theory, research, and practice* (2nd ed., pp. 500–517). Hoboken, NJ: Wiley.

Knapp, S. J., & VandeCreek, L. D. (2006). *Practical ethics for psychologists: A positive approach.* Washington, DC: American Psychological Association.

Loganbill, C., Hardy, E., & Delworth, U. (1982). Supervision: A conceptual model. *The Counseling Psychologist, 10*(1), 3–42. doi:10.1177/0011000082101002

McCarthy, P., Sugden, S., Koker, M., Lamendola, F., Maurer, S., & Renninger, S. (1995). A practical guide to informed consent in clinical supervision. *Counselor Education & Supervision, 35*, 130–138.

Park-Saltzman, J., Wada, K., & Mogami, T. (2012). Culturally sensitive mentoring for Asian international students in counseling psychology. *The Counseling Psychologist, 40*(6), 895–915.

Pettifor, J., Sinclair, C., & Falender, C. A. (2014). Ethical supervision: Harmonizing rules and ideals in a globalizing world. *Training and Education in Professional Psychology, 8*(4), 201–210. doi:10.1037/tep0000046

Pope, K. S., & Vasquez, M. J. T. (2011). *Ethics in psychotherapy and counseling: A practical guide* (4th ed.). Hoboken, NJ: Wiley.

Roth, A. D., & Pilling, S. (2008). *The competence framework for the supervision of psychological therapies.* Unpublished document. Retrieved from www.ucl.ac.uk/CORE/

Sutter, E., McPherson, R. H., & Geeseman, R. (2002). Contracting for supervision. *Professional Psychology: Research & Practice, 33*, 495–498.

Triandis, H. C. (2001). Individualism-collectivism and personality. *Journal of Personality, 69*, 907–924.

Vander Kolk, C. J. (1974). The relationship of personality, values, and race to anticipation of supervisory relationship. *Rehabilitation Counseling Bulletin, 18*, 41–46.

Van Raalte, J. L., & Andersen, M. B. (2000). Supervision I: From models to doing. In M. B. Andersen (Ed.), *Doing sport psychology* (pp. 153–165). Champaign, IL: Human Kinetics.

Whelan, J. (n.d.). *Ethics code: AASP ethical principles and standards*. Retrieved from http://www.appliedsportpsych.org/about/ethics/ethics-code/

Wilcoxon, A., Norem, K., & Magnuson, S. (2005). Supervisees' contributions to lousy supervision outcomes. *Counselor Education and Supervision, 33*, 31–49.

Yeh, C., & Huang, K. (1996). The collectivistic nature of ethnic identity development among Asian-American college students. *Adolescence, 31*, 645–661.

6 Layers of Oversight

Professional Supervision, Meta-Supervision, and Peer Mentoring

Megan K. Marsh, Thomas Fritze,
and Jamie L. Shapiro

The purpose of this chapter is to provide an overview of the primary relationships occurring within the supervisory dynamic. These primary relationships include professional supervision, meta-supervision, and peer mentoring. Each section of the chapter will include relevant literature as well as authors' reflections, including recommendations, challenges, experiences, benefits, and drawbacks to that type of supervision. Each layer of oversight, from receiving guidance and feedback from a classmate to a formal supervision dynamic with an experienced professional, has tremendous importance to the development of an aspiring sport and performance psychology consultant. Furthermore, each layer of oversight has particular nuances that can make it difficult to navigate and maximize experience and growth.

As noted in the counseling psychology literature, "supervision is an essential aspect of every psychologist's professional training and development" (Barnett, 2014, p. 1023), and supervision is also vital for trainees in the field of sport and performance psychology. As this is a relatively young field, the development and training of students is paramount, especially since many of these students will go on to train other students and young professionals in the field. Andersen and Williams-Rice (1996) shared an important sentiment on the role that general psychology may play in sport psychology: "Sport psychology is truly an interdisciplinary field and should draw from the best of both physical education, exercise science, and psychology. In the case of supervision, the field of psychology appears to have the most to offer" (p. 279). In this chapter, the various layers of supervision will be discussed, drawing largely on literature from clinical and counseling psychology. Ultimately, the supervisory relationships will be explained within the context of graduate training in sport and performance psychology. This will include explanations of dynamics among professors, doctoral students, master's students, and alumni of graduate programs.

Professional Supervision

In a general sense, professional supervision involves the supervisory oversight of an experienced (and typically licensed or certified) professional and a student (beginning or advanced). This basic definition will serve as the context for the majority of the current discussion; however, several more detailed and comprehensive definitions have been proposed. One that is particularly useful defines supervision as the formal provision (i.e., sanctioned by relevant organization/s) by senior/qualified practitioners of an intensive education and/or training that is case-focused (Milne, 2007). This process supports, directs, and guides the work of supervisees, which can include restorative (recovering from or fixing crucial mistakes) and/or normative (typical developmental processes) topics. These situations are addressed by means of professional methods, including objective monitoring, feedback, and evaluation (Milne, 2007).

Perhaps the most important aspect of successful supervision is the supervisory working alliance. Bordin (1979) has offered an extensive review on the supervisory relationship. Three components were outlined in the supervisory working alliance: mutual agreement between the supervisee and supervisor on the goals of supervision, the agreement on tasks of supervision, and an emotional bond between the two individuals (Bordin, 1979). While several supervision models have been developed (discussed later in this chapter), most would agree on Bordin's components remaining significant in order for there to be some kind of meaningful and effective supervision process. Bordin's model also identified eight goals of supervision: mastery of specific skills, enlarging one's understanding of clients, enlarging one's awareness of process issues, increasing awareness of self and its impact on process, overcoming personal and intellectual obstacles, deepening one's understanding of concepts and theory, providing a stimulus to research, and maintenance of standards of service. These tasks may change over time depending on the goal of the supervision.

Individual and Group Supervision

Prior to us delving deeper into the specific models of supervision, it is necessary to address the broad distinctions between individual and group supervision. Individual supervision includes a one-on-one dynamic between the supervisor and supervisee. However, it is not uncommon, especially in graduate programs, for the bulk of supervision to take place in a group format. Group supervision is economical and cost-effective (Bilder et al., 2014), while individual supervision tends to occur periodically for one hour and is less practical. There are certainly benefits and drawbacks to each format.

The greatest benefit of individual supervision is that it is a session that is entirely devoted to the development of the supervisee. Depending on the relationship and agreement between the supervisor and the supervisee, the content of a supervision session may include anything from personal issues of the supervisee as they affect his/her applied work to focusing exclusively on the content and process of a specific client case or session. It is a chance for the supervisee to share information that may not be as easily shared in a group setting. It is also possible, however, that the supervisee may feel less comfortable in a one-on-one meeting. Some drawbacks of individual supervision are that a supervisee does not have the input of other perspectives outside of his/her supervisor's viewpoints; therefore, one may feel forced to apply the supervisor's suggestions and may feel as if he/she is under a microscope.

Group supervision offers pros and cons as well. In addition to the cost effectiveness mentioned earlier, strengths of group supervision include support, safety, and peer impact. Each individual in the group has the potential to experience support from peers and feel the safety of everyone "being in it together." Furthermore, peers can offer useful ideas and perspectives, appropriately challenge one another's view, and offer constructive feedback. The use of video case presentation and analysis is another supervision exercise that often occurs in a group setting. Video recording eliminates the need to take notes during the session, and it also provides several opportunities for therapist self-observation and self-awareness by having one's own recorded session to review (Abbass, 2004). Supervisors have the rare opportunity to observe their supervisee's behavior in the practice setting, which allows for discussion around body language, rapport with clients, and treatment approach. Abbass (2004) discussed the potential for anxiety on the supervisee's part with video presentation, and how it is likely that this will decrease over time. Supervision through recorded sessions prepares the supervisee for future feedback settings that may be uncomfortable. This method of supervision also provides opportunities for students who may not be seeing clients yet to benefit from observing session recordings and learning from their peers.

On the other hand, groups do not always follow an ideal process. There may be group conflict among specific members of the group (Bernard, 2005). This conflict may arise for personal, philosophical, or theoretical reasons. The group format also makes the maintenance of confidentiality of client information more difficult and opens more possibilities for ethical violations. Ultimately, the maximization of benefits and minimization of deficits in the combination of individual and group supervision depends on the complex balance of skill and experience of the supervisor, maturity of the supervisees, and focus on the importance of relationships and group processes.

Integrated Development Model

Many models of supervision have been utilized, and these frameworks have helped guide the work of supervisors and improved the effectiveness of training for supervisees. For the purpose of this chapter, the authors chose to focus on the Integrated Development Model (IDM [Stoltenberg, McNeill, & Delworth, 1998]). This approach is utilized in several sport and performance psychology graduate programs and is the model utilized in the authors' program. The IDM highlights that the supervisee developmentally changes over time. While natural growth and development seem like a given, three structures can reflect the supervisee's level of development: motivation, autonomy, and self/other awareness (Brown & Lent, 2008). For a level-one supervisee, the focus is on understanding, empathy, and validation, both between the supervisee and supervisor as well as with client(s). A level-two supervisee may undergo significant conflict and stress based on previous experiences. Feeling competent enough to question other's approaches, including the supervisor's, may be an issue that emerges at this stage. Level-three supervisees are expected to have the capacity to quickly develop a relationship with clients that allows for exploration of personal dynamics. One can think of the supervisee's development paralleling therapeutic relationships and the growth that a client may undergo. Initially, the client feels apprehensive about what the therapy process is going to look like, whom their therapist is, and what secrets about themselves they may disclose. By the second phase, the client may feel as if they do not need therapy anymore, attempting to terminate. Finally, the third phase of treatment looks similar to the third stage of this supervision model, in that the client and therapist feel confident and can carry what they have learned in that relationship out with them into the world.

While the supervisee often develops a strong connection with his or her supervisor, it is important that he/she does not become too attached to that supervisor's style and methods. The role of supervisors is challenging because they are models for trainees. Supervision is an intimate learning experience where trainees commonly adopt and personalize the ethics, attitudes, and even interpersonal style of the supervisor (Van Raalte & Andersen, 2000). For a level-one supervisee (early in development), it may be completely appropriate (and sometimes required by the supervisor) to adopt the supervisor's style. This internalization process highlights the powerful role supervisors have in the education and training of future sport psychologists. As supervisees progress through the developmental levels, cultivating their own style becomes increasingly appropriate (and necessary) in order to form authentic connections with clients.

Professional Supervision in Sport and Performance Psychology

Counseling and clinical supervision models can serve as starting points for an examination of one of the most important things we do as sport psychologists: the training and supervision of future sport psychologists (Andersen & Williams-Rice, 1996). Many of the general clinical and counseling concepts highlighted previously also apply to the layers of supervision that will be discussed in regard to sport and performance psychology training models. The remaining discussion points will emphasize the different layers of supervision that are consistent with the IDM outlined previously, including professional and peer supervision as well as peer mentoring.

It is important for supervisees to understand that a supervisor will serve two purposes: advisor (providing critical analysis) and guide (providing guidance and support [Silva, Metzler, & Lerner, 2011]). Van Raalte and Andersen (2000) addressed some of the specific nuances in sport and performance psychology supervision:

> Supervision's primary purpose in applied sport psychology is to ensure the care of the athlete-client. The secondary, but still important, purpose is the development of the sport psychology trainee as a competent, knowledgeable, and ethical practitioner. Ideally, supervision helps trainees understand themselves, their strengths and weaknesses, and their needs. This understanding helps trainees appreciate what they bring to the consulting relationship that aids (and possibly hinders) their work with athletes.
>
> (p. 153)

Throughout the supervisory relationship, supervisors should ask supervisees about their history in sport psychology, what services they feel competent delivering, what skills they would like to acquire or strengthen, what types of clients they have successfully worked with, and what they see as their strengths and areas for improvement. Supervisors should help supervisees make valid assessments of their skills and determine what they need from supervision (Van Raalte & Andersen, 2000). Due to the intimate nature of this process, it is also necessary to define boundaries in the supervisory relationship. Van Raalte and Andersen (2000) stated, "Although supervision may be a therapeutic process, it is not meant to be therapy, and another role of the supervisor is to refer supervisees for counseling or psychotherapy to resolve serious personal issues that may interfere with service delivery to athletes" (p. 155).

Authors' Experiences

In our graduate program, when a student is in a consulting role, he/she is assigned a professional faculty supervisor for the academic term (in our program, a term is 10 weeks); the students are assigned to different faculty supervisors each term so they obtain multiple perspectives from supervision. The faculty supervisor conducts supervision primarily in a group context (practicum class) and provides individual supervision once per term and as needed. For each consulting session, the student-consultant writes a case note (DAP or SOAP note) in a password-protected electronic document and sends the note to the supervisor(s). This gives the student-consultant the opportunity to request specific feedback from the supervisor; it also gives the supervisor(s) enough information to decide a course of action for supervision. The student-consultant is also asked to self-reflect on each session and send these notes in a separate document to the supervisor.

Trainee's Experience (MM)

My experience with professional supervisors during my sport psychology training was highly collaborative and supportive. I look back on that time and remember feeling confident in my abilities as a consultant because of the supervision I was receiving. I appreciated that my supervisors allowed me to make mistakes and answer my own questions by trying things out, rather than always providing their advice for how they would do something. I also valued the emphasis they placed on balance and self-care, always checking in on how I was doing as a person before diving into client topics. I believe that so much of my personal growth has come from my professional supervisors. The supervisors in my sport and performance psychology program walked by my side and challenged me to step out of my comfort zone in order to actualize my potential as a performance consultant and, ultimately, as an individual.

Trainee's Experience (TF)

Looking back on my most significant experiences with professional supervision, I see there are key aspects that I valued highly and enjoyed. The true value of these experiences can be found in acknowledging the intimidation I felt at being a novice under the guidance of such experts. The most helpful and important theme of the supervision I received was the support. The type of support—positive and constructive feedback, encouragement, and empowerment—certainly went a long way in building the personal and professional confidence that is crucial with something so new and complex as performance psychology consulting as a graduate student.

Another aspect of supervision that I fondly look back on was the enhancement of my critical thinking abilities. Each supervisor had a unique way of sparking new and additional ways of thinking and evoking creativity in regard to my applied work. Often, this came from a simple "Did you think about . . . ?" or a well-placed "What do you think would happen if . . . ?" Not only did questions such as these vastly improve my consulting, but the new insights also made my head spin in a way that brought a smile to my face.

In conjunction with these invaluable experiences, I also have regrets. I wish I would have played a more active "sponge" role in seeking out opportunities (e.g., regular meeting times, class time, email, etc.) to soak up knowledge from my supervisors. I have a greater awareness now that supervision is a time to take initiative and risk in asking any and all questions related to professional and personal growth areas and goals that can lead to improved performance psychology consulting work.

Professional's Experience (JS)

Being a professional faculty supervisor has been an extremely rewarding, yet challenging, part of my job. In small group supervision, I have all students share what they are doing in their field placements and spend extra time for those students who want feedback from the group on a particular issue or challenge they are facing in their consulting. Second-year master's students have to present two cases throughout the year where they conceptualize the case, discuss interventions used, reflect on the work, and show a video of their work with the client. During individual supervision sessions, I focus less on the content of their consulting and more on the growth and development of the supervisee.

My supervision style comes from a balance of person-centered theory (Rogerian) and cognitive-behavioral theory (CBT). Depending on the developmental level of the student and using the IDM, I may be more directive (CBT, for students in an early phase of training) or student-led (asking them questions to guide them to a course of action, for students later in their training). My general method is to allow the students to give feedback to each other first, and then I add my perspectives. I strive to get the students to think about why they chose to do a particular intervention with a group or individual and to incorporate their theoretical orientations into conceptualizing cases and interventions. I also like them to reflect on how their own thoughts, feelings, and behaviors may have affected the consulting relationship and intervention(s).

The most rewarding aspects of supervision for me include watching the students' growth as consultants throughout the program, the bidirectional aspect of learning that occurs between the students and me, and sharpening my own consulting skills by thinking about what I would do if I were in their shoes. I also enjoy the discussions in our small group that offer different perspectives on case conceptualizations and courses of action. I find that the challenges of being a supervisor include the inability to give supervisees the individualized attention they may need due to having a large number of supervisees, questioning my guidance (hence the importance of having colleagues for consultation, which I am fortunate to have), addressing ethical/legal issues that come up in students' consulting, and having difficult conversations with students who may not be meeting expectations as a consultant. Since responsibility for client welfare ultimately falls to the supervisor, a supervisor must limit or remove students from their consulting placement if they are not competent or meeting expectations for their developmental level.

Meta-Supervision

The following section will focus on meta-supervision. Alternative terms for meta-supervision include "peer supervision," "layered supervision," and "supervision of supervision" or "sup of sup." The basic structure of meta-supervision involves a beginning-level student being supervised by an advanced student, and the advanced student's supervision of the beginning student being supervised by a professor (or credentialed professional). For the purposes of this chapter, we will refer to the faculty/professional supervisor as "professional supervisor," the advanced student supervisor as "peer supervisor," and the beginning student as the "supervisee."

The purpose of meta-supervision is twofold: to provide an opportunity for an advanced student to gain experience with providing supervision and to enhance the development of the beginning-level student. It is important to consider supervision as a competency to be trained, and meta-supervision is a critical aspect in this process. In the revised version of the American Psychological Association's competency benchmarks for professional psychology, supervision was included as a specific area in which practitioners must become progressively more competent before entry to practice (APA, 2011). Falender et al. (2004) proposed that a doctoral student's training should include opportunities to supervise under supervision in order to further integrate knowledge, skills, and values in a way that will begin to establish competence for supervision as the doctoral student approaches graduation.

A beginning-level student's development may be enhanced by meta-supervision because of the unique relationship that is possible in such a context. Delini (2013) suggested that "because master's students are closer to doctoral students, it is possible that they may feel less anxious and therefore more satisfied when in supervision with doctoral student supervisors" (p. 9). The same study found that "[master's level] supervisees reported their overall satisfaction with supervision [by a doctoral student] as being in the range of good to excellent on average" (p. 8). Later in this section, personal experiences and reflections will build off this finding. Lastly, because there are three parties involved in meta-supervision (professional supervisor, peer supervisor, and supervisee), there are three individuals who are able to grow professionally. A group of professionals agreed and stated, "As we attend to the development of our trainees, we must continue to attend to our own development" (Granello, Kindsvatter, Granello, Underfer-Babalis, & Hartwig Moorhead, 2008, p. 44).

Thus, the peer supervisor and the professional supervisor have the opportunity to grow as practitioners when involved in meta-supervision.

Meta-Supervision in Sport and Performance Psychology

In the field of sport and performance psychology, meta-supervision is beginning to be used in graduate schools that have beginning-level and advanced-level students who both participate in applied sport and performance psychology consulting. Silva et al. (2011) noted that becoming a peer supervisor can be complicated and uncertain because it is the first time the individual is attempting to guide and develop a new professional in the field. As time passes, the advanced student starts to feel more competent in the supervisory role and becomes more motivated to provide supervision to the beginning student. This mimics the processes explained earlier by the IDM (Stoltenberg et al., 1998). Supervision should also be considered a specific competency for sport and performance psychology practitioners and trainees. For this reason, sport and performance psychology graduate training programs must provide opportunities for meta-supervision utilizing appropriate models. Additionally, there may be factors related to developing supervision as a competency unique to sport and performance psychology. One such supervisory factor to be aware of is that of supervisory defaults (Barney & Andersen, 2014). Barney and Andersen (2014) explain the concept in comparison to coaches whose coaching style largely resembles the coaching styles of their own coaches. The key takeaway for supervisors regarding this phenomenon is that emulating a previous supervisor can be beneficial to a supervisee (assuming his/her supervision experiences were positive), or it can be a significant detriment if based on negative experiences.

If a sport and performance psychology graduate program chooses to emphasize the IDM, it is important to note that the developmental stages may not look linear in a real-life scenario. This means that an advanced student supervising a beginning student may have advanced to level three, accepting his or her role as a peer supervisor and feeling more autonomous; however, if a complicated case presents itself, such as an athlete who becomes suicidal, the student may turn to the professional supervisor and revert back to level two until the problem is resolved. The context surrounding each of these case examples is crucial to consider when looking at the development of the peer supervisor and supervisee.

Authors' Experiences

Trainee's Experience (MM)

My first opportunity to have a peer supervisor engaged in meta-supervision was during the second year of my master's program. It was an interesting case in which I was working with an athlete who had developed an eating disorder. This was a rare supervisory situation because, based on consultation with our professional supervisor, we decided the best course of action was to refer the eating disorder treatment to my peer supervisor (who was developing competency in working with individuals with eating disorders). Concurrent with the eating disorder treatment, I continued consulting with the client on performance issues under the ongoing supervision of the peer and professional supervisors (meta-supervision can get complicated to describe!). While most meta-supervision experiences look slightly different than this one, I still found it extremely beneficial to work with an advanced student and hear her perspective on the case. I often felt inspired and rejuvenated to work with my client after I would meet with my peer supervisor and discuss our coordination of care.

Since the time of the above example, I have graduated from the master's program and am now in a Psy.D. program. I am now in the "other chair" as a peer supervisor (being supervised by a professional supervisor) of a beginning student. This has proven to be an irreplaceable opportunity and experience. I recall feeling nervous when I first met with my supervisee because I was unsure of what I had to offer her that she did not already know. I enjoyed our meetings, but I remember walking away from our supervision sessions thinking that there was not much I could help her with, especially since we were not that far apart in training level. Over time, my relationship with this student changed, and I found myself collaborating on team issues with her in a way that did not necessarily feel like supervision, but rather peer consultation. By the same token, I was bringing things to light that she reportedly had not thought of before, like sticking with certain topics that her athletes shied away from or avoided (e.g., fear of failure). I have thoroughly enjoyed this opportunity to provide supervision while also getting supervised by a professional in the field. There is also something rewarding about having my own supervisor commend me for the feedback and comments I am providing, which allows me to feel more competent and excited to fill this supervisory role.

Trainee's Experience (TF)

I have been lucky enough to be a recipient of supervision from a peer supervisor engaged in meta-supervision as well as participate in meta-supervision as a peer supervisor. Both experiences were invaluable and very helpful for my development as a sport psychology consultant. As a recipient, I did not really know what to expect at first. I wondered how available my peer supervisor would be and how much I would get out of the experience. However, my peer supervisor went to great lengths to make herself available in person, phone, or video chat. I was also quickly comforted by learning that my peer supervisor was there to largely support me, offer perspectives or ideas, pose questions, and act as an extra safety net (which luckily was unneeded) in the case of significant mistakes. The best thing of all was that I felt as if I had the eyes of two more experienced consultants on my work, each stimulating me with their own unique way of approaching things. Proverbially, two heads are better than one—and I could not agree more with this sentiment as it pertains to supervision.

I am also passionate about my first experience as a peer supervisor. The beginning student I was supervising had been my "shadow" when I was a second-year master's student. When I graduated she "took over" the team I had been consulting for. Thus, as I became her peer supervisor, I had intimate knowledge of the team, the culture, and many of the individual athletes. This could not have been more helpful as it provided much more context for the work she was doing. My goal as a peer supervisor was to help in whatever ways were needed most. I met with the student to explicitly outline what she did or did not want and did or did not need. For each session she would have, she would send me her case notes; I would review them, provide feedback to answer any specific questions she had (highlight things she did well), and offer suggestions on how she may choose to delve deeper into something in the future. Periodically throughout the year, I would check in with the student in person to spend time talking about her current case(s) and ensure that I was being most useful and helpful for her and her work. I truly enjoyed being in this role, and, as many professors and supervisors attest, I believe I learned as much from her as she learned from me.

The most interesting thing about the professional supervision I received of my supervision was that it felt a lot like the professional supervision I had received of my own applied work. Early on, I felt more reliant on my professional supervisor for guiding my supervision. I needed help with considering how to go about creating a strong supervisory relationship with my supervisee as well as helping my supervisee identify specific goals for her applied work. Later on in the supervision of my supervision, my supervisor was much more "hands off" and would simply check in to see how things were going and pose questions or comments to refine what I was doing with my supervisee.

Professional's Experience (JS)

Since providing individualized attention to supervisees is a challenge as a professional supervisor, getting our Psy.D. students and alumni involved as peer supervisors has helped address this issue. This also helps our program maintain strong connections to our alumni, while providing training for supervisors in the field of sport and performance psychology. Many of our students have said that the extra attention and guidance they receive from their peer supervisor has been invaluable.

The method I use for meta-supervision includes reading the feedback that the peer supervisors provide to the supervisees, and then I provide feedback on the feedback. I also offer resources about supervision to the peer supervisors and check in with them periodically (in person or via email or phone) about how supervision is going. This process does take quite a bit of extra time and energy since I am reading two sets of notes (the supervisee's and the peer supervisor's) and spending time training the peer supervisors. Ultimately, we feel that the benefits of meta-supervision significantly outweigh the costs, and we are continually refining and improving our process of meta-supervision.

Peer Mentoring in Sport and Performance Psychology

Peer mentoring occurs when a beginning student shadows a more experienced student. Mentoring pairs typically consist of a slightly more experienced, though still beginning, practitioner (e.g., second-year graduate student) and a less experienced student who shadows the mentor (e.g., first-year graduate student). It is important to note here the shift in language from "supervision" to "mentoring." The importance is due to the differential implications of supervision vs. mentoring. The focus of peer mentoring is more informal, supportive, collaborative, and "hands on learning," while professional and meta-supervision are more formal and evaluative, and more weight is placed on the supervisor in terms of client welfare. There are several benefits to a peer mentoring relationship that can include, but are not limited to, the informal nature, the openness of the relationship, the ability of the mentor and mentee to relate on a similar level, gaining information about the student perspective, and helping the mentee build better social connections (Watson, Clement, Blom, & Grindley, 2009). In addition, students reported that advantages of peer mentorship are that peers are easily accessible for feedback in a timely manner, are less threatening than the more experienced supervisor, are easier to relate to, and have similar experiences in their development as consultants (Yambor & Thompson, 2014). On the other hand, there can be challenges associated with peer mentoring as well. Having a shadow while still relatively novice as a consultant can put the mentor in an uncomfortable position of feeling the need to be "on" for the mentee. Also, the mentee may be inexperienced enough to believe that "this looks easy" and "I could do better." However, as the relationship strengthens, mutual respect is often developed, and feelings of recognition for the skill of the mentor and acknowledgement of the mentor's own experience and competence in responding to the mentee's questions result from this process.

There are certain risks to the peer mentoring relationship that one can probably imagine when students are advising one another. Mentors are more likely to select mentees based on the mentee's perceived ability and potential, rather than on the mentee's need for help (Allen, Poteet, & Russell, 2000). This potential problem that Allen et al. point to does not allow for students to work on their areas of weakness. Mentors may also favor mentees that they prefer socially outside of the classroom, rather than functionally analyzing the potential costs and benefits to working together in a collaborative consulting setting. Some training programs do provide a more pragmatic approach to setting up peer mentoring relationships. An example would be having the students select their mentors on the first day of classes before individuals get a chance to form opinions and biases of one another. Our program focuses on matching pairs with similar interests and goals (e.g., working with teams versus individuals). One quality required when selecting mentees is a high motivation and learning orientation; Allen (2004) argues that even very high-ability protégés will be difficult to mentor if they lack a desire or willingness to learn. Other disadvantages to peer mentorship that have previously been reported are a lack of self-awareness, peers behaving in potentially unethical ways, overconfidence in ability, individuals further along in the program demonstrating a sense of entitlement, and general personality conflicts (Yambor & Thompson, 2014). All of these potential concerns are areas to be aware of when working with a peer mentor.

While some programs build the process of choosing peer mentors/mentees into their curriculum, Allen (2004) has also suggested that mentees may need to be proactive in finding a mentor. For those students seeking experience and direct training in sport and performance consulting skills, it would be highly beneficial for them to reach out to a colleague who is starting to consult and ask if they would be open to having a shadow. While this may be an unnerving process, the potential mentor would likely be flattered and possibly open to the opportunity to advance his or her training by providing mentorship to another student. Also, as mentioned previously, the rewards and benefits to peer mentorship are ongoing. Mentees that receive more career development (advice, feedback) tend to also receive more psychosocial benefits, such as emotional support and confidence building (Burke & McKeen, 1997). The peer mentoring relationship also prepares the mentees for future supervisory relationships by getting them more comfortable with feedback, criticism, and open collaboration.

"Peer consultation" is similar to peer mentoring in that supportive feedback is highlighted and there is no evaluative function. Consultation emphasizes the choice to accept or reject the suggestions of others (Bernard & Goodyear, 1992). We use mentoring here to indicate that there is a (however slightly) more experienced member of the dyad (designated the mentor) and a less experienced member of the dyad (the mentee). Peer consultation involves no hierarchy whatsoever, and it occurs formally in our program during group supervision and informally through a variety of means both inside and outside of the classroom. Furthermore, as trainees transition into professionals, it is essential to set up a peer consultation network for continued growth and development as well as ethical conduct.

Authors' Experiences

Trainee's Experience (MM)

My experience in my graduate program was an extremely positive one when it came to finding a peer mentor. Coming from a figure skating background, I wanted to gain experience observing a sport that was similar to mine, but that also could provide new challenges. I ended up shadowing a second-year master's student who was working with a synchronized figure skating team as well as a gymnastics team. I was skeptical of the process at first and felt as if I could be in her role conducting these sessions, rather than sitting back and observing. It was the reflective processing and planning we did together before and after sessions that helped our relationship and collaboration grow. I found that as I asked questions and was curious about why she tried a certain intervention in that specific moment, she would explain her thinking to me, which would open up my views of how to approach performance breakdowns. Similar to how the process was described previously, I gained more respect for my mentor, and started to feel as if I could attempt some of these consulting interventions with athletes myself.

Looking back, I see that this relationship prepared me for several other professional encounters that I would face over the next few years. I have gone on to study clinical psychology at the doctoral level, and I have received feedback from faculty that I am extremely open to supervision and seem to apply others' suggestions to my practice. I also have found it helpful to reach out to a third-year student as a first-year in the program, which was very similar to the first-year/second-year dynamic I had with my mentor in the master's program. This allowed me to network with field placement sites and potential clients that my mentor had worked with, as well as grow from her experiences and challenges that she shared with me. I do not think this experience would have been as meaningful to me if I had not been exposed to the peer mentoring opportunities in my master's program. I am forever grateful for these relationships and will continue to seek peer mentorship throughout the rest of my academic and professional career.

Trainee's Experience (TF)

As a first-year master's student, I initially chose a different path than many of my peers. Rather than doing consistent, immersive shadowing of a second-year student, I was coaching at the high school level. The relatively few experiences I had with shadowing, however, were quite informative and valuable. I quickly saw how difficult it was to keep an entire team (big or small) engaged with the session. I also learned how creative team sessions could be, blending social skills and fun in the pursuit of team cohesion. Because of having a lower quantity of shadowing experiences, I had to make the most of my opportunities to indirectly learn from my peers. This took the form of listening intently during practicum classes when second-years would talk about their recent consulting experiences and when first-years would discuss their recent shadowing experiences. It also took on another form that is a different layer of peer mentoring—learning from my peers within my cohort and "co-consulting."

When beginning my own mental performance consulting sessions, I really wished I had had more shadowing experiences. I felt as if I did not know what I was doing, and it would have helped to have witnessed more group sessions to learn some more "dos" and "don'ts." However, I also learned that this anxiety of feeling as if I did not know what I was doing was still pretty normal, regardless of the amount of shadowing experience. My anxieties were further allayed by the opportunity to "co-consult"—facilitate a group session with a peer—as an early second-year master's student. I believe the co-consulting dynamic is an ideal form of peer-to-peer consultation and collaboration as it provides an appealingly formal and informal, as well as supportive, situation to "learn by doing." It also calls for attention to detail in planning and executing sessions and defining roles (e.g., who will say what and when).

Eventually, it became time for me to have first-year students shadow my sessions. My experiences with shadows were almost entirely positive. My shadows were individuals who were hungry to learn (and thus respected my knowledge) and were constructively honest with their feedback and ideas of what could have been done differently in a session. It is surely not uncommon for first-year students to be overconfident in their knowledge and skills and skeptical of the abilities of the second year; however, the culture of the master's program was to acknowledge these thoughts and feelings as they come up in order to be cognizant of whether it is enhancing or inhibiting the peer mentoring relationship and the growth of both students. Such a culture would not have been possible without the foresight, guidance, reinforcement, and experience of the faculty.

Summary

Like clinical and counseling psychology, supervision within the field of sport and performance psychology is a staple of training and continual professional growth. Professional supervision is a competency in all fields of psychology, including sport and performance psychology. Thus, there is utility in looking to clinical and counseling psychology for guidance in specific models and ways of conceptualizing supervision and its multiple levels. The dynamics of peer mentoring and meta-supervision offer tremendous opportunity for the growth of young professionals. Making supervision processes explicit, intentional, and based on relevant research allows sport and performance psychology trainees to gain multiple perspectives and maximize professional growth. Immersing oneself in each level of supervision—peer mentoring, meta-supervision, and professional supervision—throughout one's professional career not only aids in the solidification of academic knowledge but also enriches professional practice.

From this chapter, it is important to understand the following structures and processes:

- Structures
  - Professional supervision
    - Individual supervision
    - Group supervision
  - Meta-supervision roles and primary directions of influence
    - Professional supervisor → peer supervisor → supervisee
    - Professional supervisor → peer supervisor
    - Peer supervisor → supervisee
  - Peer mentoring
    - Mentor → mentee/"shadow"
  - Peer consultation
    - Co-consulting
    - Formal (e.g., group supervision)
    - Informal (e.g., outside of school discussions)
    - Professional network
- Processes
  - Building an effective supervisory working relationship
    - Supportive and evaluative
  - Finding a match that is developmentally appropriate
    - Level of training and comfort level
  - Selecting an appropriate supervision model
    - Fitting for supervisor and supervisee
  - The development of a supervisor in meta-supervision
    - Influence from professional supervisor
    - Influence on supervisee

- Peer mentorship selection and dynamics
  - How mentors select mentees
  - How mentees select mentors
  - How mentors and mentees grow with each other

References

Abbass, A. (2004). Small group-videotape training for psychotherapy skills development. *Academic Psychiatry, 28*(2), 151–155.

Allen, T. D. (2004). Protégé selection by mentors: Contributing individual and organizational factors. *Journal of Vocational Behavior, 65*, 469–483.

Allen, T. D., Poteet, M. L., & Russell, J. E. A. (2000). Protégé selection by mentors: What makes the difference? *Journal of Organizational Behavior, 21*, 271–282.

American Psychological Association. (2011). *Revised competency benchmarks for professional psychology*. Retrieved from http://www.apa.org/ed/graduate/revised-competency-benchmarks.doc

Andersen, M. B., & Williams-Rice, B. T. (1996). Supervision in the education and training of sport psychology service providers. *The Sport Psychologist, 10*, 278–290.

Barnett, J. E. (2014). Introduction: The (hopefully) essential primer on clinical supervision. *Journal of Clinical Psychology, 70*(11), 1023–1029.

Barney, S. T., & Andersen, M. B. (2014). A supervision model utilizing peer mentoring and consultation teams in the provision of applied sport psychology. In J. G. Cremades & L. S. Tashman (Eds.), *Becoming a sport, exercise, and performance psychology professional: A global perspective* (pp. 339–346). New York, NY: Psychology Press.

Bernard, J. M. (2005). Tracing the development of clinical supervision. *The Clinical Supervisor, 24*, 3–21.

Bernard, J. M., & Goodyear, R. K. (1992). *Fundamentals of clinical supervision*. Needham Heights, MA: Allyn & Bacon.

Bilder, C., Hanley, S., ONeil, A., Shapiro, J., Cowart, S., Deihl, R., & Aoyagi, M. (2014, October). *Comprehensive supervision structure of graduate students: Benefits, limitations, and future directions*. Symposium presented at the Association for Applied Sport Psychology Conference, Las Vegas, NV.

Bordin, E. S. (1979). The generalizability of the psychoanalytic concept of the working alliance. *Psychotherapy: Theory, Research, and Practice, 16*, 252–260.

Brown, S. D., & Lent, R. W. (2008). *Handbook of counseling psychology* (4th ed.). Hoboken, NJ: John Wiley & Sons Inc.

Burke, R. J., & McKeen, C. A. (1997). Benefits of mentoring relationships among managerial and professional women: A cautionary tale. *Journal of Vocational Behavior, 51*, 43–57.

Delini, F. M. (2013). Supervision by doctoral students: A study of supervisee satisfaction and self efficacy, and comparison with faculty supervision outcomes. *The Clinical Supervisor, 32*, 1–14.

Falender, C. A., Erickson Cornish, J. A., Goodyear, R., Hatcher, R., Kaslow, N. J., Leventhal, G., . . . & Sigmon, S. T. (2004). Defining competencies in psychology supervision: A consensus statement. *Journal of Clinical Psychology, 60*(7), 771–785.

Granello, D. H., Kindsvatter, A., Granello, P. F., Underfer-Babalis, J., & Hartwig Moorhead, H. J. (2008). Multiple perspectives in supervision: Using a peer consultation model to enhance supervisor development. *Counselor Education & Supervision, 48*, 32–47.

Milne, D. (2007). An empirical definition of clinical supervision. *British Journal of Clinical Psychology, 46*, 437–447.

Silva, J. M., Metzler, J. N., & Lerner, B. (2011). *Training professionals in the practice of sport psychology* (2nd ed.). Morgantown, WV: Fitness Information Technology.

Stoltenberg, C. D., McNeill, B. W., & Delworth, U. (1998). *IDM supervision: An Integrated Development Model for supervising counselors and therapists*. San Francisco, CA: Jossey-Bass.

Van Raalte, J. L., & Andersen, M. B. (2000). Supervision I: From models to doing. In M. B. Andersen (Ed.), *Doing sport psychology* (pp. 153–163). Champaign, IL: Human Kinetics.

Watson, J. C., Clement, D., Blom, L. C., & Grindley, E. (2009). Mentoring: Processes and perceptions of sport and exercise psychology graduate students. *Journal of Applied Sport Psychology, 21*, 231–246.

Yambor, J., & Thompson, M. (2014). A supervision model utilizing peer mentoring and consultation teams in the provision of applied sport psychology. In J. G. Cremades & L. S. Tashman (Eds.), *Becoming a sport, exercise, and performance psychology professional: A global perspective* (pp. 285–292). New York, NY: Psychology Press.

7 Initial Experiences in Practica

Foundations, Experiential Learning, and Insights

Emily Tonn, Kensa Gunter, and Bob Harmison

Over the past decade, sport psychology researchers and practitioners have been increasingly focused on providing information to help students and early career practitioners in navigating applied sport psychology experiences. These sport psychology professionals have shared personal accounts of their early applied experiences related to providing mental skills training, developing a professional philosophy, and personal development of the practitioner (Collins, Evans-Jones, & O'Connor, 2013; Lindsay, Breckon, Thomas, & Maynard, 2007; Rowley, Earle, & Gilbourne, 2012; Tod & Bond, 2010; Tonn & Harmison, 2004). Additionally, developmental models, primarily from the field of counseling, have been presented as a way of understanding the professional identity development of sport psychology practitioners (Ronnestad & Skovholt, 2003; Tod, 2007; Tod & Bond, 2010), the importance of supervision during training experiences has been reiterated (Knowles, Gilbourne, Tomlinson, & Anderson, 2007; Tonn & Harmison, 2004), and specific techniques such as reflective practice have been highlighted as practices that could yield significant benefits during the training process (Cropley, Miles, Hanton, & Niven, 2007). In sum, significant efforts have been made to identify and provide information that will help neophytes in their preparation and approach to their first applied sport psychology experiences.

Research has shown that effectiveness related to providing sport psychology services is a function of practitioner characteristics including being personable, knowledgeable about sport and sport psychology, flexible, and a good communicator, as well as having a capacity for empathic understanding (Cropley et al., 2007; Orlick & Partington, 1987; Petitpas, Giges, & Danish, 1999). Researchers also have identified the capacity to establish a good working alliance (Cropley et al., 2007; Petitpas et al., 1999) as being an integral factor that impacts the effectiveness of sport psychology service provision. A comprehensive examination of this literature suggests that there are many factors for novice sport psychology consultants to consider when preparing for their first applied experiences. However, in spite of all of the information that has been presented, practitioners in training are likely still to experience unexpected scenarios and challenges during their initial experiences as they traverse the road to becoming a sport psychology professional.

In this chapter, the first and second authors provide their retrospective accounts of their first sport psychology practica. Although focused on a similar training experience, their accounts differ in that one author (Emily) was pursuing an M.A. in Sport-Exercise Psychology while the other (Kensa) was a doctoral student in a Clinical Psychology program with a concentration in Sport-Exercise Psychology. Furthermore, one account is focused on the direct application of services while the other is more focused on the personal and experiential aspect of being a practicum student. Both perspectives provide valuable insights that the authors hope will make the path through initial practica experiences appear to be a less daunting and possibly more enjoyable journey.

The Students

I (Emily) have always been involved in athletics, playing numerous sports in my youth such as softball, basketball, volleyball, and track. From among these, I decided to work hard at being a good basketball player. As it turns out, I was a four-year starter for a Division III college, a two-time All-Conference selection, the conference's most valuable player my senior year, and selected to four different All-America teams. Upon graduating, I enrolled in a sport psychology graduate program that was primarily applied in its focus, which suited me and my educational goals perfectly. Over the course of my master's program, I was exposed to a variety of classes that emphasized different aspects of sport psychology (e.g., motor learning, sport psychology research and theory, psychopathology). My program included various courses that involved critical thinking and influenced the development of my views and beliefs about my approach to sport psychology. In addition, I opted to take courses in counseling theory and multicultural counseling, which allowed me to develop additional skills and self-awareness. I currently am teaching Sociology, Psychology, and Advanced Placement (AP) Psychology at a high school in Arizona. I also have 11 years of experience coaching volleyball and basketball within all of my years of teaching. Sport psychology has played an integral role in my coaching style with the emphasis largely being on team-building skills as well as setting a foundation for mental toughness. My degree in sport psychology has allowed me to see some success with my teams over the course of my coaching career.

I (Kensa) participated in competitive sports from the age of 8 throughout my high school years primarily in the sports of swimming and basketball. When I entered college, my plan was to become a physical therapist. Having sustained numerous ankle injuries during my basketball career, I thought that this was an ideal way to combine my personal interests and experiences with my future occupation. Over time this plan changed, and I became more interested in the field of psychology and trying to understand the intricacies of human behavior. Ultimately, I ended up at a doctoral program where I pursued a Psy.D. in Clinical Psychology with a concentration in Sport-Exercise Psychology. I chose this program because I wanted to learn about clinical topics (e.g., psychopathology, psychological assessment), and I also wanted coursework related to sport psychology (e.g., psychological aspects of injury, mental skills training). This program not only offered coursework but also provided practicum experiences in both areas. I truly believe that completing a sport psychology practicum was an invaluable experience that helped in setting the stage for my sport psychology career. I currently am a licensed clinical psychologist and designated as a Certified Consultant through the Association for Applied Sport Psychology. I work in private practice in Georgia providing clinical and sport psychology services to adolescent and adult populations. I also serve as a sport psychology consultant for various athletic organizations.

Applications of Science to Practice

Theoretical Orientation and Philosophy: Emily

Given my lack of a foundation and training as a helper, my initial thoughts and approaches to doing sport psychology as a consultant in training were based on my experiences as a competitive athlete. About halfway through my first year of graduate study, my theoretical and philosophical approach to working with athletes began to take shape as I completed a required course in cognitive-behavioral theory and therapy. In this course, I learned for the first time about the intriguing relationship between a person's thoughts, feelings, and behaviors and began to formulate an understanding of how psychological skills could be utilized by athletes to alter this dynamic relationship and enhance performance. This learning and formulation has extended beyond my practicum experience and into my coaching and teaching career as well. As a high school varsity head coach, I have utilized mental training on a number of occasions and helped my athletes to understand the relationship that exists between their cognitive approach to performance and ability to perform. Likewise, in the classroom with my Advanced Placement students, we often discuss how awareness of their thoughts can either help or hinder their performance on exams.

My initial attempts to teach mental skills to individual athletes were grounded in my philosophy that athletes have the ability to control their thoughts, and ultimately their performance as a result. When I worked with these athletes, I educated them regarding the level of control that they possessed over their performance by providing them with sufficient knowledge about psychological skills and then helping them integrate these skills into their training and preparation. Ideally, I attempted to assist athletes in the process of behavioral change by not working harder than them to achieve their desired behavior change and leaving the responsibility for change to them in the end. I wanted athletes with whom I worked to understand their level of control over their performance and appreciate the effort needed on their part to bring about the desired behavioral change (e.g., talk with me about their situation, do homework assignments, practice specific skills).

Looking back, my theoretical orientation and philosophy highly influenced how I worked with a team of athletes in a number of ways. First, I adopted a psychological skills training approach to teach athletes the basic mental skills (e.g., self-talk, relaxation, imagery, and goal setting) that had been associated with peak performance in the sport psychology literature (Hardy, Jones, & Gould, 1996; Williams & Krane, 2001). This approach allowed athletes to gain knowledge about specific psychological skills and provided opportunities for them to use those skills during practice and competition and achieve desired results. Second, I opted to teach the "what" and "how" of each psychological skill (e.g., relationship between anxiety, muscle tension, and performance) in a team setting and then individualize the application of the skill with those athletes who expressed such an interest. A third goal of mine was to work collaboratively with each athlete (i.e., working *with* athletes and not *for* athletes). This required a solid foundation of rapport, trust, and understanding between the athletes and me when helping them to develop solutions as opposed to fixing their problems. Knowing that I would not work individually with every athlete on the team, I attempted to involve each athlete in the group activities and convey my support for them in achieving their desired performance goals.

My first experience as a sport psychology consultant was influenced by a number of factors related to my theoretical orientation and philosophy. Understanding my personal viewpoint for the way in which I wanted to help athletes was crucial to developing some level of success for myself. Gaining a clear perspective of cognitive-behavior therapy, realizing that athletes need to perceive that they were in control of their thoughts and performance, implementing psychological skills training, and utilizing a collaborative effort approach with athletes helped me to ultimately aid them in finding success.

Theoretical Orientation and Philosophy: Kensa

My initial sport psychology practicum experience took place within the athletic department of a midsized Division I institution, and I was assigned the responsibility of providing performance enhancement services to athletes and teams across the entire department. Prior to beginning my sport psychology practicum, I had taken several courses in counseling theory and counseling skills as well as some foundational courses in sport psychology.

My applied experiences consisted of a semester-long externship in a maximum security women's prison, a practicum at an eating disorders treatment program, and a practicum in the behavioral health services unit of a sheriff's department. These applied experiences working with clinical populations heavily influenced my mindset as I approached my sport psychology practicum.

While I recognized that applied sport psychology work would look and feel different from clinical work, I was much more attuned to working from the perspective of helping people to fix or address problem areas rather than working on performance enhancement or teaching new skills. Due to this mismatch between the methods used and my personal values and beliefs (Lindsay et al., 2007), I experienced feelings of incongruence and insecurity. Whereas I felt as if I was growing and making progress in my identity as a clinician, being faced with this new experience triggered old anxieties that were more characteristic of a novice stage of development. One of the ways I attempted to manage these feelings of insecurity was to focus on my theoretical orientation and to allow it to guide my work as a consultant.

Cognitive-behavioral therapy (CBT [Beck, 1995]) was the theoretical orientation I used in my applied sport psychology work. I was drawn to the central premise that changing an individual's patterns of thinking (e.g., cognitive distortions, maladaptive schemas) inevitably results in behavioral and emotional changes that impact an individual's response to various situations. This translated to an increased internal locus of control for those with whom I worked and was consistent with my belief that it was important to help individuals (and eventually teams) become their own agents of change to facilitate long-lasting growth. I also appreciated the psychoeducational quality of CBT because it provided a framework in which I could teach skills and incorporate mental skills training relevant to the individual's or team's needs. Additionally, this teaching component helped clients to become more aware of their thought processes and how these affected their overall performance and emotional and behavioral functioning. Lastly, I liked the inclusion of homework within the CBT model as it helped to reinforce the work done during training sessions by increasing athletes' accountability for their consultation experiences and application of the skills discussed in practice and competitive situations.

In addition to CBT, I incorporated multicultural theory (MCT [Sue & Sue, 2003]) into my applied sport psychology work. Incorporating MCT allowed me to gain a more holistic picture of the athletes and the environments in which they were operating while also understanding how the intersection of these factors were potentially impacting the clients (Kontos & Breland-Noble, 2002). In my clinical and sport work, it was important for me to understand the context(s) because doing so often provided greater insight into individual behavior (Parham, 2005). As an African American female, I am aware of the impact of various cultural factors on my own experiences, and, thus, I am conscious of this reality for the people with whom I work as well. Culture creates the lens through which we see the world, and "worldview" refers to the way individuals perceive their relationships to the world (Sue, 1981). When considering cultural factors within a sport context, I examined not only individual demographic factors but also the athletes' worldview and sport-related factors, such as the culture of their sport, their specific team, the athletic department, and the university.

Embracing a specific theoretical orientation, being aware of cultural contexts, and having some clarity about my personal philosophy helped me to establish my footing in the beginning stages of my practicum experience. Directed observation (e.g., observing practice with the intention of gathering additional information about team and individual dynamics) became another core skill that helped to increase feelings of comfort in my new role and provided additional insight regarding what was needed and how I could be beneficial.

I relied heavily on individual and group supervision to fill in some of my gaps in knowledge regarding working with sport populations, and I also began reading more sport psychology texts outside of the required readings for class to further supplement my experience and growing knowledge base.

Opportunities, Challenges, and Growth Areas

Emily

There were many opportunities and challenges over the course of my initial practicum experience that allowed for growth in a number of areas. I particularly was excited (and anxiety-ridden) about the opportunity to try my hand at psychological skills training and team building and learning how to incorporate these into a team setting. However, along with feeling excited and anxious, I was faced with a number of challenges—some for which I was prepared and others in which I had to make decisions that required considerable thought and an understanding of the consequences of my actions.

Opportunities

For my practicum experience I was the performance enhancement consultant for a junior college women's basketball team and worked with the team for a total of seven months. At the onset I met with the coaching staff to discuss our expectations for my experience with the team, various psychological skills to enhance the athletes' development, and critical group dynamics that needed to be addressed. I also conducted an informal needs assessment with the coaching staff and the previous year's practicum student regarding the mental skills they thought would benefit the team as well as areas of possible concern for the upcoming season. Eventually, I settled on the psychological skills of goal setting, self-talk, relaxation, imagery, and distraction control to provide the athletes with a solid foundation for the psychological preparation for performance (Hardy et al., 1996; Williams & Krane, 2001). I also chose team building as an intervention strategy to improve the group dynamics (e.g., cohesion, complimentary roles) of the team due to the positive benefits as noted in the sport psychology literature (e.g., Hardy & Crace, 1997) and discussed by Janssen (1999) as being important to the team's success.

Although I was excited about teaching psychological skills to the athletes and implementing various team-building activities with the team, I experienced a fair amount of anxiety about doing so effectively from time to time throughout my practicum experience. As a first time consultant, I was not always sure how to best manage these extreme differences in my excitement/anxiety feeling states. My internal angst was noticeable to me the first time I began working one-on-one with athletes who wanted individualized help with specific psychological skills. Initially, I put a lot of pressure on myself to find "quick fixes" to the problems that the athletes were presenting to me. It was so common for me to become overly concerned with techniques and wanting these athletes to perceive me as competent that I would not actually pay attention to what they needed until several sessions into our work together.

My supervisor helped me to realize that I needed to take the focus off my internal anxieties and concerns and simply listen to the athletes. In supervision, I learned that this type of self-focus and anxiety as a first-time consultant was par for the course; understanding that what I was experiencing was normal was the first step toward me becoming a more effective helper. Removing the focus from myself resulted in me allowing the athletes to talk about their situations more and establishing a stronger rapport with them. Our individual sessions became more of a partnership in designing personal performance plans rather than "quick fix" meetings. As these "partnerships" were forming, I gained insight into the fact that feeling competent as a consultant meant more than just intervening. It meant taking a step back and really listening to the athletes. It meant providing guidance while teaching athletes how to find the best avenue for themselves. As a coach and teacher, I have found this to be true as well. As a coach, my intent is to give as much support to my athletes as needed while allowing their own perspectives and creativity to influence their performance and success. As a classroom teacher, I aim to foster and encourage student growth as opposed to providing "quick fixes" and giving answers.

During the early part of the season, I was somewhat intimidated at the idea of conducting team-building activities. My experiences interacting with the team as a whole were limited at the beginning, and I felt very nervous prior to my talks with the team. I was a wreck at times, experiencing a shortness of breath, sweating, racing heart, and even self-doubt! Despite feeling fully prepared to conduct these team-building activities, I would irrationally convince myself that I was not ready. At times during an activity I found myself overly focusing on athletes who appeared to be bored and worrying about how I was going to justify the reasons for doing the activity in the first place.

Despite my initial angst and feelings of intimidation, conducting team-building activities emerged as one of my strongest areas of intervention. I overcame these negative thoughts and feelings by forcing myself to be in situations, such as being in front of the team, that were uncomfortable for me. In addition, my fears of leading these team-building activities dissipated as a result of completing a course in team dynamics as well as having discussions with my supervisor and peers in my practicum group seminar. In my team dynamics class, I learned about specific team-building exercises from the course instructor who also modeled how to facilitate the activities and process the learning that took place. In individual and group supervision I was able to process my first couple of team-building meetings and worries I had about doing and saying the right things. I eventually realized that team building was about the athletes and not about me; any derived benefit to me would be an additional plus. All I needed to do was simply focus on how I could facilitate their learning versus my insecurities as a consultant.

Challenges

When doing anything for the first time, challenges can often arise. There is a specific learning curve that must take place before a level of comfort (and hopefully a feeling of expertise) can set in for someone. Traveling with the team, my professional role, and boundary issues were three areas that presented significant challenges for me during my initial practicum experience.

TRAVELING WITH THE TEAM

I had the opportunity to accompany the team on several out-of-state tournaments and learned firsthand what to expect when traveling with a team as a consultant. I found out that a lot can happen when you spend a significant amount of your waking day with a team. Being "on the road" created challenges for me in how to best relate to the athletes and provide effective sport psychology services.

Before my first trip, I remember wanting to be as prepared for anything as I possibly could. In my mind I wrestled with what I was going to take with me (e.g., books, visualization scripts, self-talk logs), and I even made sure that I had ample supplies of gum for the athletes to chew during the games. Seeking my supervisor's advice prior to going on this trip proved to be invaluable. We discussed various situations, such as time on the bus and team dinners, that would provide opportunities for me to become a part of the team. We also reviewed times that would require me to make choices to maintain the professional nature of my relationships with the athletes, such as should I see a movie with the team if invited or meet with athletes in my hotel room. When I look back, I can now see that I was overly concerned about being ready for anything, especially with aspects that had very little to do with my role (e.g., providing gum). I now understand that being prepared means having resources to which you can turn if needed while simultaneously being creative yet professional when it comes to working with athletes. I apply this same principle in my current work as a coach and teacher.

PROFESSIONAL ROLE

My experience in and knowledge of basketball facilitated my work with the team, but at times it also complicated my relationships with the players and coaches and added complexity to my role. I anticipated that there would be times when I would disagree with the coaching philosophy. In addition, the coaches occasionally encouraged me to contribute to their conversations regarding the technical aspects of the game.

Knowing that my lone role within the team was to develop the athletes' mental skills, I struggled at times with this self-imposed limit as I strongly desired to be an asset to the coaches. Although I felt comfortable within my established role as a performance enhancement consultant, I also was nervous and unsure if the athletes would accept me and talk with me about their performance issues. To illustrate, there were times during practice when the athletes would make mistakes and the coaches would get upset with them. These were moments where I believe I could have stepped up and said something related to the technical aspects of the game or the mental state of the athletes. Despite knowing the sport so well, I often would feel uncomfortable being in this position. More often than not, I made the decision to simply step back and observe, not knowing if this was the right choice or not and being more concerned about not confusing the athletes regarding my role as their "mental" coach.

BOUNDARY ISSUES

Although I did not experience too many situations in which I had to contemplate my boundaries as a consultant, the most challenging issue in this regard was related to my wanting to be part of the team in the worst possible way. At times, I struggled with my decision to remain somewhat of an outsider of the team while very much wanting to participate in the group and be accepted by the athletes. There were times in which I was invited to participate in the group, such as being a part of a skit that the athletes were acting out in front of the group during one of our road trips. However, I was committed to the idea that I wanted the athletes to perceive me as a professional who could relax and have fun, but only to a certain extent.

In supervision, I learned some useful guidelines when trying to determine the appropriate relationship boundaries with athletes, such as observing how the coaches interact with the athletes and then distancing myself by one or two degrees. So I might pat a player on the back or clap from a distance after observing the head coach hug the player after hitting a game-winning shot. Ultimately, I decided to take this more conservative approach in the various situations I encountered. Although it took a little longer for me to fit in with the group using this approach, maintaining these types of relationship boundaries allowed me to solidify my identity and role with the team and helped me to gain respect from the athletes and coaches for the long haul.

Growth Areas

As it turns out, being a first-time consultant was not as terrifying as I thought it was going to be. I attribute this mostly to my education, training, and openness to new ideas. Going into my practicum experience, I believed I had acquired a solid knowledge base regarding applied sport psychology and felt confident in my skills to deal with the performance issues that would come my way. I quickly discovered that putting theories and mental skills into practice was completely different than reading and learning about them. However, with experience and guidance and support from my supervisor, I began to feel more comfortable with myself. This initial experience working with athletes laid the foundation for what my future entailed— coaching and teaching. I have learned that no matter what knowledge you have, sometimes you are forced to think on your feet, ask for guidance from your peers and mentors, and get feedback from those with whom you are working. I utilize every resource at my disposal to ensure the success of my athletes and students and to make sure that they always get the "best" version of me as their coach and teacher.

My supervised practicum experience proved to be significant in my growth as a sport psychology professional. Reflecting on my experience allowed me to increase my self-awareness regarding how I provided sport psychology services to athletes in a team setting, which has been identified in the literature as an important step in developing competence as a consultant (Holt & Strean, 2001; Simons & Andersen, 1995). I do wish that I would have spent more time reflecting on my services throughout my experience versus after. I think that it is important to evaluate one's own performance in anything, especially when working with individuals. From this experience, I have learned how critical self-awareness and evaluation are in my personal growth as a coach and teacher. Taking time to examine specific aspects of my coaching style, philosophy, and tactical approach has allowed me to identify my strengths and weaknesses throughout my career. The same rings true for me as teacher. Every lesson I teach can be improved through careful attention and evaluation.

Kensa

I was very excited and anxious about starting my applied sport psychology experience during the fourth year of my doctoral program. I had been working with clinical populations for the last few years, and I was finally at the point where I had the chance to do what I came to school to do—work with athletes. But could I do it? Would I be effective? Could I simultaneously balance the clinical and sport psychology consultant hats—was that ethical? Would they accept me and view me as someone who could actually help them improve their performance? Anxiety-ridden excitement—that is how I emotionally entered my first practicum experience.

Opportunities

My sport psychology practicum experience primarily consisted of individual consultations with athletes across a number of teams within a Division I university athletic department. I also conducted mental skills training sessions with teams and engaged in consultations with coaches, including regular consultation meetings with the coaching staff of one of the teams with which I worked. In all of these experiences, the most significant opportunity was having the chance to apply my book knowledge into practice and get a realistic feel for what applied sport psychology was all about. For me, teaching mental skills (e.g., self-talk, goal-setting, imagery) became a process that required a collaborative effort between the consultant and the athlete to transfer the skills discussed "in session" to tangible action steps in a live sport situation. From this perspective, in concert with "doing the work," my practicum experience afforded me the opportunity to increase my professional toolkit to expand my idea of applied sport psychology to include working with teams and coaches beyond solely equipping them with mental skills for individual performance.

EXPANDED KNOWLEDGE: TEACHING

The skills needed to teach someone a new technique or strategy are different than the skills needed to identify a problem and talk about it. During my early experiences of teaching mental skills to athletes and teams, I talked too much and provided more information than was necessary. I wanted them to know everything I knew about the subject as I tried to prove myself and force my credibility, and I felt that more information was better. Through trial and error and gaining more understanding about athletes' needs, I learned that the most important information from the athlete's perspective included the what, how, and why: (a) What do you want me to do? What skill do you want me to employ in practice/competition to address the performance block that has been identified? (b) How do you want me to do it? How do you want me to incorporate this mental skill into my physical practice or routine? (c) Why is this the skill that you chose to address this specific performance issue?

Using this relevance-based approach forced me to be more streamlined in how I presented information, which helped in communicating my desired message to athletes. When interventions were unsuccessful, using this approach helped us to identify where the breakdown in communication may have occurred. Expanding my teaching skills further facilitated my understanding of the connection between the mental and physical sides of sport and why I chose certain skills and interventions, and all of this helped with feeling more competent and secure in my professional identity as a consultant.

BEYOND INDIVIDUAL CONSULTATION

The second-most significant opportunity afforded me by this experience was realizing that sport psychology work involved more than working with individual athletes and included having the chance to gain experience working with teams and coaches. Individual counseling was the modality I most often used in my clinical practica experiences, which in structure is similar to individual sport psychology consultations. Working with teams and coaches was a very new experience and another opportunity for me to develop additional skills. A combination of sources proved to be helpful in navigating this new terrain; individual and peer supervision and knowledge gained from my sport psychology and some of my clinical psychology classes proved to be particularly beneficial. Specifically, my group dynamics and therapy and family therapy courses were helpful in conceptualizing some of the interactions that were observed among team members and between coaches and teammates.

It is important to note that I initially viewed coaches more as bosses than as clients in that they had the power to allow me access to their teams or not. Although this was true, viewing them in this way certainly impacted my presentation when they were present, resulting in increased feelings of anxiety and pressures to perform. However, through supervision, experience, and integrating some of the clinical knowledge previously mentioned, this perspective shifted so that they were viewed as clients, and I was able to see them as a part of the team system rather than as separate from it. An unexpected benefit of working with teams and coaches was that it enhanced the work with individual athletes. As previously mentioned, understanding culture and environmental context often provides insight into individual behavior (Parham, 2005). This insight contributed to increased understanding from a big-picture perspective, which allowed me to intervene in a more pointed and intentional way.

Challenges

CLINICAL VS. SPORT PSYCHOLOGY

The most significant challenge for me during this initial practicum experience was balancing the roles of being a student-in-training in both clinical psychology and sport psychology. As a clinician, I was more comfortable with the notion of helping people to work through problems, but as a sport psychology consultant I questioned my skills and abilities and reverted back to thinking that my role was to "fix" their problems and to prove myself as a professional. Using Ronnestad and Skovholt's (2003) counseling development model as a guide, I realize now that I was experiencing an internal conflict between feelings of confidence and readiness in my role as a clinician versus feelings of apprehension, anxiety, and self-doubt related to my new role as a sport psychology consultant.

Rather than exploring my professional philosophy in both the clinical and the sport domains, I erroneously made the assumption that the helping frame of sport psychology would mirror the frame of clinical psychology. This clinical frame was defined as one-on-one or group therapy that occurred in an office whereby the clinician obtained detailed information about the client's background and presenting concerns and then worked with the client to address the identified problems. Although the sport frame included some individual consultations in an office as well, it also involved meeting in the locker room, in the gym, on the practice field, or in the athletic training room; meeting with the team with the coaches present; or meeting only with the coaches. All of these experiences challenged me to think about what it meant to be a sport psychology consultant and how to balance this with my role as a clinician.

As I attempted to make clinical and sport psychology coexist, I experienced a host of questions and concerns about ethics specifically related to confidentiality and multiple relationships. I was quite uncomfortable with the idea of working with clients in public spaces (e.g., meeting at the track to address a mental block, addressing mental skills questions at practice in front of teammates) because of how this could negate any sense of confidentiality and potentially impact the working relationship. I also was concerned about functioning in multiple roles (e.g., serving as a consultant for an individual athlete and also the coaching staff) and how this would be perceived by the athletes and coaches. Despite obtaining the necessary authorizations for release of information and obtaining consent from the athletes to provide services in nontraditional settings, there was an internal struggle and what I called a professional identity conflict between my clinical and sport psychology selves.

This issue was processed a great deal in individual supervision throughout the duration of my practicum experience as it was difficult for me to grasp the concept of providing ethical services in these different settings. The ethical issues were examined, my concerns were addressed, the potential implications were explored, and my supervisor provided examples from his professional experiences in which it had been extremely beneficial to provide services within the field of play. Ultimately, I was able to address this conflict by placing an emphasis on obtaining consent, being very clear about the purpose of meeting in a nontraditional setting, and taking care during that meeting of maintaining the confidentiality of what was discussed. If the athlete was not comfortable with it, it did not happen.

However, the athletes generally welcomed meeting in the sport environment and actually appreciated the effort to integrate the mental skills into their physical activity.

CULTURAL IDENTITY

The second-most significant challenge for me was related to my concerns regarding whether or not I as an African American woman would be viewed as someone who had the knowledge and skills to help athletes and teams improve their athletic performance. While I held other cultural identities, my racial and gender identity were the two that were most salient for me at the time. This thought stemmed from a larger concern about whether or not I would be accepted within the larger sport psychology community.

When I began my sport practicum in 2004, my impression of sport psychology as a field was that it was largely dominated by White men, which is supported in the literature (Cogan & Petrie, 1996; Parham, 2005). Additionally, there were very few African American students in my cohort, classes, and practicum placements, and I did not have any African American professors or supervisors during my doctoral training. Researchers have found that African American doctoral students are often faced with navigating the challenges of interacting in spaces in which they are not traditionally represented (Torres, Driscoll, & Burrow, 2010), which can lead to frustration, self-doubt, feeling as if they are racially invisible in classroom environments (Solorzano, Ceja, & Yosso, 2000), and general feelings of cultural and racial isolation (Lewis, Ginsber, Davies, & Smith, 2004). I experienced all of those feelings and realities during my doctoral training, and, despite my passion and enthusiasm, I was uncertain about where I fit within the sport psychology profession. I had encountered similar feelings and experiences at other times in my life, most notably during my time as a competitive swimmer. Looking back, some of the dynamics (e.g., self-doubt, cultural and racial isolation, questions about acceptance due to my racial identity, feeling the need to prove my worth and capabilities) were the same.

Unfortunately, I did not take these concerns to my supervisor, who happened to be a White male. Why? There are a several reasons, but the unpolished truth is that I did not want to have to justify or explain my experience as it related to my racial identity. Even more importantly, I did not want to risk having my cultural experience dismissed or not being treated as a significant and salient part of my overall experience as a developing sport psychology professional. Furthermore, the impact of the consultant's intersecting cultural identities on the consultant's experience was never really discussed in my classes and supervision. So despite my personal struggle, I did not broach the subject because navigating these identities did not seem to be a challenge for any of my peers. I did not want my experiences to be dismissed for fear of being seen as "playing a race card" or making an issue where there was none. Also, highlighting my insecurity related to cultural identity and acceptance while simultaneously dealing with the anxiety of shifting from clinical to sport psychology–related work felt inconsistent with the confident and capable perception that I was trying to convey and was a vulnerability that I was not willing to share with my supervisor.

I needed support, understanding, and validation without the prerequisite of explanation. So, instead, I discussed these concerns with my family, friends, peers, and other professors who I thought might understand my experience. Researchers suggest that it helps to establish space in academic and/or social settings characterized by educational, emotional, and cultural support whereby African American students can vent frustrations and hear from others who have had similar experiences—a space where their experiences are validated and viewed as important knowledge (Solorzano et al., 2000; Solorzano & Villalpando, 1998). Processing my experiences in this way helped tremendously in my process of resolving the internal conflict and feeling more confident and secure in my cultural identities. In retrospect, it likely would have been very helpful to address my concerns with my supervisor as well, as it would have given us the chance to explore how holding these concerns impacted my work. It also may have provided an opportunity for my supervisor to think about cultural identity and professional development in a different way. I am certain that many students navigate this journey related to their cultural identities (e.g., racial, sexual, religious, ability status, etc.), and supervisors of our work can benefit from participating in our struggles.

Growth Areas

My primary areas of growth should be apparent above as each was woven into the discussion about opportunities and challenges. Specifically, I grew as a consultant during my first practicum experience in the expansion of my clinical/consulting skill set to include teaching and working with teams and coaches, the integration of the identities of clinician and sport psychology consultant, broadening the idea of the way in which my services could be delivered while maintaining ethical and legal standards of practice, and becoming more comfortable and confident in my ability to conceptualize a case from a performance-enhancement standpoint and intervene effectively. I also realized more clearly the importance of engaging in self-examination and reflection. You have to be clear about who you are as a professional (or who you want to be) to be able to help anyone. I attempted to address various personal concerns and anxieties (e.g., my cultural identity) in an effort to minimize their impact on my work. Hindsight being 20/20, I could have used supervision to further explore some of my concerns and anxieties to add to my attempts. As a new consultant, you are not going to know everything and may experience a host of different thoughts and feelings. It will be important for you to be able to identify "your stuff" (e.g., struggles, buttons, insecurities, fears, challenges) so that you can better understand and work through it as needed to be the best consultant you can be.

The only other growth area that I would add would be creativity. From my perspective, there is a level of creativity involved in the process of providing sport psychology services. Athletes can present with the same performance concern, and yet the intervention or the mental skills used to assist them can be very different. Creativity is needed to truly individualize mental skills training plans so that the athlete can apply them and receive the intervention as intended. At the beginning of my first practicum experience, I had not reached the point in my training where I embraced creativity. There was too much concern about doing things "right" (e.g., applying an intervention according to the textbook) and not making mistakes. This probably was developmentally appropriate, but also contributed to some of the anxiety that I experienced. I am thankful that I had a supervisor who pushed me beyond this point so that, at the end of the practicum, creativity was viewed as an important and necessary skill.

Advice to Future Trainees and Final Thoughts

If I Could Go Back in Time . . . : Emily

Since my experience as a new trainee, there have been several accounts of people documenting their own adventures as neophyte consultants that I would have found useful throughout my time with my team. For example, Lindsay et al. (2007) discussed the importance of considering a variety of options with regard to personal approaches and working with athletes. I am not sure that I did that. I was drawn to CBT and thought that psychological skills training just made sense, so that was what I did. Looking back, I probably did not spend enough time in reflection of my own personal beliefs. It should be noted that emphasis on personal reflection early on can help with congruence between a new trainee's methods of practice and personal philosophical approach (Lindsay et al., 2007). Poczwardowski, Sherman, and Ravizza (2004) also pointed out that it is important to focus on philosophical areas to provide better delivery of sport psychology services and that this can be done by having the trainee explore questions related to personal beliefs and values with regard to behavior change.

Additionally, hearing more personal accounts from other neophytes would have been useful. In one such account (Woodcock, Richards, & Mugford, 2008), a trainee discusses listening to her supervisor's initial experience with regard to his professional journey that highlighted his personal anxieties, strengths, weaknesses, and tools that he used along the way. The consultant explains how once she had time to reflect on the supervisor's experience, she realized that the lesson was about taking the focus off the athletes and tools that should be utilized and directing it toward getting to know yourself (e.g., strengths and weaknesses) to understand how to better develop as a consultant. I never did this. I did not take time to sit down and reflect with my own supervisor about his experience, nor did I make "getting to know myself better" a priority. In hindsight, I have learned that core beliefs are instrumental in guiding professional and personal behavior. If I would have taken the time necessary to really understand my own philosophy, coupled with my personal life and sport experiences, I could have done an even better job as a consultant.

Woodcock et al. (2008) also discussed the significance of trainees evaluating their strengths and weaknesses by reading their journal entries throughout consultation. They claim the purpose for this is to boost personal confidence and eliminate doubt. I kept very thorough journal entries for my entire practicum experience, and I cannot remember even a handful of times that I went back to read about things that I had done well (or not so well). I think that if I would have made even a slight effort to look at my journal, I could have learned from some of my mistakes as well as gained confidence in my abilities for things I was doing well.

If I Could Go Back in Time . . . : Kensa

If I had an opportunity to repeat my first practicum experience, the primary thing that I would do differently would be to spend more time thinking about my professional philosophy and what being a sport psychology consultant meant to me. As defined by Poczwardowski et al. (2004), professional philosophy encompasses several factors including the consultant's beliefs and values concerning the nature of reality, the nature of human behavior change, and also his or her potential role in influencing clients toward mutually set intervention goals. According to Poczwardowski et al., the foundation of an individual's professional philosophy rests in his or her personal core beliefs and also includes a theoretical paradigm concerning behavior change, model of practice and the consultant role, intervention goals, and intervention techniques and methods. I explored these elements in the context of my clinical identity but simply tried to adapt my clinical identity within the sport psychology realm. In retrospect, I may have experienced less conflict between these identities had I intentionally taken the time to develop my philosophy as a neophyte sport psychology consultant and explore what it would mean to integrate these identities and philosophies under one professional identity umbrella.

In an effort to be intentional about fostering continued growth throughout the practicum, I would have kept a journal documenting success, failures, and my reflections about the experience of being a new consultant. Certainly I discussed my practicum experiences in individual and group supervision, but this additional component of reflective practice would have afforded the opportunity for increased self-examination, self-evaluation, increased self-awareness, and effective practice (Cropley et al., 2007; Knowles et al., 2007).

Final Thoughts

There is an abundance of advice that we could offer first-time consultants. We both experienced many situations over the course of our practica that allowed room for learning, reflection, and growth. If we had to select the most important pieces of advice to offer to those just beginning their journey into the world of sport psychology consulting, the central themes would surround self-reflection and the importance of supervision.

As stated throughout this chapter, trainees can benefit tremendously from the process of self-reflection regarding their practicum experience. Providing sport psychology services to athletes in a team setting is a complex process, and developing competence in such a setting requires learning how to deliver effective presentations, facilitate group work, fit into the group while maintaining a professional identity, and meet the needs of individual athletes. For us, it was not until we removed ourselves and reflected on our individual experiences as trainees that we realized how influential our initial practicum was in the development of our competence. Trainees are encouraged to engage in reflective practice during and after their practicum to gain deeper insight and self-awareness (Holt & Strean, 2001).

It is also important to acknowledge the significance of supervision and the role a supervisor can play in the development of a trainee in sport psychology. Whether a new trainee is enrolled in a master's program or doctoral program, supervision is critical throughout the entire process. As we have documented throughout this chapter, supervisors can be utilized in a number of ways, and trainees should take advantage of all of the time and advice they can get! Our practica may have been vastly different as consultants, but both of our supervision experiences offered support and guidance as needed. There were times of question, confusion, and anxiety, but the support offered during these times was crucial and helped in transforming these uncomfortable experiences into meaningful growth opportunities. During supervision, we also were challenged to think critically about ourselves, which ultimately allowed each of us to build self-confidence and become more independent as practitioners.

In closing, we want the neophyte to remember that a practicum is a time for learning. Everyone has to start somewhere, and, in the world of sport psychology, trainees cannot just walk into a group of athletes and know what to do in every situation. And guess what? That's okay. There are going to be many mistakes that are made and many things that are done well. In the end, as long as reflection and growth have happened, well, you are on your way.

References

Beck, J. (1995). *Cognitive therapy: Basics and beyond*. New York: The Guilford Press.

Cogan, K. D., & Petrie, T. A. (1996). Diversity in sport. In J. L. Van Raalte & B. W. Brewer (Eds.), *Exploring sport and exercise psychology* (pp. 355–373). Washington, DC: American Psychological Association.

Collins, R., Evans-Jones, K., & O'Connor, H. (2013). Reflections on three neophyte sport and exercise psychologists developing philosophies for practice. *The Sport Psychologist, 27*, 399–409.

Cropley, B., Miles, A., Hanton, S., & Niven, A. (2007). Improving the delivery of applied sport psychology support through reflective practice. *The Sport Psychologist, 21*, 475–494.

Hardy, C. J., & Crace, R. K. (1997). Team building [Special issue]. *Journal of Applied Sport Psychology, 9*, 1–10.

Hardy, L., Jones, G., & Gould, D. (1996). *Understanding psychological preparation for sport: Theory and practice of elite performance.* Chichester, UK: Wiley.

Holt, N. L., & Strean, W. B. (2001). Reflecting on initiating sport psychology consultation: A self-narrative of neophyte practice. *The Sport Psychologist, 15,* 188–204.

Janssen, J. (1999). *Championship team building.* Tucson, AZ: Winning the Mental Game.

Knowles, Z., Gilbourne, D., Tomlinson, V., & Anderson, A. G. (2007). Reflections on the application of reflective practice for supervision in applied sport psychology. *The Sport Psychologist, 22,* 109–122.

Kontos, A. P., & Breland-Noble, A. M. (2002). Racial/ethnic diversity in applied sport psychology: A multicultural introduction to working with athletes of color. *The Sport Psychologist, 16,* 296–315.

Lewis, C. W., Ginsber, R., Davies, T., & Smith, K. (2004). The experiences of African American Ph.D. students at a predominately White Carnegie-I research institution. *College Student Journal, 38,* 231–245.

Lindsay, P., Breckon, J., Thomas, O., & Maynard, I. (2007). In pursuit of congruence: A personal reflection on methods and philosophy in applied practice. *The Sport Psychologist, 21,* 335–352.

Orlick, T., & Partington, J. (1987). The sport psychology consultant: Analysis of critical components as viewed by Canadian Olympic athletes. *The Sport Psychologist, 1,* 4–17.

Parham, W. D. (2005). Raising the bar: Developing an understanding of culturally, ethnically and racially diverse athletes. In M. Andersen (Ed.), *Practicing sport psychology* (pp. 211–219). Champaign, IL: Human Kinetics.

Petitpas, A. J., Giges, B., & Danish, S. J. (1999). The sport psychologist-athlete relationship: Implications for training. *The Sport Psychologist, 13,* 344–357.

Poczwardowski, A., Sherman, C., & Ravizza, K. (2004). Professional philosophy in the sport psychology service: Building theory on practice. *The Sport Psychologist, 18,* 445–463.

Ronnestad, M. H., & Skovholt, T. M. (2003). The journey of the counselor and therapist: Research findings and perspectives on professional development. *Journal of Career Development, 30,* 5–44.

Rowley, C., Earle, K., & Gilbourne, D. (2012). Practice and the process of critical learning: Reflections of an early stage practitioner working in elite youth level rugby league. *Sport and Exercise Psychology Review, 8,* 35–50.

Simons, J. P., & Andersen, M. B. (1995). The development of consulting practice in applied sport psychology: Some personal perspectives. *The Sport Psychologist, 9,* 449–468.

Solorzano, D., Ceja, M., & Yosso, T. (2000). Critical race theory, racial microaggressions, and campus racial climate: The experiences of African American college students. *Journal of Negro Education, 69,* 60–73.

Solorzano, D., & Villalpando, O. (1998). Critical race theory, marginality, and the experience of minority students in higher education. In C. Torres & T. Mitchell (Eds.), *Emerging issues in the sociology of education: Comparative perspectives* (pp. 211–224). Albany, NY: State University of New York Press.

Sue, D. W. (1981). *Counselling culturally different: Theory and practice.* New York: Wiley.

Sue, D. W., & Sue, D. (2003). *Counseling the culturally different: Theory and practice* (4th ed.). New York: John Wiley & Sons, Inc.

Tod, D. (2007). The long and winding road: Professional development in sport psychology. *The Sport Psychologist, 21,* 94–108.

Tod, D., & Bond, K. (2010). A longitudinal examination of a British neophyte sport psychologist's development. *The Sport Psychologist, 24,* 35–51.

Tonn, E., & Harmison, R. J. (2004). Thrown to the wolves: A student's account of her practicum experience. *The Sport Psychologist, 18,* 324–340.

Torres, L., Driscoll, M. W., & Burrow, A. L. (2010). Microaggressions and psychological functioning among high achieving African-Americans: A mixed-methods approach. *Journal of Social & Clinical Psychology, 29,* 1074–1099.

Williams, J. M., & Krane, V. (2001). Psychological characteristics of peak performance. In J. M. Williams (Ed.), *Applied sport psychology: Personal growth to peak performance* (pp. 162–178). Mountain View, CA: Mayfield.

Woodcock, C., Richards, H., & Mugford, A. (2008). Quality counts: Critical features for neophyte professional development. *The Sport Psychologist, 22,* 491–506.

8 Reflections of Advanced Doctoral Students

Challenges and Lessons Learned From Our Sport Psychology Consulting

Alex Auerbach, Joey Ramaeker, Shelly Sheinbein, Alexandra J. Thompson, and Trent A. Petrie

What would it be like if there were a single agreed-upon road map for successfully undertaking (and completing) the journey to become a sport psychology consultant? What if, from the start, we had known the exact steps to take to become competent, the ways to respond so we never felt uncomfortable or vulnerable, and the right answers to all the challenging questions and situations we would face so we would never make a mistake? In many ways, knowing the steps to take would have made our professional (and personal) lives much easier. Yet such a road map also would have made for a boring, unstimulating, and inauthentic experience. . . . It would have deprived us of the breadth of opportunities (and mistakes) that would allow us to grow and develop and define who we each would become as sport psychologists.

In reflecting on our journey, which ranges from the second to fifth year in a counseling psychology doctoral program (with sport psychology specialization), we have realized that our training has been a process . . . one that has form (and direction), but also one that has been shaped by each of us individually. And though we recognize the individuality of each of our paths, we also acknowledge the experiences and learning that have been shared and are common to all of us as graduate student consultants (GSCs). In this chapter, we discuss four key areas in our growth and development—ethical and professional issues, trust and credibility, multiculturalism, and professional identity—yet adhere to the idea that GSCs, through their experiences and training, ultimately will define who (and how) they will be as sport psychologists.

Ethical and Professional Issues

Consider the following scenario. A GSC is preparing to depart with the team for an away game when one of the team's coaches asks if he would have time to speak after the team arrives at the hotel. Once at the hotel, the GSC meets the coach in the lobby. The coach says, "My guy is really having a tough time. He told me that he's been talking to you, so what did you tell him to do? What do you think is wrong with him?"

In this instance, the GSC reminded the coach of the limits of confidentiality and how important respecting this boundary is to maintaining the athlete's engagement and commitment to treatment. This type of interchange is not uncommon in the world of sport consulting and presents several professional and ethical challenges that can be difficult to navigate (see Chapter 3). In this section, we identify three common professional/ethical issues—boundaries (and multiple roles), limits of competence, and being vulnerable in supervision—and discuss ways in which GSCs may successfully think through and navigate them.

Boundaries and Crossings

Sport psychologists, like psychologists working in the military and rural communities, often immerse themselves in the environment and interact in ways that are not typically found in traditional therapeutic settings, such as observing athletes at practice or conducting an intervention during a bus ride to a competition. Such interactions generally represent boundary crossings, which are deviations from the traditional and accepted practice that may or may not benefit the client (Speight, 2012). When GSCs cross boundaries, as often occurs in the practice of sport psychology, they may experience challenges as they try to balance the realities and demands of the sport environment with the ethical standards and principles they must follow. For example, the authors have attended doctors' appointments with athletes (at the request of athletic trainers or the athlete themselves) to support them before or after surgery, traveled with teams to away competitions where they shared meals with the team, and attended social functions at coaches' houses. Although some of these behaviors initially felt uncomfortable and unusual, the authors' presence at these and other related activities communicated that they were a committed part of the team and could be trusted and relied on to assist the athletes and coaches in areas of performance and life. Although boundary crossings can be unnerving and scary for GSCs because there often are no clearly defined sets of behaviors (or rules) to follow, these crossings may be necessary for the GSC to function effectively in the sport environment and may offer opportunities to provide services that are needed for that athlete, team, or coach (Aoyagi & Portenga, 2010). Thus, the end result may be a strengthened and deepened relationship with the team and the development of trust that allows the GSC to best serve the team and its mission.

There are times, however, when boundary crossings (in the form of multiple roles) may be confusing to all involved and result in harmful (if unintended) behaviors. GSCs often assume other roles on campus, such as course instructor or clinician at the university's counseling center, which increases the possibility of the GSC having multiple roles with a given athlete. Unknowingly, athletes on a team the consultant is working with may be assigned by their academic advisor to a class section that the GSC is teaching, or the GSC may see them coming out of the office of a "nonsport" counselor at the counseling center. One of the authors had an athlete from the team she worked with enrolled in a class she taught, which created the complication of how to objectively grade the athlete's work while simultaneously providing mental skills training to her and her team. In this situation, the author discussed the potential role conflicts with the athlete who had enrolled in her class and, when it became clear she could not switch sections, set up a system within the course where another graduate teaching assistant graded all of her assignments.

Within a sport psychology consulting context, boundary crossings and multiple relationships are nearly unavoidable. Fortunately, ethics codes, such as the one provided by the American Psychological Association (APA, 2010), provide a set of principles and standards that GSCs can use to guide their decision-making in such situations. However, GSCs may have more difficulty navigating personal boundary challenges, which may be indirectly addressed by ethical principles and standards but ultimately require personal/professional choice. For example, GSCs' personal boundaries may be challenged when coaches fail to realize the multiple demands on graduate students' time and expect the GSC to be present at practices and competitions like typical sport graduate assistants (GAs). An expectation in the world of sport is that every coach, athlete, and extended staff member will go above and beyond, spending whatever time is needed (or determined by the head coach) to improve the team's and the athletes' performances. Coaches may hold GSCs to the same expectations, which may create stress and strain in other areas of the GSCs' lives (and with their other responsibilities). Given that many GSCs work with a team as part of a graduate practicum course and are not being paid for their services, it is necessary to establish realistic expectations for the working relationship between the consultant, coaches, and athletes, and to define the GSCs' roles and how their time can best be used by the team. For example, it may be beneficial to hold a meeting to orient coaches and athletes to the consultant's role with the team at the start of services, or utilize a contract that clearly defines the consultant's offerings for the organization.

When one of the authors began working with the university's football team, the coaches asked the consultant to chart plays in the press box, assist with play cards at practice, make copies, and generally serve as a football GA might. The author was spending far more time with the team than required by his sport practicum class, and, in the end, his sport psychology skills and knowledge were not being fully utilized. With the help of his supervisor, the author was able to effectively communicate with the coaches about his role as a GSC and how he could bring unique and needed assistance in this role. Through the rest of the season, the author used every interaction with the coaches as an opportunity to educate them about his position and role, and how he could best help them accomplish their performance goals. Now in his third year with the team, the benefits of this educational process are paying off in terms of improved (and clarified) relationships with the coaching staff and players and the effective implementation of his skill set. GSCs are responsible for defining their professional roles and skills, and they should talk with coaches about the services they are able to provide prior to beginning the consultation (Aoyagi & Portenga, 2010; Moore, 2003).

Consulting Within the Bounds of Our Competence: The Pull to Do More!

Being a GSC is like being a kid in a candy store. . . . There are so many things to see and try, and it can be hard to resist the temptation to do everything! By the time GSCs start their sport psychology practica, they likely have taken several sport psychology classes and maybe even watched an advanced consultant present to a team or work with an athlete-client on mental skills. Now, once assigned to a team (or an athlete-client), they want to help them. . . . They want to "do" something and demonstrate that they are competent and can help the team/athlete/coach succeed!

Nearly all of the GSCs who work with the authors, as well as the authors themselves, have felt the pull to "do" . . . to teach the "canon" of mental skills (e.g., imagery, goal setting) or to jump in and offer solutions for perceived problems on the team (even before fully understanding the relationship dynamics of the athletes and coaches). At best, such approaches are likely to be minimally effective and, at worst, backfire on the GSC. The authors have learned that taking the time to get to know the team and its "needs" first often results in more beneficial (and effective) future interactions. The need to spend time developing strong relationships with the coaches, team, and individual athletes is paramount for being an effective GSC (Halliwell, 1990; Sharp & Hodge, 2013).

Even when GSCs are patient and have focused on "being" (and developing relationships) first, the allure of addressing all of a team's needs can be strong. Coaches may ask GSCs to present information on a topic about which they have minimal understanding (e.g., teaching their athletes mindfulness when the GSCs have had no formal training in this area). In such situations, the desire to please the coach (and do what he/she wants) can be powerful and may lead GSCs to practice outside of their current bounds of competence. When faced with such situations, GSCs should simply acknowledge that they do not know the answer (or have the skill to immediately address the need) and offer to find out more information by talking with their supervisor and peer GSCs. Although responding in this manner may be uncomfortable and seem counter to being a "knowledgeable" GSC, admitting what is not known and practicing within one's competence is the best, and most ethical, course of action.

Another area in which GSCs may be pulled to do more concerns the recognition and treatment of the athlete-client's mental health concerns. For GSCs who are being trained in sport science, providing mental skills training to an athlete is well within their bounds of competence. But, if an athlete-client discloses a mental health concern, even in the context of a strong consulting relationship, GSCs must recognize their limits and make a referral to a mental health specialist. For GSCs who are in an integrated psychology and sport science program, the challenge may not be competence or ability to help with the mental health concern; rather, the question is whether working with the athlete-client in this manner may undermine the GSC's effectiveness with the team. For example, a peer colleague of the authors began working with a student-athlete, individually, from her team on issues related to performance anxiety. Within a few sessions, however, the athlete-client brought up and wanted to talk about a variety of severe mental health concerns. Although the consultant, under the guidance of her supervisor, could have addressed these concerns, she decided that treating this athlete-client might interfere with her work with the team and coaches. Thus, she decided to refer the athlete to the university's counseling center where the athlete could receive in-depth treatment and still interact comfortably with the consultant as part of the team.

Broadening Competence Through Supervision

Working with an athlete-client, team, and/or coaching staff may reveal to GSCs all that they do not know, especially as they consider the responsibilities they have. Throughout their training (and even into their careers as professionals), GSCs can benefit from taking a growth-oriented perspective to learning, in which failure and mistakes are embraced as chances to learn, and the desire to take on new challenges outweighs the fear of appearing unskilled and vulnerable (Dweck, 2006). In taking such an approach to consulting, opportunities will arise from GSCs' missteps and provide them with the chance to reflect on their own development, skills, abilities, and areas of improvement.

Learning to trust themselves as consultants is a dynamic process that will fluctuate throughout their professional life (and certainly throughout training!). When GSCs are unsure of how to proceed and whether or not they are qualified to intervene in a certain way, discussing their concerns with supervisors can help them make decisions about treatment that are in the best interest of their clients. Supervision is a place where they can be vulnerable (i.e., reveal themselves fully without sense of shame [Brown, 2012]), which can facilitate honest and deep discussions of the progress and challenges they are facing in their work (Watkins, 2012). GSCs' supervisors also can help them find their blind spots—things they don't know about themselves but may be apparent to others—which is essential for them to grow and develop, both personally and professionally.

Establishing Credibility Through Trust

In counseling and psychotherapy, trust is defined as a "belief by a person in the integrity of another individual" (Larzelere & Huston, 1980, p. 595), and developing it is a key component to creating a strong alliance that is characterized by empathy, positive regard, and nonjudgment (Gilbert, 2008). In sport consulting, trust is equally important. GSCs are only as effective as the relationships they form with their athletes and coaches, and developing trust is one of the key tenets to being credible in this role (Sharp & Hodge, 2013).

For one of the authors, the importance of developing a trusting relationship became clear when she was assigned to a team where the coach had worked extensively with GSCs over the years. Prior to her involvement with the team, the coach had enlisted GSCs to teach his athletes mental skills and, ostensibly, to provide him with input regarding his coaching effectiveness. Although he was very open to the former, he was reticent to receive the latter. Thus, the author focused on developing a relationship with him first and foremost . . . starting with exploring his history in the sport, learning about his coaching philosophy, and discussing his life goals and values. Over time, as the coach came to trust her (and thus see her as more credible), he began to regularly ask her for help, be vulnerable, show emotion, and fully invest himself in the relationship. In this section, we detail factors that contribute to GSCs developing trusting, and thus credible, consulting relationships, including being present, being integrated and intentional, and communicating effectively with experienced coaches.

Being Present

As we mentioned briefly in the preceding section, a common problem for many overeager, high-achieving, often Type-A GSCs is the desire to *do something* when working with a team, athlete-client, or coach. As a result, GSCs can forget that simply *being present is doing* sport psychology. According to Carl Rogers (1957; Rogers, Gendlin, Kiesler, & Traux, 1967), in *being present*, counselors are open, genuine, accepting, self-aware, and connected with their clients on a personal level, qualities that research has shown to have moderate positive effects within the therapeutic relationship (Kolden, Klein, Wang, & Austin, 2011). In being present in this way, GSCs bring a perspective that is different from almost everyone else in the sport environment. They do not determine playing time, return to play following injury, or employment status. Instead, GSCs create open, genuine, inviting relationships where they are present to listen and support in a nonjudgmental manner. Sport is often a high-pressure, demanding, judgmental, chaotic environment, so it can be powerful for athletes and coaches to have someone who can listen attentively, support them emotionally, and help them be the best they can be and enjoy what they are doing.

GSCs also may be the only individuals in the sport organization who are willing to acknowledge that everyone in the system has emotional reactions and that their feelings may influence (positively and negatively) their performances as coaches, athletes, and athletic trainers. Further, taking the time to ask about the *person*, and not just the outcome, can serve as an excellent model for how everyone in the system can relate to each other and can help to validate GSCs' interest in everyone as individuals and not just performers. For example, in the midst of a competition, an athlete was severely injured and required immediate medical attention. Because the athletic trainer needed to remain with the team for the duration of the competition, one of the female authors, who had been at the competition as well, traveled with the athlete to seek emergency medical treatment. The author stayed with the athlete, just listening and helping her remain calm and as relaxed as possible throughout the medical treatment. Although the author took the athlete through some breathing exercises when she was starting to panic, it was being fully present and talking with the athlete as a person that was helpful to her, the athletic trainer, and, in the end, the coaching staff.

Being Integrated and Intentional Within the System

In addition to being present, learning how (and why) the sport system functions as it does is necessary if GSCs are going to accurately conceptualize the team's dynamics and develop an effective approach to intervening and helping each level of the system. Thus, GSCs need to focus on integrating themselves into the sport system and paying attention to how each level functions (Fletcher & Wagstaff, 2009), including at the organizational (i.e., sport organization as a whole), intergroup (i.e., groups within the system, such as the coaching staff, medical staff, and administration), intragroup (i.e., within each group in the system, such as the team itself), and individual (within each athlete or coach) levels.

Although all of the authors have gained entry with their teams through the head coaches (and have worked extensively with them), they have learned how important it is to take the time and energy to attend to all the levels within the system and to develop unique relationships with each of their teams' assistant coaches, graduate assistants, and athletic trainers. One of the authors developed a close working relationship with the team athletic trainer at the initial onset of her sport consultation. In their first meeting, the athletic trainer provided his general impressions of the team as well as offered his specific concerns for individual athletes. Through this relationship and his guidance, the author was able to be more intentional in providing support for the athletes (individual level of the system), such as by reaching out to them directly to inquire how they were doing with specific issues (e.g., injury rehabilitation). She also understood, however, the importance of accurately assessing how well the team (as a unit) and the coaching staff (as a unit) functioned, and thus she paid attention to those systems as well. As a result, she determined that the team would benefit from developing emotion regulation and communication skills, and that the coaching staff would benefit from being more cohesive and respectful (and inclusive) of each other's ideas, particularly those being offered by the assistants.

Being integrated is essential, but, without being intentional, GSCs may become lost within the system and be less influential than they could. Thus, GSCs must be purposeful in how they spend their limited time and energy when working with a team. Good uses of time may include (a) observing practices and the interactions among players, coaches, and other staff members that occur; (b) talking with and building relationships with other team personnel (e.g., athletic trainers) to ask how they are doing and obtain information on how they see the structure and function of the system; (c) traveling with the team; and (d) offering in-the-moment mental skills training, such as during practices or during appropriate breaks at competitions. One of the authors traveled extensively with her team during the winter break between semesters, which provided many opportunities to bond and develop trust as they worked through the hardships that often occur when being on the road. She was very intentional in how she spent her time, such as eating meals with coaches, playing games (e.g., cards) with the athletes during layovers in airports, checking in with specific athletes, and just making herself visible and available throughout travel. She knew that these shared experiences would strip away the sport personas that act as protective shields and allow her to get to know the athletes and coaches as more than performers. Being intentional allowed for these experiences in which she could develop a sense of common humanity with the athletes and coaches.

The Baby-Faced GSC: Communicating New Ideas to the Experienced Coach

As young female GSCs, two of the authors have worked with male head coaches who were in their fifties and had more than 30 years of coaching experience each. These coaches had built successful programs and were considered accomplished in their respective sports; they had established what they considered to be effective approaches to coaching and were not always open to feedback from others (even from their own assistant coaches). In fact, they thought they should know how to handle almost any situation that arose on their teams and with their athletes. To the authors, each coach was intimidating in his own way. As one of the coaches said to the author's supervisor, "Taking advice from someone that young . . . that's hard to do!"

For GSCs, remaining confident in their knowledge and skills can be challenging when interacting with seasoned coaches, some of whom have been coaching for more years than the GSCs have been alive! GSCs may be afraid of how coaches will perceive them, how valued their opinions will be, and/or how well they will be able to translate their sport psychology theories and philosophies into practical advice that will work in the real world of sport—all of which can interfere with their ability to be emotionally and fully "present" with the athletes and coaches. Thus, a first step for GSCs is to develop a solid understanding of their coaches' values and philosophy. . . . What is important to the coach (e.g., winning at all costs, developing relationships with athletes, teaching skills and strategies)? What type of program are they trying to build, and how does the GSC fit into that? When GSCs explore (and understand) these areas with their coaches, they establish an environment in which their work may be valued and integrated into the team's system. For example, early in one of the author's training, she assumed all coaches would contribute whatever time needed to improve their athletes' performances. She offered one coach what she thought were a number of great ideas to improve their athletes' accountability, motivation, and confidence. However, the coach repeatedly did not implement them. As she came to learn, the coach prioritized a work–life balance and spending time with family, and her recommendations meant devoting more time to the athletes than he was willing to do. Once she better understood his values, she was able to strategize more collaboratively and effectively with him on how to reach the same outcomes.

A second step for GSCs is to be available to help the coaching staff with difficult situations or solve problems when they arise, such as helping an athlete who is struggling in her or his game, or directly intervening with an athlete-client who is experiencing mental health concerns. In the early stages of working with one of the authors' teams, the author was able to develop a close and consistent relationship with an athlete-client with whom the other coaches had struggled to connect. As a result, the author was able to help the athlete adjust her attitude and be more open to the coaches and their feedback. Through this situation, the author demonstrated to the coaches that she had well-honed relational skills and could be an asset to the program. This situation also helped the author feel more confident and comfortable in her role and position on the team. As she continued to work with the team, the athletes and coaches started to approach her for assistance with both personal and sport performance–related issues, and she became an integral part of the coaching staff.

A third step for GSCs is to develop a philosophy for how they will work within a sport organization and facilitate performance excellence (Poczwardowski, Sherman, & Ravizza, 2004). Such a philosophy would guide sport psychology practice in the same way that coaches' values and philosophies ought to direct how they develop and run their programs. For GSCs, the philosophy would provide guidance for effective in-the-moment decision-making, a structure for setting the short- and long-term goals of the consultation, direction for how to handle difficult and challenging professional and ethical situations that may arise when working within sport systems, and the foundation for being viewed as a credible, consistent, and trustworthy consultant. For one of the authors, her sport psychology conceptual framework is grounded in relational theory (e.g., Jordan, 2010), which stems from her belief that authentic, honest human connections foster personal growth and development and provide the foundation of performance excellence. Although her personal beliefs and values provide the foundation for her framework, it also has been influenced by the coursework and counseling experiences she has had during her master's degree and currently in her doctoral program. This framework guides her role such that she puts greater emphasis and priority on relationships with those involved in the sport system than on teaching the use of mental tools, for instance. Thus, her intervention goals always begin with the development of a close, trusting working relationship, which then is the foundation for all of the subsequent systemic and individual interventions she might put into place (e.g., teaching mental tools, improving coach–athlete communication, developing leadership).

Becoming a Culturally Sensitive GSC: A Process of Growth

During her first year consulting with a Division I track and field team, an author's team of GSCs included a White male, a Chinese-American male, and two White females (one of whom was bisexual); none had any previous experience in track and field as either an athlete or a coach, though all had been competitive athletes in other sports. All the consultants were younger than the head coach, who was African American, as were the majority of the athletes on the team; there also were international students hailing from countries such as Israel and Australia. As this situation illustrates, there are many dimensions to athletes', coaches', and GSCs' sociocultural identities, which are defined through their values, beliefs, and attitudes, and expressed through their communications and their behaviors. Some sociocultural categories with which individuals identify include race, gender, religion, age, education, income, sexual orientation, ability status, and sport, to name a few. Although some of these identifications may be immediately obvious, others may not be as apparent or must be shared overtly by the person. Thus, in order to become a multiculturally aware and sensitive sport consultant (see Chapter 11), GSCs must not make assumptions about athletes' and coaches' sociocultural identities, but rather listen and remain open to what they reveal and how they define themselves. To help GSCs in this process, we discuss four areas—privilege, multicultural perspective-taking, microaggressions, and self-reflection—that have been meaningful in our own development as multicultural sport psychology consultants.

Privilege

McIntosh (1988) defined privilege as an invisible, weightless package of unearned assets that provides advantages and protection against discrimination in many contexts such as financial, social, and governmental. Although race, specifically being White (of European descent generally), is one of the most common privileges discussed within counseling psychology (Kiselica, 1999; McIntosh, 1988), other privileges exist and influence social interactions. Being heterosexual, being male, having financial means, and being a college graduate, to a list a few, are privileges that bestow opportunities and/or shield individuals from indignities.

For GSCs, acknowledging their own privilege can be challenging because, if done, feelings of guilt or unfairness may arise (McIntosh, 1988). However, by acknowledging privilege and power differences, GSCs can empower athletes and coaches who may come from marginalized cultures or backgrounds (McGannon & Johnson, 2009; McGannon & Metz, 2010). When a White male GSC acknowledges that he has privilege in relation to his sex and racial status compared to the African American female athlete with whom he is working, he creates a safety and openness in the relationship where the athlete may feel more comfortable discussing issues related to these dimensions.

Recognizing privilege (McIntosh, 1988) also means acknowledging ethnocentrism, which is defined as judging another culture based on the values and standards of one's own (Kiselica, 1999). GSCs who grow up in Western individualistic cultures may espouse independence, assertiveness, and control of thoughts and feelings, which, if applied universally, might limit the effectiveness of their work with athletes or coaches whose cultural views are different from their own. For example, a White male peer of the authors, whose general approach was individualistic and born out of his experience growing up in an affluent suburban home, had assumed that all student-athletes who were on scholarship used their money for themselves and their personal needs. This assumption was challenged by his supervisor and peers, who helped him recognize his ethnocentrism and how this view kept him from truly understanding the experiences of some of the athletes on his team who came from lower SES households and who were sending money home to their parents and families each month. With this new awareness, the GSC has been able to better understand the lives of his athletes; establish genuine, trusting relationships; and assist them in reaching their performance goals.

Multicultural Perspective-Taking

Prior to being trained in multicultural counseling, GSCs may adopt a culturally blind (or universalist) approach to consulting, viewing all people as being equal and treating them the same regardless of their background or identity (e.g., race, sexual orientation, gender [Butryn, 2010]). Although the intentions behind this perspective are often positive, the result may be oppression, invalidation, and silencing of athletes and coaches, particularly those from more diverse backgrounds (Sue et al., 2007). For instance, over the course of several months, one of the female authors worked separately with two female distance runners (individually)—one White and one Hispanic. Each runner was having trouble managing pain and communicating with her White female coach. Initially, she conceptualized the runners' situations very similarly, relying on a universalist perspective. However, in doing so, she had not acknowledged cultural differences, as well as the presence and/or absence of privileges that were likely influencing her relationships with each one. As she became more culturally aware, her subsequent interventions became more multiculturally congruent and effective, such as when she acknowledged one of the athlete's collectivistic cultural upbringing and discussed the influence of family pressure on her athletic performance and experience of pain. Although taking a multicultural course is an excellent approach for increasing cultural awareness, and one done by all the authors, GSCs also would benefit from additional supervision in multiculturalism from a supervisor with this competency, being open to diverse personal experiences, traveling to different regions within the United States (as well as internationally), and reading books that introduce, promote, and/or celebrate diversity, to list a few.

Taking a multicultural perspective also means understanding that numerous sociocultural identities may exist within one individual and thus create a complex interaction of values, attitudes, and beliefs. In such instances, no one identity may be prominent, some of the identities may conflict, and/or individuals may be working through which identities will be most influential. As an example, one of the female authors worked with an athlete-client who was struggling with finding a way to successfully integrate (and manage) religious, academic, and athletic identities. All three identities, and their respective demands, pulled for the athlete-client's time and energy, which left her confused, exhausted, and frustrated. The author helped her by openly discussing the different parts of her identity, validating her experiences and feelings, and examining how she could honor (and integrate) each part of herself rather than trying to live one identity at a time. Helping athletes understand and accept their different identities can be challenging because they may believe that prioritizing one identity invalidates the other or that two (or more) cannot coexist within the context of society (e.g., being religious and gay/lesbian). However, by being culturally sensitive, GSCs can help athletes move to a place of awareness and acceptance that benefits them as individuals and performers (Haldeman, 2004).

Microaggressions

Subtle or brief verbal, behavioral, or environmental indignities, whether intentional or unintentional, that communicate hostile, derogatory, or negative slights and insults toward an aspect of individuals' minority status are microaggressions (Sue et al., 2007). Sue et al. (2007) described two types that often occur outside the consciousness of the aggressor: (a) microinsult (e.g., behavioral or verbal remarks that convey rudeness or demean a person's racial heritage or identity) and (b) microinvalidation (e.g., verbal comments or behaviors that negate the thoughts, feelings, or experiences of reality for a person of color). The third microaggression is often conscious, and referred to as a microassault (e.g., name calling, avoidant behavior, or purposeful discriminatory actions intended to hurt the victim). Regardless of the type, microaggressions often demean individuals' cultural values and communication styles, reinforce color blindness, misattribute behavior, and/or impair the development of interpersonal relationships.

Because race often is a visible aspect of individuals' sociocultural identities, it is an area in which microaggressions occur. For example, a female author was supervising a male Hispanic peer who was a junior consultant on her consultation team. The author was the senior consultant and thus responsible for providing direction and feedback, including the timely completion of his case notes. In her role, she assumed that the lateness of his notes was simply a lack of commitment to his GSC role and communicated that to him. In doing so, she unintentionally negated his experiences (i.e., microinvalidation), which included his need to attend to issues within his extended family. Through their discussion, she came to realize how her assumptions had undermined their relationship (and thus her supervision of his work), which likely influenced why he had not shared his family struggles with her from the start. GSCs also need to remember that microaggressions are not limited to those involving race, and may occur in relation to any part of their athletes' and coaches' sociocultural identities, such as age, religion, gender, sexual orientation, ability status, or sport.

In contrast, GSCs also can be recipients of microaggressions, which presents other challenges. For instance, a short male Vietnamese peer of the authors was told during his first meeting with the head coach of the volleyball team (who was tall and White) that he "did not know the sport." That was a true statement; he had not played volleyball, and his knowledge at the time was limited. However, past consultants, all of whom had been tall White men, had not known the sport either, but the head coach had not raised this concern with them. When such microaggressions occur, GSCs must decide how to respond (if at all). Recognizing that microaggressions have occurred, which may be subtle and difficult to detect, can be challenging. Thus, it is helpful for GSCs to discuss their experiences with peers and supervisors to gain perspective on what has happened and to figure out how to navigate the situation. Although microaggressions that are directed toward GSCs by athletes and coaches may be painful and disorienting, reflecting on such experiences can help GSCs decide how to approach athletes and coaches about what has occurred with the focus on creating a more culturally aware and sensitive environment.

Self-Reflexivity

Schinke, McGannon, Parham, and Lane (2012) defined self-reflexivity as a type of introspection used to enhance awareness of individuals' situations and subsequently help them become more receptive to different perspectives. Self-reflexivity is a critical technique for increasing multicultural sensitivity and learning how to handle differences in values, cultures, and beliefs, to list a few, that inevitably arise during sport consultations (Cropley, Hanton, Miles, & Niven, 2010; Schinke et al., 2012). Yet being self-reflexive is challenging for GSCs to do because of their lack of experience and insight. Thus, GSCs must make a commitment to engage in this introspective process, by themselves as well as with their peers and supervisors, and to work to understand how their own values, biases, social position, and self-identity categories may influence the consultation process, including being able to develop a strong relationship with athletes and coaches (McGannon & Johnson, 2009; Ryba & Schinke, 2009; Schinke et al., 2012). As discussed previously in the chapter, differences in biases, backgrounds, and interests between GSCs and their clients can affect the course of consultation if not acknowledged; however, by recognizing these differences, GSCs can monitor the influence of their value system and maintain the focus on the client (Schinke et al., 2012). Overall, improving multicultural sensitivity, awareness, and competence is ongoing and occurs through trial and error, quality supervision, and a diverse range of consulting experiences; it is a process to which all GSCs should commit.

Professional Identity

By entering the field of sport psychology and taking on the rigorous academic and practical training that it entails, GSCs have made the decision to become professionals. However, this process extends beyond acquiring a comprehensive knowledge base, understanding applicable ethical standards, conducting relevant research, and implementing effective interventions; it requires developing the *identity* of a professional as well.

Across many professional fields (e.g., medicine, journalism, counseling), the development of an identity has been recognized as a vital component of training (Deuze, 2005; Fagermoen, 1997; Mellin, Hunt, & Nichols, 2011; O'Connor, 2008; Pratt, Rockmann, & Kaufmann, 2006). Such identity development represents a dynamic, lifelong process through which GSCs integrate their professional (e.g., academic knowledge, acquired skills, accepted ethical principles) and personal (e.g., previous experiences, personality, values and beliefs) selves, and subsequently align themselves with their field's community (Gibson, Dollarhide, & Moss, 2010). Auxier, Hughes, and Kline (2003) described this identity development as a series of cycles through which students develop internal evaluation processes by oscillating between dependence and autonomy in their conceptual learning (e.g., coursework), experiential learning (e.g., applied experiences), and external evaluations (e.g., supervision). Through this process, GSCs identify and clarify, and subsequently reclarify, their self-concepts as helpers and have opportunities to integrate their own values, beliefs, and experiences into their coalescing professional identity (Auxier et al., 2003).

Developing and solidifying a professional identity can be a challenging and complicated process for GSCs. The paradox of being a student yet taking on increasing levels of responsibility in professional activities as service providers underlies this challenge. One author felt mixed emotions during his first year of sport practica when his team's head coach asked him for his "professional opinion" regarding how to best address a problem on the team. On one hand, he felt valued, accepted, and trusted by the coach. Yet there was also a sense of anxiety and self-doubt: how could *he* offer a "professional" opinion when he was just a student? Within this section, we highlight some of the common challenges GSCs face as they navigate the overlapping roles of student and emerging professional.

Professional Philosophy

Recognizing and articulating a professional philosophy as a sport psychologist is one challenge for GSCs as they develop their identities in the field (Poczwardowski et al., 2004; see also Chapter 1). Sport consultants' professional philosophies are reflected in their comprehensive approach to consultation, ultimately guiding how they behave with their clients (e.g., ethics, interventions). Importantly, core values (e.g., respect for autonomy) and beliefs (e.g., free will vs. determinism) represent the foundation upon which a professional philosophy is built; it informs their choice of theoretical orientation, models of practice, and understanding about their roles and responsibilities. These personally held convictions (e.g., values) are thought to develop outside of one's role as a GSC and are rooted in personal experiences and/or culture, making them inherently unique to the individual.

GSCs' sport psychology practica represent opportunities for, and obstacles to, developing their professional philosophy. GSCs are placed with teams where they may be given considerable responsibilities to deliver sport psychology services, such as teaching mental tools, collaborating with coaches to develop their own values/philosophy, and/or providing mental health care to athlete-clients, yet they remain under the guidance, as well as scrutiny and evaluation, of their more experienced and licensed (or credentialed) supervisors who are ultimately responsible for the work they are doing. Because of this power differential, many GSCs may be required, or feel compelled, to take on the philosophy of their supervisors, potentially limiting their ability to bring into play their own beliefs and values (Nelson, Barnes, Evans, & Triggiano, 2008). Strict adherence to a supervisor's philosophy may interfere with the self-reflexivity and experimentation that facilitates the growth of a GSC's professional philosophy.

As GSCs advance through their training and begin to develop their professional philosophy, they may experience some disconnect between their own, and their supervisor's, beliefs. Left unresolved, this incongruence (or internal conflict) may negatively affect their work with their athlete-clients, coaches, and teams and hinder the formation of an integrated professional identity (Lindsay, Breckon, Thomas, & Maynard, 2007). In working with a youth athlete-client, one author experienced such a conflict with his supervisor—the author advocated for teaching the athlete mental skills, whereas the supervisor suggested that the consultation focus on how to improve the parents' communication style (i.e., to alter the motivational climate). Their approaches simply emerged from their different life experiences (e.g., the supervisor was a parent whose children had extensively played sports, whereas the consultant was childless), yet it did create some self-doubt for the author (e.g., "Is my approach wrong?"). Because the author's and his supervisor's goals for the consultation were similar (e.g., increase athlete's fun and confidence), they were able to resolve their different approaches in supervision. Each discussed his approach, provided a rationale, and outlined a course of consultation; ultimately, they agreed upon a plan that drew from both perspectives. For the author, talking about these differences in supervision exposed him to a new viewpoint and required him to articulate his own, a process that both encouraged self-reflection and facilitated his professional growth.

Talking the Talk

Learning to speak professionally represents an important integration of personal (e.g., verbal style) and professional (e.g., using domain specific terminology) dimensions. O'Byrne and Rosenberg (1998) emphasized the importance of acquiring professional language, stating that, through practical and supervisory experiences, "[t]he supervisee is socialized in the language of therapeutic discourse, value orientations, and modes of thinking and problem solving that are characteristics of the profession" (p. 36). Thus, learning to "talk the talk," and doing so with confidence, is part of GSCs' professional development.

In classes and other professional contexts, speaking technically (i.e., using domain-specific professional terms or concepts) reflects competence and aligns GSCs with the larger professional community. Yet, in their applied work, GSCs need to learn how to translate their field's technical and theoretical language/knowledge into a form that makes sense to (and has meaning for) their athletes, coaches, and sport administrators. During a discussion with his coaches about motivation, one author struggled with translating what he knew about goal orientations (and motivational climates) into language that made sense to the coaches and that provided concrete ideas on how they could help their athletes. His message never quite "hit home" with the coaches in the same way it did when discussing the topic with his classmates. Supervision, both formal and informal, is a mechanism through which GSCs develop technical professional language as well as identify ways to communicate effectively with athletes and coaches (O'Byrne & Rosenberg, 1998); it helps them learn to "talk the talk" in both domains! Supervision provides a space where GSCs can use professional language to discuss their work (and thus increase their theoretical and technical competence), yet also think through how they may communicate most effectively with their athlete-clients, such as by engaging in role plays or identifying ways to more effectively relay important concepts (e.g., metaphors, integration of sport specific terminology). All the authors have found supervision to be an essential mechanism for them becoming "native speakers" of sport psychology.

Peer Supervision: The Ultimate Identity Paradox

For GSCs, being a peer supervisor (see Chapter 6) can be a confusing yet rewarding experience. The confusion emanates from engaging in behaviors that are associated with a professional role (e.g., providing advice/guidance to a person in training), while still identifying as a student themselves. GSCs may ask themselves, "How can I help another student develop her or his skills, when I am still developing myself?" Further, because most GSCs have not had formal training in the supervisory role, they will have limited knowledge, abilities, experiences, and understandings to guide how they interact with and provide feedback to their peer supervisees. Thus, GSCs may experience some degree of self-doubt about their knowledge base and vulnerability in their role, and thus hesitate when providing peers with constructive feedback or take on a more directive, authoritarian supervisory style.

Yet being a peer supervisor can lead to professional growth and development, particularly in relation to one's identity. Taking on this role can be empowering and result in a reflection on (and integration of) GSCs' professional accomplishments and the development of their professional identity. Simply obtaining experience as a supervisor can alleviate the discomfort associated with this identity paradox and mark a shift toward professional self-validation (Gibson et al., 2010; Nelson, Oliver, & Capps, 2006). The authors of this chapter all have served in the role of "senior consultant" within their program, a position that requires them to mentor and supervise a "junior consultant" (i.e., a less experienced doctoral or master's level GSC). During his third year with his team, one author and his junior GSC were confronted with an ethical situation that was having a negative influence on their team's performance and cohesion. In his role as peer supervisor, the author spent extra time with the junior GSC answering her questions regarding the events that had unfolded and ensuring that she understood the reasons behind why they had intervened as they had. Although at times he felt pulled to be the expert and have the answers to all her questions, he realized that his emerging professional philosophy included acknowledging his limitations and blindspots and being comfortable with not immediately knowing the best course of action (Ladany & Lehrman-Waterman, 1999). Thus, he created an open environment in which they could talk freely about the process and collaborate together on how to proceed with the team. He modeled this openness during their formal supervision each week as well, which helped the junior consultant feel more included and confident in her own developing professional self. Being a peer supervisor helped him to *feel* like a professional because it provided opportunities to impart acquired practical knowledge and/ or share experiences from which the junior consultant could learn. Through their discussions as well as his reflections and sharing, the author was able to make strides forward in the development of his professional identity.

Conclusion

The decision to become a sport psychologist represents the start of a journey to becoming a professional. It represents a commitment to continued growth and development—a process that is facilitated by a willingness to be vulnerable and acknowledge mistakes, an investment in multiculturalism, a self-reflexive approach to learning, and a lifelong promise to being part of formal and informal supervision experiences. Being GSCs can involve exhilarating, yet humbling, experiences . . . ones that have direction but ultimately are determined through their opportunities and training (and GSCs' responses to these experiences). We have recognized our direction but, like other GSCs, know our paths are still being shaped as we gain new experiences and are exposed to new ideas. Enjoy the journey.

References

American Psychological Association. (2010). Ethical principles of psychologists and code of conduct. Retrieved from http://apa.org/ethics/code/index.aspx

Aoyagi, M. W., & Portenga, S. T. (2010). The role of positive ethics and virtues in the context of sport and performance psychology service delivery. *Professional Psychology: Research and Practice, 41*(3), 253–259.

Auxier, C. R., Hughes, F. R., & Kline, W. B. (2003). Identity development in counselors-in-training. *Counselor Education and Supervision, 43*(1), 25–38.

Brown, B. (2012). *Daring greatly: How the courage to be vulnerable transforms the way we live, love, parent, and lead.* Garden City, NY: Avery.

Butryn, T. M. (2010). Integrating whiteness in sport psychology. In T. V. Ryba, R. J. Schinke, & G. Tenenbaum (Eds.), *The cultural turn in sport psychology* (pp. 127–152). Morgantown, WV: Fitness Information Technology.

Cropley, B., Hanton, S., Miles, A., & Niven, A. (2010). Exploring the relationship between effective and reflective practice in applied sport psychology. *Sport Psychologist, 24*(4), 521–541.

Deuze, M. (2005). What is journalism? Professional identity and ideology of journalists reconsidered. *Journalism, 6*(4), 442–464.

Dweck, C. (2006). *Mindset: The new psychology of success.* New York, NY: Random House.

Fagermoen, M. S. (1997). Professional identity: Values embedded in meaningful nursing practice. *Journal of Advanced Nursing, 25*(3), 434–441.

Fletcher, D., & Wagstaff, R. D. (2009). Organizational psychology in elite sport: Its emergence, application, and future. *Psychology of Sport and Exercise, 10*, 427–434.

Gibson, D. M., Dollarhide, C. T., & Moss, J. M. (2010). Professional identity development: A grounded theory of transformational tasks of new counselors. *Counselor Education and Supervision, 50*(1), 21–38.

Gilbert, P. (2008). Psychotherapies. *Medicine, 36*(9), 496–498. doi:10.1383/medc.32.8.67.43173

Haldeman, D. C. (2004). When sexual and religious orientation collide: Considerations in working with conflicted same-sex attracted male clients. *The Counseling Psychologist, 32*(5), 691–715.

Halliwell, W. (1990). Providing sport psychology consulting services in professional hockey. *The Sport Psychologist, 4*, 369–377.

Jordan, J. V. (2010). *Relational-cultural therapy*. Washington, DC: American Psychological Association.

Kiselica, M. S. (1999). Confronting my own ethnocentrism and racism: A process of pain and growth. *Journal of Counseling & Development, 77*(1), 14–17.

Kolden, G. G., Klein, M. H., Wang, C. C., & Austin, S. B. (2011). Congruence/Genuineness. In J. Norcross (Ed.), *Psychotherapy relationships that work* (pp. 187–223). New York, NY: Oxford University Press.

Ladany, N., & Lehrman-Waterman, D. E. (1999). The content and frequency of supervisor self-disclosures and their relationship to supervisor style and the supervisory working alliance. *Counselor Education and Supervision, 38*(3), 143–160.

Larzelere, R. E., & Huston, T. L. (1980). Toward understanding interpersonal trust in close relationships. *Journal of Marriage and Family, 42*, 595–604.

Lindsay, P., Breckon, J. D., Thomas, O., & Maynard, I. W. (2007). In pursuit of congruence: A personal reflection on methods and philosophy in applied practice. *Sport Psychologist, 21*(3), 335–352.

McGannon, K. R., & Johnson, C. R. (2009). Strategies for reflective cultural sport psychology research. In R. J. Schinke & S. J. Hanrahan (Eds.), *Cultural sport psychology* (pp. 57–75). Champaign, IL: Human Kinetics.

McGannon, K. R., & Metz, J. L. (2010). Through the funhouse mirror: Understanding access and (un)expected selves through confessional tales. In R. J. Schinke (Ed.), *Contemporary sport psychology* (pp. 153–170). Hauppauge, NY: Nova Science Publishers.

McIntosh, P. (1988). White privilege: Unpacking the invisible knapsack. Excerpt from *White privilege and male privilege: A personal account of coming to see correspondences through work in women's studies*. Wellesley, MA: Wellesley College Center for Research on Women.

Mellin, E. A., Hunt, B., & Nichols, L. M. (2011). Counselor professional identity: Findings and implications for counseling and interprofessional collaboration. *Journal of Counseling and Development: JCD, 89*(2), 140–147.

Moore, Z. E. (2003). Ethical dilemmas in sport psychology: Discussion and recommendations for practice. *Professional Psychology: Research and Practice, 34*(6), 601–610.

Nelson, K. W., Oliver, M., & Capps, F. (2006). Becoming a supervisor: Doctoral student perceptions of the training experience. *Counselor Education and Supervision, 46*(1), 17–31.

Nelson, M. L., Barnes, K. L., Evans, A. L., & Triggiano, P. J. (2008). Working with conflict in clinical supervision: Wise supervisors' perspectives. *Journal of Counseling Psychology, 55*(2), 172–184.

O'Byrne, K., & Rosenberg, J. (1998). The practice of supervision: A sociocultural perspective. *Counselor Education and Supervision, 38*, 34–42.

O'Connor, K. E. (2008). "You choose to care": Teachers, emotions and professional identity. *Teaching and Teacher Education, 24*(1), 117–126.

Poczwardowski, A., Sherman, C. P., & Ravizza, K. (2004). Professional philosophy in the sport psychology service delivery: Building on theory and practice. *Sport Psychologist, 18*(4), 445–463.

Pratt, M. G., Rockmann, K. W., & Kaufmann, J. B. (2006). Constructing professional identity: The role of work and identity learning cycles in the customization of identity among medical residents. *Academy of Management Journal, 49*(2), 235–262.

Rogers, C. R. (1957). The necessary and sufficient conditions of therapeutic personality change. *Journal of Consulting Psychology, 21*, 95–103.

Rogers, C. R., Gendlin, E. T., Kiesler, D. J., & Traux, C. B. (Eds.). (1967). *The therapeutic relationship and its impact: A study of psychotherapy with schizophrenics*. Madison, WI: University of Wisconsin Press.

Ryba, T. V., & Schinke, R. J. (2009). Methodology as a ritualized eurocentrism: Introduction to the special issue. *International Journal of Sport and Exercise Psychology, 7*, 263–274.

Schinke, R. J., McGannon, K. R., Parham, W. D., & Lane, A. M. (2012). Toward cultural praxis and cultural sensitivity: Strategies for self-reflexive sport psychology practice. *Quest, 64*(1), 34–46.

Sharp, L., & Hodge, K. (2013). Effective sport psychology consulting relationships: Two coach case studies. *The Sport Psychologist, 27*, 313–324.

Speight, S. L. (2012). An exploration of boundaries and solidarity in counseling relationships. *The Counseling Psychologist, 40*(1), 133–157.

Sue, D. W., Capodilupo, C. M., Torino, G. C., Bucceri, J. M., Holder, A., Nadal, K. L., & Esquilin, M. (2007). Racial microaggressions in everyday life: Implications for clinical practice. *American Psychologist, 62*(4), 271.

Watkins, C. E., Jr. (2012). Psychotherapy supervision in the new millennium: Competency-based, evidence-based, particularized, and energized. *Journal of Contemporary Psychotherapy, 42*, 193–203.

9 Working With Individual Clients

Jessica D. Bartley, Adam M. O'Neil,
Steve Portenga, and Mark W. Aoyagi

In this chapter, we bring our experiences as two early career sport psychology consultants to our peers. While you read, we encourage you to listen to the questions that we ask and not necessarily the answers that we give. This chapter is not meant to be a protocol for how to work individually with clients. These are *our* experiences! We see our roles as active learners of our clients' passions and expertise. They are, after all, the experts of their own lives, and we are fascinated by the experience that an individual takes when choosing to pursue a difficult task. Our roles are to be astute listeners, to deeply appreciate the process of the person's development, and to offer support and training of evidence-based mindset skills when appropriate. This approach does not change when we are working with teams. We believe that in order to have an authentic and productive relationship, it is vital to protect our relationship to the best of our abilities. Throughout the chapter, we invite you to reflect on our developmental approach as we discuss the process of sitting down across from our first individual clients. Notice the focusing on the self and on the client, and the ways in which we balance the two.

Premeeting/Session Logistics

Where Did the Referral Come From?

After we have been referred a client (and this includes self-referrals), one of the first questions that we like to ask is how the person learned about us. We can gather a lot of information from clients' responses to this question. What is their drive to see us (e.g., autonomous or controlled motivation)? How do they articulate the reason for reaching out (e.g., focusing on problems or performance)? What words and tone do they use to describe their current situation? How do they talk about the conversation with the referral source when they learned about us? In the first conversation with the client, we find that asking the client early on how they heard about us can quickly build a sense of rapport. Overall, where the referral came from (e.g., self-referral, athletic director, coach, parent, colleague) can greatly influence how we work with an individual client.

What Is Your Role With the Individual, Team, and Organization?

This can quickly lead to more questions. Are you contracted by the organization, team, or individual? Are you contracted for performance? Are you contracted for performance and clinical services? Are you a coach who provides sport psychology techniques? There can be a number of roles that might allow you the opportunity to provide sport psychology services to an individual client.

With these roles, we think informed consent should be openly discussed early on so that clients are informed of our scope of practice. For example, I (AO) feel it is important to discuss with clients that I have a master's degree, what that means for the client, and that I am not an independently licensed psychologist in California (yet!). I typically talk about the nature of the relationship being based in a mental skills training model rather than a psychotherapeutic model. I (JDB) have a different conversation since I am a licensed psychologist, but I am also quick to explain what my role with the team is (e.g., contracted by the athletic department, a team, a parent) and what that means for the relationship. Since I have the competency to address mental health concerns as well as performance, I also try to be very clear about what we are addressing and when I would need to refer (e.g., when something has fallen outside of the scope that we agreed upon).

In our initial consultations, we thought talking about confidentiality would be an awkward moment, but we have come to appreciate the sense of safety and boundaries that it cultivates for everyone involved. We think of confidentiality as being more about information and privacy. So, early on in the process, it is important to talk with our clients about how confidentiality is an important element of our job to secure not only the information from our meetings but also the nature of our relationships in public. Even though this is clearly articulated in our intake paperwork, it is important to have a brief conversation about it as well. We tend to tell adult clients something like, "OK, so let's get clear about the nature of our conversations. It's my job to keep secure all of the information you share with me. If you want to share the details of our conversations, like with your coaches or trainers, that's up to you—just trust that I can't do that, and that is to protect you." Another way that we might say it, especially if we are consulting with a team in public settings, might be, "When you see me speaking with someone else in your social circles, I can't talk about you, or what you and I have talked about, with them. Your coaches are also included in this, and part of my agreeing to work with the team was contingent upon their respect and appreciation for confidentiality." I also say something like, "If we run into each other in public settings (e.g., on the sideline, at a grocery store in our community . . .), I'll follow your lead. If you want a high-five, I'll high-five. If you're around friends and you want to pretend we didn't see each other, that's OK with me, too." These are not pithy statements, or things to say to try to act "cool" or to speak the language of younger clients. Rather, talking about *how* confidentiality and privacy are upheld demonstrates early on that you are thinking of their safety and that you want what's best for them. Beyond fostering collaborative exploration with the client, we think it also models boundary setting, professionalism, and foresight on the part of the consultant.

Mark: While I agree wholeheartedly with the above points, with experience I have come to appreciate some additional nuances to confidentiality. One such nuance is that confidentiality can be divided into two aspects: content and contact (Welfel, 2012). Content confidentiality addresses the information shared by the client within the bounds of the professional relationship. This information is the client's and is never to be shared without the client's awareness and consent. On the other hand, I believe sport and performance psychology (SPP), following in the footsteps of general psychology, has perhaps limited itself by being overly protective of contact confidentiality. Contact confidentiality refers to the existence of the professional relationship, and in my experience the way contact confidentiality is approached can be anxiety-provoking to clients as well as limiting those who might seek our services. The way that I have seen contact confidentiality be anxiety-provoking is when its importance is stressed to clients in a way that gives clients the impression that SPP consultation is secretive with the corresponding implication that there is something socially undesirable about it. Clearly, this only serves to reinforce the social stigma that may be attached to SPP consultation. Furthermore, this can limit access to services by discouraging current clients from sharing their experiences with teammates or other people with whom they have a relationship. Many clients with whom I have had the privilege of providing services have indicated they would never have sought out services had so and so not worked with me (or another SPP consultant) and told them it was a positive experience. Consistent with my beliefs that SPP consultants should be trying to maximize good as well as avoid harm (Aoyagi & Portenga, 2010), I believe it is important to discuss contact confidentiality in a way that makes clients feel empowered (rather than stigmatized) for seeking out consultation as well as empowered to decide for themselves whether to share the existence of their consulting relationship with whomever they choose (without implicit messages that disclosing they have received SPP services is undesirable). Thus, I am fully supportive of consultants upholding their responsibility of contact confidentiality; I just encourage all SPP consultants to be thoughtful about how they communicate this to clients such that clients are not influenced to believe that they must be secretive or protective of the existence of the relationship.

In the age of technology, an important consideration is how clients can contact you when you are not in each other's company, such as through texting, phone conversations, and meetings via Skype, Zoom, FaceTime, and Microsoft Lync. I (AO) find that it is important to provide clients with my direct contact information at the onset of the relationship. Providing my direct contact information shows a willingness to trust, to be available, and to invite concepts of approachability early on in the relationship. It can also model for my potential client what it looks like to be open, curious, and clear with boundaries and expectations. This decision only came with extensive discussion with my clinical supervisors, an awareness of the legal and ethical guidelines and best practices, and a personal weighing of pros and cons by offering this to clients.

Were There Clear Directions Provided and Information About Parking?

We learned early on that first impressions go a long way. If the clients have to park in an expensive lot in order to see us or if they can only find one-hour parking in a metered space, it is not surprising when they begin to check their phones about 40 minutes into the meeting to make sure they are not ticketed. Wouldn't it be amazing if your client came in with one less source of anxiety? Our advice is to talk about the parking situation in the initial phone consultation, even briefly.

What Happens in the Time Before the Session?

In the same sense, we feel it is imperative to discuss where the client can first meet us. Do you have a waiting room? Are you sharing your office space with another professional? Put yourself in the mindset of someone coming in who might not know who you are, what you look like, and how the process typically plays out. Think strategically about the feel of your waiting area as well. What magazines best reflect an element of your practice? If you play music, what is the vibe you want to create? A lot of this, in our opinion, is based more on knowing who you are and what you are all about from a professional sense instead of trying to manipulate an environment that appeases your clients. Being you can be felt before the client ever meets you!

Is Paperwork Sent Beforehand?

Most institutions and organizations in mental and behavioral health settings have started using electronic paperwork that must be completed immediately prior to the first appointment. If possible, we lean toward sending clients an electronic version of our intake paperwork before meeting for the first time. For the client, they are afforded with time and space to complete the form. It also provides them with the opportunity to read the notice of privacy practices, confidentiality, and our roles, and much more. For our purposes, when a client brings in a completed intake form, it helps to kick-start our conversations. It also reflects the time that the clients took to think deeply about both their current situation in life and also some of their character strengths. We both use intake forms that have been molded over the years with the influence of various supervisors. Because requirements and processes for intakes can vary greatly depending on the setting you are working within or the training program you are in, we suggest talking to your supervisors about their expectations for the intake process and what they want you to use as an intake form.

How Do You Set Up the Room?

The setup of the room reflects how you want to be perceived. Do you want to be perceived as warm? Confident? All-knowing? For us, the setup of the meeting room is an important element to consider. Do you have two chairs? Or should there be three or four chairs? How close should the chairs be together? Is there a table? Artwork? Personal pictures?

We both determined early on that we felt most comfortable in a conversation when we were sitting directly across from another person. From observing our clients behavior (e.g., whether they pushed their chairs back or were leaning in) we try to arrange the chairs about three feet apart from each other. We have found that other chairs in the room are important, too, especially when a client decides to bring another person in for the first consultation, such as when a younger client wants to bring his or her parents into the conversation. We both have decided that we prefer to walk with a client to our meeting room and offer them to enter before we do. We want clients to feel as if they have a sense of belongingness and autonomy. Once I (AO) enter the room, I tend to offer the clients to sit anywhere they like, and I simply adjust accordingly by sitting in the chair across from them. Another option that I (JDB) utilize is having my chair across from a couch. I usher clients into the room and ask them to be seated on the couch. I usually make a joke about the stereotypical therapist's couch and tell them they can sit up and have a face-to-face conversation. Thus, having a couch has rarely been an issue. In fact, many clients enjoy having extra room to get comfortable while talking. Depending on the size of the room, I will have additional chairs as well.

Aside from the seating arrangement, we enjoy having inspirational quotes and a few personally relevant artifacts in the room, which often invite questions or comments at the beginning of the conversation. However, we find that establishing a focus in the first few minutes is important, so we do our best to limit visual distractions like a cluttered desk. While we have suggested several things about the setup of the room, we also want to highlight how various cultures might perceive an office (e.g., how close we sit, artwork, etc.). For more information on cultural differences, please see Chapter 11 on multicultural issues.

Before the First Session

We both value being on time for the first meeting. Clients have carved time out of their busy schedules to make this first meeting happen, and it is important to honor that—especially for that first meeting! If your conversations with people tend to run longer than the allotted time (often 45 to 50 minutes), then schedule appointments farther apart so that you have enough buffer time to get closure on your conversations, write down process notes while they are still fresh, mentally regroup, and prepare to be present with your next client. Plan for extra time to do this after intake sessions as there will be a lot of information that you want to take note on during your first interaction.

Steve: A small but useful tip is to put a clock in your office that you can see from your chair without having to turn your head. If you sit in a couple of chairs, then have a couple of clocks. Most people find it hard to check their watch in session, so don't rely on that. You'll be much better at starting to wrap up a session in time if you can keep an eye on the clock. Remember that as much as it may feel like you're not honoring someone's issues by ending a session on time, you're not honoring your next client if you run over into his or her session and start late.

Let's consider what to wear for that first meeting with a new client. What is an appropriate attire for this meeting? Do you want to dress more "professional," or is a "casual" approach just right for this meeting? What is your style? I (AO) remember trying to look like influential mentors and supervisors in my graduate training and beyond, and consequently I was left feeling like a blend between all of my mentors. Stylistically, they all dressed "casual-business," in that order. Eventually I just began wearing what I thought was most comfortable for me, especially if my schedule had me working in various environments for very long days. I landed on my style of wearing clean sneakers, nice jeans, and a button-down shirt with rolled-up sleeves that I feel are just fine for meeting clients at skate parks, team practices on the beach, meetings in indoor athletic gyms, and in my office space.

While we both appreciate comfort and approachability, I (JDB) might wear something more professional, particularly when working with a male team or client. I hope to be perceived in a professional manner and feel as though attire can play a huge part in perception—particularly for a female. And for better or worse, attire can also provide the wrong impression—if you want to be perceived that you are there to work, watch what you wear!

Early on in the First Session

How do you want the client to experience the first meeting? How do you make the client feel comfortable? For both of us, we think the first eight seconds is an exciting time! We've come to appreciate these moments more and more with each client. For me (AO), it is important to use my clients' names when addressing them, to make a warm connection with eye contact, and to shake their hands. One thing that I have noticed in preparation for writing this chapter is that I often thank my clients, right at the outset, for taking the time to meet with me. For most clients, I also like to hint that what they are about to experience is often a fun process, and I prefer to ask them if they are ready to get started in a tone that reflects my authenticity and excitement. This is part of my style that has been grooved with practice, and my awareness of verbal and nonverbal tendencies has increased from both supervision and comments made by my clients after the relationship has been established.

Steve: Many beginning sport psychologists have feelings ranging from concern to fear to panic regarding what they say in their first session. They are often worried that they may say something so wrong that their client gets up and leaves in the middle of a session. I have never heard of a client doing such a thing. Early on when supervising a new trainee, I try to mention Bordin's (1994) tear-and-repair process. Research has shown that saying something "wrong" does not have to be terminal if the therapist is willing to talk about what he or she said and model an openness to talk through difficult situations (e.g., Kivlighan & Shaughnessy, 2000; Safran, Muran, Samstag, & Stevens, 2001; Stiles et al., 2004). In fact, a willingness to talk about the consulting relationship can actually lead to a stronger alliance, where clients trust they can talk about anything with the consultant. So don't be afraid of saying the wrong thing as long as you're willing to talk about your relationship with your clients.

In the Room for an Individual Session

How Do You Get Started After Entering the Room?

In the spirit of honoring our clients' time and desires, we both inquire relatively early on in the conversation what brings us together today. As we are listening, we find our minds are highly present; we closely observe tone of voice, word choice, thought flow, and the way clients explain the worlds in which they live. For example, does the client seem to be an optimist? Do they demonstrate an internal locus of control regarding their current situation? Are they psychologically gritty? We encourage clients early and often to expand and explore their psychological orientation with as much clarity as they can. We do our best to match clients' nonverbals, such as leaning in when they lean in, sitting back when they sit back, getting comfortable when they get comfortable, and nodding when they nod.

Mirroring a client is one skill that we remember learning about early in graduate training. Actively using your own nonverbal behaviors to help shape the conversation is another skill that we learned by actually "doing the work." I (AO) noticed through the help of video supervision that I developed the skill to convey open nonverbal behaviors when my clients convey closed-off gestures, such as sitting comfortably and breathing deeply in response to seeing my clients sitting with crossed arms. It isn't exactly something that I feel that I had to train in graduate school. Rather, I think it developed with time and with experience working with clients. I think being fully present in the room with someone is the greatest gift we can offer our clients, and being "authentically me" helps to establish my own place in the room by controlling the things that I can control.

We both have a genuine interest in people, and our inquiries are guided by theories of motivation (e.g., self-determination theory [Ryan & Deci, 2000]), holistic development (Wylleman & Lavallee, 2004), and cultural influence (Hays, 2009). For us, it is important to understand our clients through these scientific lenses, but these are certainly not the only options available (see Chapter 1 on developing a theoretical orientation to performance excellence).

Depending on the elements contained in your TOPE, structured and unstructured intakes have been developed to assist in the initial interviewing process. While more needs to be done in regard to having structured and unstructured interview guides for sport and

Table 9.1 Selected Structured Intake Protocols

- Aoyagi, M. W., Poczwardowski, A., Statler, T., Shapiro, J. L., & Cohen, A. B. (2016). The performance interview guide: Recommendations for initial consultations in sport & performance psychology. Manuscript submitted for publication.
- Taylor, J., & Schneider, B. A. (1991). The sport-clinical intake protocol: A comprehensive interviewing instrument for applied sport psychology. *Professional Psychology: Research and Practice, 23*(4), 318–325.
- Hays, P. A. (2009). Integrating evidence-based practice, cognitive-behavior therapy, and multicultural therapy: Ten steps for culturally competent practice. *Professional Psychology: Research and Practice, 40*(4), 354–360.
- First, M. B., Williams, J. B. W., Karg, R. S., & Spitzer, R. L. (2015). *Structured Clinical Interview for DSM-5 Disorders (SCID-5-CV)*. Arlington, VA: American Psychiatric Association Publishing.
- DiNardo, P. A., Brow, T. A., & Barlow, D. H. (1994). *Anxiety Disorders Interview Schedule for DSM-IV: Life Time Version: Client Interview Schedule*. Boulder, CO: Graywind Publishing.
- Wylleman, P., & Lavallee, D. (2004). A developmental perspective on transitions faced by athletes. In M. Weiss (Ed.), *Developmental Sport Psychology: A Lifespan Perspective* (pp. 507–527). Morgantown, WV: Fitness Information Technology.
- Bystritsky, A., Khalsa, S. S., Cameron, M. E., & Schiffman, J. (2013). Current diagnosis and treatment of anxiety disorders. *Pharmacy and Therapeutics, 38*(1), 38–57.

performance populations, there is a new semistructured interview, the Performance Interview Guide (PInG), that we wish we had as a resource when we started consulting (Aoyagi, Poczwardowski, Statler, Shapiro, & Cohen, 2016). Coincidentally, the PInG is a structure that we already adhere to, but it may have accelerated our growth if we had a similar structure to guide intake interview questioning. While it is beyond the scope of this chapter to discuss the similarities and differences of "structured" (e.g., formal) and "unstructured" (e.g., asking open-ended questions, following where clients take you) interviews, we have provided some references to more structured intake examples in Table 9.1. You don't have to follow a structure, but a structured intake may help to guide you. Our most important advice about the intake is to ask yourself, Why am I asking these questions? What am I trying to understand about this client? The answers to these questions should be driven largely by your theoretical orientation to performance excellence (TOPE).

Let's say that you align closely with the notion that performance excellence is driven or determined by emotional factors, which could be informed by research and theoretical models such as emotional intelligence, channeling passion toward a craft, and/or the pursuit of happiness in life. One theoretical model that may influence your thought process is the Resonance model for performance excellence and life engagement (Newburg, Kimiecik, Durand-Bush, & Doell, 2002). If this is the case, you may develop a process of inquiry pertaining to the articulation of your clients' dreams or visions in their performance domain and in life; their training practices; their response styles to internal, external, and situational barriers; and ways that they revisit their dreams. Using established models allows the opportunity for educating clients in the session how they can see their performance process. Having a rich understanding of the nuances of established theory, research, and clinical practices that make up your TOPE isn't the whole story, though. It is the appropriate application of the best available research and practices that fit the unique characteristics and preferences of your client that determines the effectiveness of the consultancy relationship.

Do We Allow Questions About Ourselves?

We have learned that there is an art of vulnerability in the first session (see Rempel, Holmes, & Zanna,1985; Simpson, 2007; Wieselquist, Rusbult, Foster, & Agnew, 1999).We both like to offer an open yet brief discussion of who we are, what our backgrounds are, and maybe a few nuggets on our personal history that are relevant to the building of a new relationship with a client. At first, I (AO) was thrilled to answer questions that my early clients had of me. Looking back, I was so ego-focused. I have decided to take a different path nowadays. I really try to be mindful that this is *their* time, so I want to be able to honor that by spending our moments together working on what *they* want to accomplish. It is rare to hear someone say that they want to learn all about me when I ask them, "So, what do you want to tackle today?" Personally, we have both learned to inquire about where questions about us originated for them.

Defining the Issue(s)

During our training, we both sought supervision whenever we could. We also reached out to professionals in the field in our local and regional communities. One lesson that has remained engrained in our thought process when meeting with a client for the first time is to consider three questions: What is the presenting issue? What is the real issue? Who is the client? We find that this is a great structure to guide how to perceive the presenting issue. The reader (you!) might read these questions and assume that the purpose is to identify the problem or what is wrong with the client. However, we see it through a solution-focused lens:

What is the issue?

Translated in our minds, we are thinking about:

- To what extent are the apparent barriers to performance casting a shadow over this person's inherent character strengths and resources?
- If this person were a relative, what would we suggest in regard to training an optimal mindset?

What is the real issue?

Translated in our minds, we are thinking about:

- How is this person conceptualizing his or her current situation? What words does this person choose to use, and, importantly, what is it that is not being said (e.g., all the good stuff)?
- Is the timing for sport psychology right for this client right now? In other words, what is going to be best for this client in the immediate future?
- What might be causing or exacerbating the presenting issue that the client is unable or unwilling to recognize, confront, or discuss?

Who is the client?

Translated in our minds, we are thinking about:

- To whom are we ultimately responsible (client, parent/guardian, coach, athletic director)?
- What does this mean for confidentiality and boundaries (who will be told what and under what circumstances)?

- Who is this client most closely linked to in terms of social support?
- Who else might really help this client to invest in sport psychology right now (e.g., a nutritionist, a medical consultant, a sleep specialist, etc.)?
- How do we make the largest impact for this client?

Steve: These are great questions to keep in mind when working with clients. It is always important to be aware of your role, whether you're working for an organization, team, or the individual. There is a lot of great scholarship and research in the field of consulting psychology that highlights the importance of identifying your client (e.g., Newman, 1993; Newman, Robinson-Kurpius, & Fuqua, 2002). And it is vital to keep in mind that the "issue" our clients describe may not be the actual "issue" that needs to be worked on. Although our clients are experts on themselves and their experiences, they are not often experts in the realm of performance psychology—which is why they are coming to us! So, as important as it is for us to understand how they describe their "issue," we must rely on our training to see if there is a "real issue" below the surface.

Conceptualizing the Client/Issue(s)

How are we conceptualizing the client? What theories are we using? Think about the bigger picture, the broader scope. Problem definition is difficult (if not impossible) without theory. Do you actually know what's going on first? Often, novice consultants don't conceptualize in theory, but interventions. Upon reflection, we noticed something about the arc of case conceptualization that we have taken since initial studies at the University of Denver. Early on, while we were still studying for our master's degrees, we remember being highly focused on the appropriate application of interventions—we just wanted to try out imagery, meditation, relaxation strategies, and confidence development techniques, to name a few. Interactions were *about us* practicing a new craft *on* a willing client. After graduation, and early on in our applied careers, we noticed that having a clear understanding of the psychological theory that underpinned interventions became the focus of our attention. This reflected our general interest in the origins of mindset training, and we found that a solid understanding of various key theoretical paradigms helped us to free up our creativity and confidence when working to develop individualized mindset training programs and drills. Looking back, we feel that at times the interaction was *either* about us *or* about the client and that we were providing more *education* than training of mindset principles. At this point in our careers, there is a much deeper appreciation for the importance of evidence-based research—namely, what could work best, why it could be really good for this client, and what limitations are important for both of us to consider when using applied drills and interventions. Using an analogy, we feel as if early on we took a shotgun approach, hoping to hit some target. At this level of our applied experience and clinical training, we have a much deeper appreciation for a sniper approach—using evidence, insight, and active collaboration with clients to come together in the pursuit of hitting their optimal target. To build on the sniper metaphor, our TOPE (see Chapter 1) would be analogous to the scope—the lens through which information is filtered, allowing us to hone in on the most important aspects of the oftentimes vast amount of information at our disposal.

Steve: I think this is one of the biggest shifts that occurs in the development of a young practitioner, especially in the field of sport psychology. Most students' training is focused far more on interventions than on a thorough understanding of the psychology of high performance. Thus, augmented by trainees' desires to be helpful and to "do" something, their thought processes naturally focus on interventions. However, the most elaborate, creative intervention will not benefit the client if it does not address the actual issue the client needs to work on. This seems to be one of the most difficult things for students in our practicum to get comfortable with. At the beginning of the year, many of them roll their eyes when I jump in after a 5- to 10-minute discussion of interventions and ask what they are actually trying to solve. By the end of the quarter, they realize that it is far more important to spend the time to come up with an accurate assessment and conceptualization than to work on an intervention. In fact, research confirms that expert consultants spend more time working on problem identification than on intervention planning (Brown, Pryzwansky, & Schulte, 2006). So come up with cool, creative interventions. Just make sure that they are actually beneficial to the client you're working with!

Wrapping Up

Could you summarize the content up to this point? Ask what they want to talk about next week? Assign homework? Imagine this: It is the last few minutes of the initial conversation. Hopefully things went pretty well, and you notice that there might be a warmer temperature in the room, figuratively speaking. How do you think you would end the conversation? When we first began, we were both afraid to stop the session. Right around the 58th-minute marker, I (AO) discovered that is when my client and I would both find our groove. What it led to were many apologies for being a few minutes late with other clients waiting for me, and rushed endings that unfortunately did not have a chance to be unpacked with the time, space, and respect that they may have deserved. Over time, we have developed the following strategy for ending sessions. We like to thank our client for coming in to do this work, and to encourage them to explore what resonates most for them (and to write it down!) before starting their cars and heading home. At the end, we ask if they have any parting questions for us, and we provide a closing statement, such as "This is the time that we have for today—come on, I'll walk you out."

Through supervision, we've learned more about the importance of offering a statement like this to clients at the end of a meeting. It provides closure, and it is important to verbally state that we are leaving this experience together. It is also another opportunity to model what it looks like to set and hold boundaries and demonstrate respect for both the client's and our own time. We have found that this type of statement sets up the hallway conversations to genial topics and reduces the likelihood of bringing up sensitive topics when reaching for the doorknob.

Mark:　As Adam and Jessica have done an excellent job illustrating, the consulting setting is a novel and often-intimidating setting that requires consultants to be thoughtful about how to orient their clients. I find that the close of the session is one of the most potentially awkward and also fruitful aspects of consulting. Particularly in an initial session, I find it helpful to verbally "walk" the client through the transitions. Thus, if we have scheduled a 50-minute session, at 40 minutes I'll provide a brief acknowledgement that we have 10 minutes left. This gives clients an opportunity to address anything that they might be hoping to get to. With five minutes left I'll say something to the effect of, "With our last five minutes, I'd like to check in with how you are doing?" Typically, clients will give a brief reply, and I'll ask them to elaborate. I'll specifically ask about what worked for them today, what they enjoyed, and anything that didn't work or they would like to see differently next time. Additionally, I'll inquire about any topics we didn't get to that they would like to discuss next time, or if there is anything else they feel would be helpful for me to know. This provides a nice closure where the power is shifted to clients, and there is a gentle reminder that this is their time, they are in charge, and the benefits they experience will be a result of their efforts and intentions.

Parting Thoughts

From Adam: First, as a consultant, you'll find your groove soon enough. But if you are nervous, not grounded in the session, not there for your client, or not present, then you are making the session about you and not them. Second, we can all sniff out a phony. Get really clear with your consulting philosophy, know your guiding theoretical frameworks inside and out, and keep in mind that you may be sitting down with someone who might just change the world in some powerful way.

From Jessica: First, you can't be your supervisor, your professor, or anyone else! And you shouldn't be! You can only be you! And related to AO's parting thought, be patient because you will find your own style! You might try out a few things, and you will only discover what works through trial and error!

Good luck and have fun!

References

Aoyagi, M. W., Poczwardowski, A., Statler, T., Shapiro, J. L., & Cohen, A. B. (2016). The performance interview guide: Recommendations for initial consultations in sport & performance psychology. Manuscript submitted for publication.

Aoyagi, M. W., & Portenga, S. T. (2010). The role of positive ethics and virtues in the context of sport and performance psychology service delivery. *Professional Psychology: Research and Practice, 41*(3), 253.

Bordin, E. S. (1994). Theory and research on the therapeutic working alliance: New directions. In A. O. Horvath & L. S. Greenberg (Eds.), *The working alliance: Theory, research, and practice* (pp. 13–37). New York: Wiley.

Brown, D., Pryzwansky, W. B., & Schulte, A. C. (2006). *Psychological consultation and collaboration: Introduction to theory and practice* (6th ed.). Boston, MA: Allyn & Bacon.

Hays, P. A. (2009). Integrating evidence-based practice, cognitive-behavior therapy, and multicultural therapy: Ten steps for culturally competent practice. *Professional Psychology: Research and Practice, 40*(4), 354–360.

Kivlighan, D. M., & Shaughnessy, P. (2000). Patterns of working alliance development: A typology of client's working alliance ratings. *Journal of Counseling Psychology, 47*(3), 362–371.

Newburg, D., Kimiecik, J., Durand-Bush, N., & Doell, K. (2002). The role of resonance in performance excellence and life engagement. *Journal of Applied Sport Psychology, 14,* 249–267.

Newman, J. L. (1993). Ethical issues in consultation. *Journal of Counseling & Development, 72,* 148–156.

Newman, J. L., Robinson-Kurpius, S. E., & Fuqua, D. R. (2002). Issues in the ethical practice of consulting psychology. In R. L. Lowman (Ed.), *The Californica school of organizational studies handbook of organizational consulting psychology: A comprehensive guide to theory, skills, and techniques* (pp. 733–758). San Francisco: Jossey-Bass.

Rempel, J. K., Holmes, J. G., & Zanna, M. P. (1985). Trust in close relationships. *Journal of Personality and Social Psychology, 49*(1), 95–112.

Ryan, R. M., & Deci, E. L. (2000). Self-determination theory and the facilitation of intrinsic motivation, social development, and well-being. *American Psychologist, 55*(1), 68–78.

Safran, J. D., Muran, J. C., Samstag, L. W., & Stevens, C. (2001). Repairing alliance ruptures. *Psychotherapy: Theory, Research, Practice, Training, 38*, 406–412.

Simpson, J. A. (2007). Psychological foundations of trust. *Current Directions in Psychological Science, 16*(5), 264–268.

Stiles, W. B., Glick, M. J., Osatuke, K., Hardy, G. E., Shapiro, D. A., Agnew-Davies, R., Rees, A., & Barkham, M. (2004). Patterns of alliance development and the rupture-repair hypothesis: Are productive relationships U-shaped or V-shaped? *Journal of Counseling Psychology, 51*, 81–92.

Taylor, J., & Schneider, B. A. (1992). The sport-clinical intake protocol: A comprehensive interviewing instrument for applied sport psychology. *Professional Psychology: Research and Practice, 23*(4), 318–325.

Welfel, E. R. (2012). *Ethics in counseling & psychotherapy: Standards, research, and emerging issues* (5th ed.). Belmont, CA: Cengage Learning.

Wieselquist, J., Rusbult, C. E., Foster, C. A., & Agnew, C. R. (1999). Commitment, pro-relationship behavior, and trust in close relationships. *Journal of Personality and Social Psychology, 77*(5), 942–966.

Wylleman, P., & Lavallee, D. (2004). A developmental perspective on transitions faced by athletes. In M. R. Weiss (Ed.), *Developmental sport and exercise psychology: A lifespan perspective* (pp. 503–523). Morgantown, WV: Fitness Information Technology.

10 Working With Groups

Engaging, Communication, and Impacting Both Individuals and Teams

Mike D. Lewis, Angus L. Mugford, and Taryn K. Morgan

There are many aspects to applied sport psychology, but the ability to present and engage a group of people is one of the most powerful tools in the practitioner's arsenal—although presenting is just one aspect of working with groups. We must also consider the importance of other competencies such as the ability to assess needs, collaborate with leadership, design curriculum, implement programs and applied activities, present material, debrief activities, communicate and connect, problem solve, adapt, and evaluate the program. There are many subtle aspects to effective consulting, but even just within the context of working with groups and teams, a wide variety of factors are at play.

The reality is that successful consultants put in a great deal of thought, preparation, and effort, yet make it look easy. We are dealing with a complicated process, with often complex and abstract concepts, but great consultants are able to share messages that are both simple and concrete (see Chapter 2 in this book for an in-depth presentation of these issues as applied to student-consultants). Being both a "scientist" with a strong grasp of theory and an "artist" with the ability to create and adapt is a formidable challenge as a young practitioner. There often are parallels between the athletes, teams, and performers that a consultant may work with and the methods and practices utilized by both. Great performers have the ability to exhibit unyielding focus, unshakeable confidence, and an enormous amount of self-control. As a consultant, practicing and utilizing these same abilities can build a solid foundation. If your plan is to have a long, successful career in this field, mastering some of the same skills can prove to be invaluable when working with groups.

The goal of this chapter is to share practical insights, from the considerations of working with groups and teams, to specific factors that are important to engage, communicate, and impact the individuals involved. The authors of this chapter work at IMG Academy, a full-time applied performance-training center for junior athletes. Note that there is a distinction between groups and teams (i.e., individual sports like tennis and golf are groups, and the team sports are teams), since the authors work with both in a group setting. At IMG Academy, every student-athlete receives mental training in addition to physical training on a weekly basis. Be it an individual sport (golf, tennis, track) or team sport (baseball, basketball, football, lacrosse, and soccer), whether they are 10 or 18 years old, these student-athletes train in groups and work with their mental coaches in a group setting. Perhaps one of the unique aspects of IMG is the mental coach's work with a diverse group of clients. These clients range from the youth athlete to college and professional athletes, as well as parents and coaches, to corporate executives and even military personnel. Regardless of who the client is, and indeed whether in a group setting or individual session, your interaction as a consultant must be authentic and engaging, the communication must be clear, and the message must be impactful. This chapter will begin with a narrative from a neophyte consultant focusing on a scenario that captured a key learning experience and insight into his learning process. Second, we follow the perspective of core competencies of a sport psychology consultant and how this relates to the developmental journey of a neophyte practitioner. Third, we focus more specifically on the process and key aspects of engaging, communicating, and impacting clients.

The Good, the Bad, and the Ugly

It is the morning of your first mental conditioning session. In 30 minutes you are expecting a group of 30–40 basketball players, all males ranging in age from 10–18. Within this group a total of 10 countries around the world are represented: Russia, Canada, Guatemala, France, Cameroon, Spain, the list goes on. As their mental coach, you have planned out your session exactly the way you want it to run. You have designed a session that is geared toward young competitive athletes who love the sport of basketball. You have discussed your ideas with your mentor and have an organized, well-thought-out plan. You have committed yourself to delivering the best possible content and plan on hitting home three key messages that can help the athletes perform better.

It's now 15 minutes before your session, and you are relaxed and ready to get started. You go through your mental checklist: video, white board, eraser, dry erase markers, handouts, activity, pencils, and your notes written on a 3x5 index card to keep you on track.

It's now five minutes after the scheduled start time, and no one has arrived. As you are waiting, your coworkers pass by looking at their watches, asking, "*Don't you have a session in here at 10am?*" or "*Where is everybody?*" These basic questions become annoying, and you begin to doubt if anyone will even show. Just as you complete that thought, a young boy about 12 years of age strolls in sucking on a large smoothie through a straw, in no hurry, wearing socks and sandals, swag backpack, Beats by Dre headphones, and looking down at the giant smartphone in his hand. You eagerly approach ready to introduce yourself. The young man never even looks up, grabs a seat, and, about one minute later, removes his left earphone and in an accent you have never heard before says, "*Is this Mental?*" You reply, "*Yes!*" and introduce yourself. Through a series of basic questions, you learn that the young athlete in front of you is from Ukraine and does not speak fluent English, and neither do the 15 other basketball players he came with. In addition, you learn they all have played only one full season of basketball, and they actually love soccer. Wow.

A few minutes pass, and the room is now beginning to fill: at first 10, then 20 more, and even more people are flowing in for a total of 67 athletes. Coaches and parents also file in, adding an additional nine people. You soon realize you do not have enough handouts and pencils for a group this size. A slight panic begins to set in. As the athletes are settling in, you hear two to three different languages being spoken. It is now 15 minutes after the scheduled starting time. You have never made use of the stage behind you, but given the size of the group you think standing on the stage is a great way to grab the attention of your audience. As you stand on the stage and begin to introduce yourself, no one is listening, you attempt to speak louder, a few conversations end, and a few "*shhhhs*" from your audience begin to quiet the room. Now you have their attention, and they are focused on you. You immediately realize that you are in a foreign place, with foreign people, standing on an uncomfortable stage, expected to deliver a Mental Conditioning Session you knew inside and out just 10 minutes ago, but somehow you cannot recall what your first slide on the PowerPoint is about.

You realize that you have their attention, and, just as you get through your introduction, someone's cell phone rings. The ring tone is the song "Wannabe" by the Spice Girls: "*I'll tell you what a want what I really, really, really want!*" The room erupts in laughter, and several conversations begin. You make several attempts to reel the audience back in, but to no avail. After a few moments, the room quiets down enough so that you can continue.

The topic of your session is "Composure." As you turn to write the word "Composure" on the white board with a dry erase marker, the marker does not write. You reach for another marker, and that one is dried up and doesn't write either. Finally, you grab an orange-colored marker that works, but it is barely visible. The athletes begin to ask among themselves what the board says and what it means. You are not too concerned with them not being able to view the white board, because you have developed a great slide deck with YouTube videos that will help hit home the message. As the questions begin, you realize that 80 percent of the audience does not speak English. The perceived language barrier gets larger and larger with each passing moment. Due to this unexpected challenge in communication, you decide this is a good time to go to the video. You think to yourself, "*They'll definitely understand Michael Jordan, Larry Bird, and Kareem Abdul-Jabbar.*" You believe everything will click once they watch the video.

The video is queued on YouTube; prior to playing the video, you built up how great the video is and how your audience is really going to enjoy it because it depicts composure at its best. You push play, and your computer freezes up. It takes about one minute for the laptop to unfreeze; and somehow one minute feels like 10 minutes. You push play, the video starts, and, about two minutes into the video, the Wi-Fi signal is lost and the video will no longer play. Rather than move on, you make the decision to try to fix the problem. Well, fixing the problem takes several minutes, and there is now an awkward silence in the room. The remaining video plays, then as it ends you begin to transition into the next part of your presentation. Several athletes are walking back and forth to use the bathroom, which causes a disruption. As you begin the next segment, you also notice the parents whispering in the back row and giving you blank stares. As you try to keep a poker face and go on with your delivery, you cannot help but to wish it were over.

Despite all of these issues, you have noticed some buy-in from a few of the athletes up front. You make an attempt to ask them a question, and you simply receive the deer in the headlight stare. The boys' attention is diverted once they hear a loud siren, and the Florida sky opens up and there is a downpour of rain. A siren signals that it is unsafe to be outside and to quickly move indoors. At a moment's notice, the doors fly open and 25 female tennis players ranging in age from 10–18 come rushing into your conference room. They are unaware a session is going on, and they could not care less; they just want to get out of the rain. At this point there is an even greater distraction to your presentation, teenage hormones! No one is listening; there is giggling, sighing, and loud talking. There is an overwhelming feeling that you have lost control of the session. There are only five minutes left, and you have not covered your take-home message.

It may seem hard to redeem many positives out of this session. The reference to the classic Clint Eastwood western movie *The Good, the Bad and the Ugly* refers to the fact that there are always positives and negatives with any experience, and the positive in this example is typical of many eager practitioners who have a passion to share their knowledge and impact others. The reality, however, is that while content is important, the art with which you engage and manage the session makes all the difference in the world.

What Competencies Are We Looking For?

While there is often an emphasis in sport and performance psychology literature on the effectiveness of interventions, there is an increasing emphasis on the development of the consultant (Cremades & Tashman, 2014; Silva, Metzler, & Lerner, 2007; Taylor, 2014). Key attributes that make up a competent consultant or clinician have been identified for some time. Indeed, if we exclude the specific requirements for licensed mental health professionals, the Association for Applied Sport Psychology (AASP) has criteria that highlight

Table 10.1 AASP Criteria for Consultant Evaluation

1	Ability to build and maintain a trusting consulting relationship in applied sport or exercise psychology.
2	Effectiveness in structuring applied work in an activity where both client and consultant have responsibilities (e.g., both parties are fully engaged in the process).
3	Ability to define the client's weaknesses and strengths and to understand solutions to those performance issues.
4	Ability to seek assistance when necessary and to implement supervisory feedback.
5	Ability to integrate theory and practice.
6	Sensitivity to the ethical and legal standards of the profession.

the perceived needs of a competent professional beyond a specific knowledge base as evaluated by a mentor, first established in 1989. These are represented in Table 10.1.

These criteria are graded from outstanding to unsatisfactory, including the ability to add consultant strengths and weaknesses. What is interesting is that the emphasis is broad enough that it can include group work, but is not specific to highlight what makes an effective consultant with groups.

Given the lack of specificity in profiles like this, the IMG team developed a Competency Profile (Mugford, Hesse, & Morgan, 2014) to help profile strengths and weaknesses for professional development for everyone from neophyte coaches to senior consultants. This helped us develop consultant awareness, improve communication between consultants and their mentor, as well as identify training protocols and goals.

Mugford et al. (2014) gave greater depth to the specific areas of group consulting, presented in the following table.

Once mastered, the aforementioned competencies can provide confidence and a firm foundation when delivering or serving a client. Beyond the requisite base of knowledge, the content of a message is not the most important aspect to deliver an effective consulting session. The previous narrative of the boys' basketball group is a good case in point. Frequently, an ineffective session is a result of a message that is too complex, abstract, and disconnected from sport performance, or boring, irrelevant, or poorly presented to an athlete. Equally as limiting is a session without clear learning objectives, where there is no action plan or assignment to follow once a session is over.

The art of being a successful presenter means that the presenter understands that communication is measured by the response that you get, not what you say. Where this is concerned, the mental coach begins to focus on *doing a little, a lot*, rather than on too much material at a superficial level. Establishing a concrete take-home message is first and foremost. Once this is identified, creating a theme that is both educational and entertaining (*edu-taining*) becomes the challenge and figuring out how the topic can be presented in this way. The clearest feedback as to the success of this is the response that you get in a group session, especially in a demanding environment that may have 100 student-athletes ranging from 10 to 18 years old, that vary in language and sport ability levels. If a group is not engaged and interested in the session, the presenter will know fast! Maintaining the balance of "entertainment" to get a group interested and paying attention creates the opportunity to "educate" and provide valuable content that translates to behavior change and improved performance. Two particularly important characteristics of group delivery will be discussed in this chapter: Connecting with Learner Motivation, and Stickiness of Message. The first focuses on connecting with a learner's motivation and using that

Table 10.2 "Total Consultant" Competencies at IMG Academy

Competency	Description	Examples
Knowledge	Demonstrate a deep and broad knowledge base within relevant fields of sport psychology, learning and behavior, and sport-specific domains. There is a further ability to integrate theoretical concepts into clear practical application.	Knowledge of sport psychology, learning, and behavior. Ability to demonstrate integration of theory and ethical practice. Performance specific knowledge.
Relationships	Ability to build and maintain trusting relationships and exhibit strong communication skills across a variety of groups, from clients and families, to peers, coaches, mentors, interdisciplinary staff, and management.	Professional relationships with clients, peers, coaches, mentors, and interdisciplinary staff. Excellent personal and professional communication skills. Generating and transforming opportunities and maintaining appropriate relationships.
Delivery	Ability to utilize strong individual counseling skills, in addition to strong group presentation skills that both entertain and educate.	Individual consulting skills such as listening skills, collaborating with clients, and providing quality strategic advice. Group presentation skills such as connecting with learner motivation, ability to facilitate discussion, and "stickiness" of sessions.
Organization/ Management	Demonstrate personal awareness, efficient planning, and organizational skills, with an ability to work well with others through developing proposals and executing team projects.	Personal and situational awareness, planning and organization, problem solving and solution design, case documentation, and reflection. Program evaluation and business proposal development.
Development	Achieve personal and professional balance, while seeking growth through knowledge, innovation, practical expertise, research, and business opportunities.	Professionally with regard to certifications, expanding research and performance knowledge, innovation, and knowledge management. Personal development through work/life balance and personal health.
Leadership	Seek opportunities to positively impact the organization and others to develop, grow, and achieve their goals.	Staff development, mentoring, organizational awareness, upward management.

Table 10.3 Group Consulting Competency Description From IMG Academy

Broad Category	Specific Characteristic
Group Consulting Delivery	Comprehension of content
	Quality of transitions and flow
	Presentation mechanics (Voice-Eyes-Gesture-Attitude [Webster, 2010])
	Connecting with Learner Motivation (Attention-Relevance-Confidence-Satisfaction [Keller, 1987])
	Ability to facilitate group discussion
	Use of media and activities
	Flexibility
	Stickiness of messages (following principles of SUCCES: Simplicity, Unexpected, Concrete, Credible, Emotion, Stories [Heath & Heath, 2007])
	Ability to present to wide variety of group populations (age, culture, ability level, sport)

motivation to deliver a compelling message. Second, the *stickiness* of the message focuses on ensuring that the message is memorable and applicable.

Learner motivation (Keller, 1987) highlighted the importance of being relevant to an audience, capturing their attention, and allowing them to feel confident that they can apply their learning experience and to feel satisfied and rewarded for their experience. This is one reason that at IMG we tend to use short videos and activities rather than lectures or complicated PowerPoints to connect with an audience. Balancing the two sides to *edutainment* takes a lot of deliberate practice and time to develop, but it's a powerful skill set once developed. In reference to Anders Ericsson's research (2009), the idea of achieving mastery as a teacher and presenter is perhaps no different than mastering many other kinds of skills. The act of deliberate practice with feedback and corrected presentation skills on a next take should not be overlooked. Hence, both repetition and quality practice should lead to improvement.

One of the newer concepts that is often key with group consulting delivery is the idea of creating *sticky* messages. *Stickiness* is a term coined by Chip and Dan Heath in their best-selling book *Made to Stick* (2007), where they used their acronym of SUCCES (Simplicity, Unexpected, Concrete, Credible, Emotion, Stories) to highlight principles that help concepts resonate and impact people. This is just as applicable to sales and marketing as it is in education. Some of the great advertising campaigns are examples of sticky concepts, with great tag lines like "melts in your mouth, not in your hand," by Hershey's M&M's in 1954. That slogan is almost 60 years old, but many people can recite easily and attribute it to M&M's. Rather than attaching this to a commercial product, we raise the reader's attention to the implications for such *stickiness*. More than only creating a slogan, there is a concept that tells a story that is simple, unexpected, concrete, and credible, and that makes an emotional connection with the audience. Challenging our staff to be creative and strong in their technical style of presenting, but to also focus on the content and *stickiness* of the messaging, creates a high likelihood of success in both the science and the art of presenting.

Engaging

Preparation is essential for any practitioner, but perhaps even more so for those with less experience. In the neophyte consultant's session described previously, having the wrong assumptions may have been a major contributing factor for the session to not run smoothly. In addition, there was a lack of awareness of what to anticipate and even prepare for that ultimately failed the consultant. While there are many facets to explaining the mechanics of a failure, we know that people do not pay attention to boring things, and, ultimately, if a client is not engaged for whatever reason, you will not be successful in facilitating change. Engaging the client is a fundamental step in the process of working with a group or individual, but it also is a skill that, once mastered, creates a foundation on which an entire professional practicing style can be built.

There is a tremendous amount of literature on how to execute the many tasks of a sport psychology consultant. Indeed, if you look at the core of counseling psychology, Carl Rogers (1951), and the foundational work on establishing rapport, these are also relevant for group environments in creating the conditions necessary for change. Acceptance of the client(s) and valuing them as human beings of worth is fundamental to building the trusting and collaborative relationship. This is demonstrated by showing empathy, providing a frame of reference, and having an idea of what they are going through. Genuineness, or being authentic, and showing an unconditional positive regard are the remaining core conditions that are central to Rogerian "person centered therapy," but are just as relevant on a group scale.

Silva et al. (2007) contributed thoughts specific to sport psychology professionals and shared six suggestions to building relationships that are both consistent with Rogers and also relevant for individual and group sessions. Additionally, these suggestions provide a great framework for engaging a client. While mentoring young coaches at IMG, we notice that many young practitioners focus so much of their time and energy on content and preparing for a session that they forget about the opportunity to develop rapport before the session even begins. In fact, we teach that the session starts as soon as the first person from the audience walks into the room.

The following six tips are commonly used by all of the mental conditioning staff at IMG when attempting to build rapport early on:

1. *Always greet the athlete with a smile.* In the prior story, perhaps the first mistake was that the practitioner did not go out of his way to greet the first athlete and make him feel comfortable. Nor did he properly greet the other athletes when they entered the room. Greeting your audience with a friendly, warm smile, both individually and addressing the group as a whole, can add instant rapport. A brief "Hi, my name is Coach . . ." can open up the door for some basic conversations and allow the audience member to feel connected with you. A sincere warm smile can immediately set the tone, especially when there may be a language barrier. A smile is a universal language that all people can relate to.

2. *Ask athletes about their day. Place the focus of the conversation on the athlete.* Most often at IMG, our athletes are coming to our sessions immediately after a sport or training session. There exists an opportunity to have a discussion about the athlete's experience thus far. If our practitioner pursued a conversation with the first athlete, he may have easily had 15 other athletes buy into his session. By asking open-ended questions like "What have you learned?" or "What would you like to learn or improve on?" can open up a discussion that is centered on the athletes and their progress.

3. *Engage the client(s) in at least three to five minutes of small talk.* This is a conversation that is not at all related to the athlete, just one that is pleasant and interesting. In the previous story, the practitioner could have started a brief conversation with the first athlete into the session about the Beats by Dre headphones. "*Ohh, I love my Beats. . . . Aren't they amazing!*" Starting a conversation on something basic yet enjoyable is a method to simply engage the client in a discussion that revolves around a commonality.

4. *Be upbeat and use some humor in the first few minutes of the small talk.* Once the above practitioner had a room full of athletes, parents, and coaches, there was an opportunity to make a humorous statement about parenting or coaching. Sometimes we can find a clever way to humorously set some ground rules. "*Please place your phones on vibrate or turn them off, I am easily distracted by catchy ringtones, like the Spice Girls! I suddenly get the urge to dance.*" (Then execute your worst dance move.) By using humor, you can immediately remove some tension from the room and send the message that you like to have fun and that you enjoy what you do.

5. *Find an easy, not rehearsed, segue into the session. If you are good at this, your audience may never realize that you are into the session.* The practitioner's topic was composure, and after setting the ground rules of cell phone use, and carrying on about dancing to the Spice Girls, a segue may have been created by simply talking about losing composure when you are required to perform, and what it may look like.

6. *Always reward the athlete for hard work and progress.* Throughout the above discussed session there may have been opportunities to involve the audience in an
   activity or if someone volunteered to help illustrate a point. At the close of that
   activity, offering a round of applause for the participant can be an effective way to
   keep the morale high throughout the session. Complimenting a volunteer on his or
   her courage to come forward and participate is a small way to reward someone. In
   closing the session, thanking the audience for their attention and participation and
   asking them to give each other a round of applause is a simple yet effective way to
   demonstrate reward and appreciation.

Halliwell, Orlick, Ravizza, and Rotella (2003) suggested that possibly the best approach
to long-term work is to blend in with the woodwork, work the area, be available, and be
patient. The opportunities to engage with an individual or the team or some key players will
present itself, thus allowing for an improved session once a rapport has been established.
Being successful at engaging the client is key, although keeping a client engaged requires a set
of skills as well. Knowing your clients and understanding the sport they play, the demands
of the sport, and common terminology all are essential to keeping the clients engaged.
Being clear on how you may approach a group of tennis athletes versus a group of football
athletes will aid you in delivering a quality session. Tennis being an individual sport may
require a delivery style that speaks to the individual performance of that athlete. This can be
illustrated through video of top tennis athletes' performances or interviews sharing specific
insight into a role model's experience. In the case of a team of football athletes, engaging
the athletes in an activity where they can witness the power of an activity as a team may be
impactful and allows the team to remain engaged as a team.

Communicating

In today's world, the technology that is readily available affords many ways to communicate a message. As practitioners, we would hope that our communication skills are strong
and that our messages *stick* and are memorable. As stated earlier, connecting with a group
of individuals is both an art and science. This can be more challenging the more diverse
a group is with different nationalities, various ages, and different sport backgrounds. As
we already stated, ultimately communication is more about the message received than the
message sent, but we typically focus on the latter and not the former.
    Looking back at the practitioner's session that opened our chapter, we can see that there
are several instances where he failed at communicating with the group that led to losing
engagement and the opportunity to impact. In fact, at certain points he created a wall
and separation between himself and the group, simply by standing on a stage and keeping
his back turned toward the group for an extended period of time. Although small, these
actions reduce the practitioner's chances to stay connected with the group. Indeed, such a
mistake can even be seen among experienced consultants/teachers/speakers.
    At IMG, we like to use the proverb "teach the student, not the lesson." The practitioners
who remove themselves from the idea that they need to teach a lesson can begin to focus
on creating a memorable experience for this specific group or client. A common practice
used among the practitioners at IMG is to begin building a group session by asking the
question, "What are the needs of this client, and what would be a helpful take away from
the session?" This allows us to create a framework where we can decide the tools, aids, and
resources focused toward a clear message. A common mistake made by enthusiastic and
well-meaning consultants is that they want to share everything and provide a lot of tools
and techniques, which ultimately gets lost in a confusing and overwhelming presentation.

Clarity of focus around a single theme and concept is often far more powerful than trying to achieve multiple objectives in a short period of time.

There are a host of resources that can be used, ranging from everyday technology, such as video, to requiring the group to participate in an activity using their smartphones or tablets, or even utilizing music. There are numerous methods to communicate ideas and concepts—for example, Skype, GoToMeeting, and Google Hangouts. The use of these resources can enable a practitioner to have a reach far beyond the classroom. Social media outlets such as Facebook, Twitter, and Instagram are all acceptable means of communication for today's client, although these methods do have limitations and a new scope of ethical and professional standards should be considered. The bottom line is that technology opens up more possibilities and can increase engagement by simply integrating something that is very normal to, and even expected from, a more tech-savvy audience.

The other end of the spectrum may allow for the practitioner to use more traditional means such as pencil and paper, dry erase white boards, handouts, or a phone call. Utilizing a theme-based message when working with a team on a long-term basis may be beneficial. Some of the traditional resources such as handouts or a workbook/manual may resonate better for this group over a period of time, as they can have a tangible point of reference. Technology is not always reliable, as our case study example highlighted between the computer freezing and Wi-Fi buffering, so it is always good to have low-tech solutions in case things go wrong. Adaptability is a key trait when working in these kinds of dynamic environments.

When looking at communication, delivery is also impacted by location and environment. Group sessions are often held in a variety of locations like conference rooms, hotels, classrooms, dugouts, locker rooms, buses, or the field. Being aware of the environment and how it may impact the group is the responsibility of the practitioner. If the session area is set up like a classroom or conference room, then the group may instinctively feel as though participation is not expected. For most athletes, moving from a training session to a quiet cool room can pose a challenge in staying alert and wakeful.

Communicating One-on-One/Subgroups

While the emphasis of this chapter has focused more on formal group sessions or meetings, the reality is that much of consulting can be informal. This is especially common in situations where a consultant is traveling with a team and doing group work, but in more informal individual settings. Ken Ravizza stated, "[B]rief encounters may take place in a hotel lobby, on a bus, in the training room, or at a meal" (Fifer, Henschen, Gould, & Ravizza, 2008, p. 370). Having a brief conversation with a client (or a few of the group members) when it is least expected tends to allow for instant rapport, which can be helpful to have higher buy-in during the next full group session. The unique environment at IMG Academy allows for frequent interaction with athletes throughout the day. These brief interactions occur constantly, in the training room, rehab room, weight room, locker room, dining hall, coach's office, sport environment, and tram. When these opportunities are presented, reiterating a previously delivered message in a new environment can result in a message that hits home. Making it a priority to be seen and heard in these unexpected places can create an open line of communication between the practitioner and the clients.

Impacting the Client

A challenging aspect for practitioners is to feel certain that we have impacted a group or an individual client. Impacting can be thought of as causing a shift in an individual's thinking, which results in an action such as helping an athlete learn the use of positive self-talk, then witnessing a shift in the athlete's performance due to the use of that skill—for example, the tennis player that embraces the challenge of playing against a high seed in a tournament and goes out on the court thinking positive, even though he or she would have previously given low effort and used negative self-talk in anticipation of losing easily. Practitioners have an opportunity to touch the hearts of athletes and inspire their minds, and doing so can be accomplished in numerous ways. Ultimately it is up to the practitioners to do their diligent practice getting to know the idiosyncrasies of each athlete, as well as the group or team, to gain an understanding of what moves them and who and what they are truly passionate about.

Generational Considerations

Tim Elmore, the author of *Generation iY* (2010), describes the opportunities and challenges for people born after 1990. Generation iY is the largest generation ever recorded and is defined as the most "connected" generation where advanced technology and information is literally at the fingertips via smartphones, tablets, and even the *internet of things*. Impacting this generation requires a great amount of creativity and versatility, and there is perhaps more of a generation gap between "iY" and others than in any generation gap before.

While this gap exists, the ability to digitally measure engagement and impact among people has become easier and helped provide insights like we have never seen before. The online platform *TED* (Technology Entertainment and Design) hosts videos held at conferences across the world where speakers engage audiences to share ideas in 18 minutes or less. Such is the popularity of this format that analysts are sharing the insights of what makes a successful talk and why these are effective (Donovan, 2014; Gallo, 2014). The emphasis of these insights is consistent with the other aspects of what has been shared in this chapter—specifically, preparing content using storytelling as a tool, delivery to elicit connection on an emotional level, and design to make the "take away" or "big idea" memorable. Nancy Duarte (2008, 2010, 2012) has written successfully on how to persuade and resonate with people by knowing how to use visual images to connect with people. Taking the time to prepare the message, develop compelling stories, and take people on a journey to inspire have been the hallmarks of an entire business and are applicable to sport psychology practitioners of all levels.

Tim Elmore discussed the importance of presenters being involved and engaged with generation iY as opposed to being the lecturer. Indeed, an acronym that he has used effectively to maximize the impact with working with generation iY is "E.P.I.C." First, "E" stands for *Experiential*, meaning that it is more effective for someone to experience a lesson than it is to be told about it. Also, the more we can create experiences for people, the more likely they are to engage. The "P" stands for *Participatory*, meaning that there is involvement and the idea that members in the audience support what they help create. By being involved and having some ownership, there is an increased connection to what happens next. The "I" stands for *Image Rich* and is consistent with the fact that we are a visually dominant society, but even more so now as mobile technology and video become greater aspects of our daily lives. As the saying goes, a picture is worth a thousand words. Last, "C" stands for *Connected*, to underscore the importance of feeling part of the group and world. This last principle calls for creating opportunities to connect with each other and talk as well as share the collective experience rather than be a receiver of a passive provision of information from the instructor.

It is often misunderstood that the consultants are responsible for all the content to engage, communicate, and impact their audience. However, by using the principles that

Duarte (2008, 2010, 2012) and Elmore (2010) identified, we can see that by setting up the conditions for dynamic experiences where both presenter and audience play roles together, you can further facilitate a successful experience and drive the outcome of the session. The process of achieving these outcomes often comes by focusing on collaborating with an audience and leveraging some of these techniques within a well-planned and executed experience to foster self-learning and collective learning.

Take-Away Messages

Working with groups can be the most rewarding, effective, and also challenging part of being an applied sport psychology consultant. There are many considerations and never-ending opportunities to improve and develop the skills necessary to effectively engage groups in sport psychology content. Part of what makes groups particularly challenging is because every group is different and the process is dynamic. Here are some of our top take-aways for consideration.

- Learn from each session, and, whether "good, bad, or ugly," make sure that you reflect on what went well and what you would do better next time, and, perhaps most importantly, identify the steps you will take to achieve success next time.
- Understand your own competencies, where you are strong, and where you need more work. Set goals and seek to train and get feedback in the aspects that are not as strong for you.
- Develop a good understanding between the two fundamental characteristics of group session delivery: content and style. With content, be sure to understand the context and motivation of your audience so you are able to focus on delivering clear messages and effective applied strategies. With style, be deliberate with the art of presenting and engaging their attention. If "edu-taining" is the concept here to remember and apply, "education" is the content and "entertaining" is the style.
- Engaging with groups involves many of the same core steps of rapport that are critical for individual relationships, too. Be able to convey empathy, and take the time to build rapport.
- Communicating is about the message received, not the message sent. Being able to shift focus from yourself to the audience is the same as the idea of "teaching the student, and not the lesson." Being able to be deliberate and focused with your purpose and key messages will help set you up for success. This approach needs naturally to consider the method, location, and "how" you deliver it, as these factors will also determine the effectiveness and impact.
- Impacting a group means that we need to do more than just share information. You need to connect and move people to maximize their openness for change. Some will be more ready and willing than others, but the quality of your work in a group setting and ability to be "E.P.I.C." (Experiential, Participatory, Image Rich, and Connected) will make a difference.

(Elmore, 2010)

References

Cremades, J. G., & Tashman, L. S. (Eds.). (2014). *Becoming a sport, exercise, and performance psychology professional: A global perspective*. New York, NY: Routledge/Taylor & Francis Group.

Donovan, J. (2014). *How to deliver a TED talk*. New York: McGraw-Hill Education.

Duarte, N. (2008). *Slideology: The art and science of creating great presentations*. Hoboken, NJ: John Wiley & Sons.

Duarte, N. (2010). *Resonate: Present visual stories that transform audiences*. Hoboken, NJ: John Wiley & Sons.

Duarte, N. (2012). *Harvard business review guide to persuasive presentations*. Hoboken, NJ: John Wiley & Sons.

Elmore, T. (2010). *Generation iY*. Atlanta, GA: Poet Gardener Publishing.

Ericsson, K. A. (Ed.). (2009). *Development of professional expertise: Toward measurement of expert performance and design of optimal learning environments*. Cambridge: Cambridge University Press.

Fifer, A., Henschen, K., Gould, D., & Ravizza, K. (2008). What works when working with athletes. *The Sport Psychologist, 22*(3), 356–377.

Gallo, C. (2014). *Talk like TED: The 9 public speaking secrets of the worlds top minds*. New York: St Martin's Press.

Halliwell, W., Orlick, T., Ravizza, K., & Rotella, B. (2003). *Consultant's guide to excellence for sport and performance enhancement*. Chelsea, Canada: Zone of Excellence.

Heath, C., & Heath, D. (2007). *Made to stick: Why some ideas survive and others die*. New York: Random House Publishing.

Keller, J. M. (1987). Development and use of the ARCS model of motivational design. *Journal of Instructional Development, 10*(3), 2.

Mugford, A., Hesse, D., & Morgan, T. (2014). Developing the "Total" consultant: Nurturing the art and science. In G. Cremades & L. Tashman (Eds.), *Becoming a sport, exercise, and performance psychology professional: A global perspective* (pp. 268–275). New York, NY: Routledge/Taylor & Francis Group.

Rogers, C. R. (1951). *Client-centered therapy: Its current practice, implications, and theory*. London: Constable.

Silva, J. M., Metzler, J. N., & Lerner, B. A. (2007). *Training professionals in the practice of sport psychology*. Morgantown, WV: Fitness Information Technology.

Taylor, J. (Ed.). (2014). *Practice development in sport and performance psychology*. Morgantown, WV: FiT Publishing.

Webster, G. (2010). *Naval education and training command: Techniques of teaching briefs* [PowerPoint slides]. Retrieved from http://www.public.navy.mil/bupers-npc/support/21st_Century_Sailor/suicide_prevention/command/PublishingImages/TechniquesofTeachingBrief.pdf

11 Multiculturalism in Sport Psychology Practice

Perspectives and Experiences of Trainees

Aaron W. Halterman, Nicole T. Gabana, and Jesse A. Steinfeldt

Multiculturalism has been referred to as the "fourth force" in psychology (Pedersen, 2001), following the psychodynamic, behavioral, and humanistic paradigms of explaining human behavior. Multicultural perspectives have provided psychologists with conceptual templates to help them understand the integral role of culture and other contextual factors on human behavior (Leung & Chen, 2009). Because sport psychologists often work with athletes and coaches from a variety of different cultural backgrounds, the field of sport psychology requires an explicit incorporation of multicultural conceptualization into its theory and practice. The integration of multiculturalism into the scientific literature of sport psychology picked up in the 1990s, when researchers began to critically evaluate the scientific and practical approaches to sport psychology, relative to other psychological fields (Duda & Allison, 1990). For example, multicultural psychology has long focused on culturally relevant aspects of identity (e.g., racial identity), while addressing the intersection of many other aspects of identity (e.g., gender, sexual orientation, age, socioeconomic status, education level). However, there has been a paucity of research on the application of these multicultural constructs within sport psychology. Thus, sport psychology practitioners would benefit from more explicitly integrating multicultural constructs into their practice because interventions that recognize cultural differences for both groups and individuals tend to produce more positive outcomes than those that ignore diversity (Parham, 1996). Furthermore, in order to most effectively train the future generation of sport psychology professionals, it is important to develop training models that incorporate a multiculturally oriented approach so that sport psychology graduate students can be more effective with the athletes, teams, and coaches with whom they work (Martens, Mobley, & Zizzi, 2000).

The purpose of this chapter is to illustrate the integration of multicultural perspectives and constructs into the provision of sport and performance psychology services. The constructs we will cover in this chapter will be divided into sections that address (a) race; (b) the experiences of international students; (c) sexual orientation; (d) gender; and (e) socioeconomic status (SES). Across each section addressing a different dimension of identity, we will introduce and integrate multicultural constructs such as (a) identity development identified by Waterman (1985) as a "self-definition comprised of those goals, values, and beliefs which a person finds personally expressive and to which he or she is unequivocally committed" (p. 6), with a particular focus on intersections of racial identity and athletic identity (e.g., athletes overly identify with sport identity, therefore not forming a strong personal identity); (b) microaggressions that refer to "the everyday verbal, nonverbal, and environmental slights, snubs, or insults, whether intentional or unintentional, which communicate hostile, derogatory, or negative messages to target persons based solely upon their marginalized group membership" (Sue, 2010, p. 24); (c) stereotype threat, which is being the target of a negative stereotype that threatens self-regard and creates significant concern and discomfort for the individuals of a stigmatized group (Crocker, Major, & Steele, 1998), including racial and academic stereotype threat (e.g., that student-athletes are less engaged and competent academically than other students) and possible compensatory strategies for gender stereotype threat; (d) issues with service provision (counseling services) across dimensions of identity (e.g., race, gender, sexual orientation) between student-athlete and clinician, coach and clinician, and/or student-athlete and coach; and (e) experiences and perspectives in clinical supervision specifically addressing multicultural issues (e.g., ways that these issues were addressed and resolved, ways these issues were not addressed or resolved, and the impact of the supervisory relationship).

Each section will incorporate some combination of these aforementioned multicultural constructs. Some sections will utilize vignettes and questions for consideration, while other sections will incorporate case study information in a more narrative form (all student-athlete names have been changed to protect their identities). This chapter has been written in a relatively informal style with the intent of increasing reader accessibility so these prominent concepts can illustrate practices and perspectives that may impact the delivery of sport and performance psychology services by advanced graduate students in athletic settings. The two primary writers of this chapter are advanced doctoral students who have received training in the provision of sport and performance psychology services to high school and college student-athletes. All of the contributing authors are former Division I student-athletes. The first author (Aaron) is a White heterosexual male doctoral student in Counseling Psychology who played collegiate and professional football, and the second author (Nicole) is a White heterosexual female doctoral student in Counseling Psychology who was a collegiate rower. We identify our names and aspects of our identity so that the reader can actively assess the interaction of the practitioner's dimensions of identity within each of the case studies presented in each section.

Issues of Racial Dynamics

In each session, I (Aaron) begin with informed consent, a discussion about how trust is paramount, and limits of confidentiality, particularly how nothing leaves the room except the *Big Four* (i.e., self-harm, harm to others, ongoing child abuse, or elder abuse). I also share limits of confidentiality with regard to signing a release form for the inclusion of members of the designated treatment team so I can readily collaborate (e.g., if an athlete is having trouble sleeping, I can consult with the team physician). I also share information about how, to the best of my ability, I try to leave my own personal judgment outside of the door, yet I am not perfect in my ability to do so. With that, I choose to share a piece about myself being a former athlete, but I acknowledge that my experiences are not their experiences—I actively try not to put myself or what I have been through athletically onto the student-athletes in any way. I choose to self-disclose more with athletes on the first day in order to help them feel more comfortable with the therapeutic process, especially if they have never been to counseling before.

My advisor frequently uses the phrase "make the implicit explicit," so I also feel that it is useful to address potentially obvious differences (e.g., race) up front with the client. In doing so, I intend to model honest disclosure, and I can also address and possibly process any reactions the client may have to these differences. I did this with one particular client, and I will share my experiences with "Ericka" in this section of the chapter. Ericka was a female biracial (African American/Caucasian) athlete at a large Midwestern university whose mother is White and father is Black. I worked with her for more than two years, but, in the beginning of our therapeutic relationship, I explicitly addressed two factors of identity (e.g., race, gender) on which we were visibly different. I said something to the effect of, "I want to take a moment and state the obvious that I am White and you identify as biracial. I wonder what kind of impact this might have on our building a relationship?" To that Ericka replied, "I grew up in a White household, my mother is White, my brothers are White, I am a mix. I come from a predominately White area. I identify pretty heavily with my White heritage." She went on to say, "You were an athlete, you had Black teammates and biracial teammates, so I think that you would understand athlete culture." In the sake of full disclosure (making the implicit explicit for the reader, here), as I was asking her this question, I felt uneasy, and uneasy might be putting it mildly at best. I was downright nervous and could feel it in my guts. However, when Ericka replied with what she said and how she said it, it sort of normalized the process and brought me back to the room and lowered the anxiety I was feeling. From there, we were able to have an open conversation about race and racial dynamics, both within the room and in her life outside of the room. We were able to build a working relationship and collaborate on how we were going to handle issues that related to race and how we were going to handle other potentially charged topics (topics that resonate deeply with us). I shared with her that I would do my best to be as informed/educated as possible, but that I was going to be learning from her since she is the expert on herself and on her racial identity.

Looking back over the course of treatment, I think one of the major issues Ericka was struggling with was her identity, both her racial identity and her athletic identity. Most if not all college student-athletes struggle with issues of identity, but for her it was more than that. For her it was navigating her racial identity, particularly the experience of "growing up White" and then being thrust into the African American athletic culture and not feeling as if she fully fit in. She often mentioned how she spent the majority of her time with Black athletes and how they were her best friends. In order to convey how much she wanted to fit into that culture, she would often use charged racial words to describe interactions she had with other athletes.

One day, coming back from winter break, I noticed that she had cut her hair short. As she walked in the door, I said something about her new " 'do" (what I call hairdos). She replied, "Yah I wanted to get my Black back." And I had no response for this. I froze. I fumbled to find the words to respond. As we began the session, I'd like to say that I was more focused on the issues she was presenting (e.g., how her break went, how she was progressing with the therapeutic homework that we agreed upon). But I did not focus on those things. I was admittedly a bit shocked because I had never heard a response like that. Now, it was not out of character for Ericka to make jokes. In fact, she was very good at using humor to deflect more serious topics, thoughts, and feelings. And I have to admit she was good at it. She was funny, and it was easy to get lost in her humor and even harder not to laugh. So in this moment I was sitting with the thought: Was this statement a harmless rapport-enhancing joke, or is she deflecting away from a deeper sentiment, or neither? In the session, after spending some time sharing how break went, I was able to insert a process statement about what she meant by "getting her Black back." She said it meant that she wanted to "get back to her roots," which lead to me asking her what it was like growing up in a White household and a predominately White community. She revealed that her father was not in her life, except by phone, and that he lived in California, raising the family that he had started after Ericka was born. But we didn't go into too much more depth than providing these details.

I brought this experience to my supervisor who was also White. We discussed how I felt when she said that and what I thought. We also discussed how I did not explore her comment in the moment, but that I chose to come back to it later, and also why I opted not to relate it back to the bigger picture. We also case conceptualized how her haircut fit with what she was going through and what purpose her behavior was serving. Ultimately, through supervision, I was able to come to an understanding of what an opportunity she had given me to explore, and how I felt as if I had dropped the ball and missed the opportunity. However, rather than leave a fumble on the ground, I went to the turf. I came back the next session and asked if we could revisit her previous comment and the meaning of that comment from a broader perspective. She reluctantly agreed, and said she was making a joke at the time, but that it was okay to discuss it further. Despite her initial hesitation, we ended up exploring deeply how her being back home in her White community over break conjured up feelings and thoughts about herself that were different than what she experienced here at school in the Black athletic community. This discussion led to deeper and more meaningful exploration of her experiences in navigating her emerging racial identity.

The point I want to share with the reader is that I was uncomfortable with her comment when she walked in the door. I think that this discomfort stemmed more from not knowing what to do with a potentially off-hand comment/joke, which concealed my true discomfort in talking about racial identity. In spite of this insight, there was a piece of me that still put on the brakes when it came to discussing race. I wish I could say I was that good of a counselor to identify it in the moment and be able to use it, and given future situations I think I would handle it more confidently and effectively. However, through engaging in supervision and exploration, I was able to use those feelings of unease with the client to help her come to a better understanding of where her behavior was coming from and what purpose it was serving. It was more than just making jokes about a haircut while walking in the door; it was an implicit invitation to explore deeply impactful dimensions of identity that were central to her emerging sense of self. And by taking the chance to open the discussion in a collaborative way, we were able to enhance our therapeutic alliance and set the norm for discussions about race and other difficult topics in future sessions.

Vignette (Racial Dynamics): Jeremy

Jeremy is an 18-year-old Black freshman football player at a small NCAA Division III college. He is a first-generation college student and is the oldest of six children in his family. Jeremy said he was glad to come to college because he has his own space; at home he shared a room with two of his brothers. Jeremy is proud of his accomplishments because it took a lot of work for him to get to college. His parents are originally from Africa and were not familiar with the college application process. In spite of his difficulties getting to school, he felt it was worth it to set an example for his younger siblings to pursue higher education. Jeremy expressed frustration with some of his teammates, who are predominantly White. Jeremy reported that he was tired of being around his teammates when they would smoke pot and drink alcohol, because he does not use substances. Jeremy felt as if he was having trouble connecting with his teammates by not participating in these activities. He said that sometimes he felt tempted to try drugs or alcohol to fit in, but he expressed confidence that he would stick to his values.

Seeing Jeremy was one of my (Nicole) first experiences as a sport psychology graduate student working with a racial minority athlete. As a White female, I tried to be mindful of the potential intersections of Jeremy's personal, racial, and athletic identities, especially during his freshman year as a college student-athlete and first-generation college student. I grew up in a predominantly White, middle-class geographical area, and I attended a high school, college, and graduate school that consisted of predominantly White students. Through the use of supervision, I knew it was important for me to be aware of how my own racial identity and cultural experiences might contribute to potential bias when working with clients from different racial backgrounds. I was trained to know that it is always important to take time to acknowledge both strengths and weaknesses of working with diverse populations in order to be an effective counselor and to grow personally and professionally.

In my short time working with Jeremy, we were able to explore how his familial and racial backgrounds shaped his emerging sense of identity, and we discussed how to integrate his personal identity with his new role as a college student-athlete. First, I asked Jeremy to tell me more about why he chose this particular college, and I inquired about his football background and interest in the sport. Together, we discussed the benefits and challenges of Jeremy's transition into college, considering topics such as homesickness, family dynamics, expectations from family, coaches, siblings, friends at home, peers, and teammates. I took time to validate Jeremy's feelings of confusion about the college environment and social pressures that came along with his new network of peers and teammates. Jeremy told me about the pressure of being the first one in his family to attend college and how he felt a responsibility to set a good example for his younger siblings. Jeremy said he especially struggled with the application process, since his parents did not have any knowledge about college or financial aid. We were able to discuss how his racial and socioeconomic background differed from many of his teammates. Sometimes Jeremy expressed frustration that his teammates never had to experience this and would never understand what he had to go through to get to college. Jeremy expressed appreciation for the opportunity to attend college for both academic and athletic purposes, and he often felt that his White teammates were "entitled" or "ignorant" people who didn't understand him.

In addition to these feelings, Jeremy disclosed that he often felt conflicted in terms of "fitting in" in college. Jeremy stated that although he does not drink alcohol or use drugs, sometimes he feels that it's what "everyone does in college." We also talked about his support network at home and at school, coping strategies for peer pressure, his personal values, and the rationale for why he chose to practice those values. From this foundation, we were able to incorporate racial issues into our discussion, such as how stereotypes of Black males might contribute to his teammates expecting him to engage in recreational drug and/or alcohol use. These initial acknowledgments of multicultural factors helped to increase Jeremy's understanding of the multiple dimensions of his identity development. In our sessions together, Jeremy also disclosed his identity as a Christian, which played a substantial role in his life and overall decision-making. By incorporating discussions of faith, I was able to gain a better understanding of Jeremy's family background, values, and future aspirations.

Questions for Consideration

1. How might you take into account racial factors when exploring Jeremy's experience of peer pressure?
2. From an identity development perspective, how might you utilize a multiculturally oriented framework to conceptualize Jeremy's freshman collegiate athletic experience?
3. How might you consider the role of potential stereotype threat in this case?
4. If Jeremy comes into the next session and reports succumbing to drug and/or alcohol use, how might you respond?

Issues to Consider When Working With International Student-Athletes

One of the biggest differences I (Aaron) have experienced in counseling athletes (in comparison to counseling nonathletes) is the athletes' expectation that I will tell them what to do—replicating a dynamic similar to that of their coaches—and the expectation that they will get better immediately. This holds true for the majority of athletes I have seen across all races, ethnicities, gender, SES, and sexual orientation. However, this dynamic has been particularly pronounced when working with international student-athletes. Many of the international student-athletes I work with come from cultures where being told what to do is the norm, and then they comply with this directive. I have often found myself being pulled into this and have given performance-enhancement strategies without doing enough exploration of the underlying issue. In these moments, I have to essentially pull back from the moment and realize I am being drawn into their cultural expectation that they would be given directives to follow.

One way to combat this is with supervision. My supervision mantra is that if I am uncomfortable or do not want to discuss something, then that is most likely the thing I need to bring up first in session. I was and still am uncomfortable being a *life coach*, a term I have deemed to best fit when athletes come in and want me to tell them what to do. Through exploration and collaboration in supervision, I was able to understand that I am not totally off base being uncomfortable with being a life coach. If I can use those feelings, I now have a good indicator in session: when I do not realize I am being drawn in, I need to remember that feeling of unease as an early indicator. Through supervision, we were also able to come up with a plan of using exploration techniques to get at what was really driving the problem behavior or issue. We decided that using Solution Focused Therapy is a nice bridge between athletes wanting me to give them directives and facilitating a process of guided exploration and self-empowerment.

The other interesting issue I have found in working with international student-athletes involves understanding language. Beyond occasional logistic difficulties with comprehension, I notice this dynamic being most pronounced not only in regard to the denotative meaning of words but also in connotation and with the use of metaphors. In counseling, we try to meet the clients where they are, so we have to agree upon shared meaning of words to reach a mutual understanding. This becomes problematic for me because I love metaphors; let me repeat, I LOVE metaphors! They are therapeutically effective across many treatment modalities (e.g., Wirtztum, van der Hart, & Friedman, 1988), and I use metaphors frequently in my personal life. My brain works in a way that if I can see something in another light or in different terms, then I can better understand it. This is problematic for someone from another culture when my metaphors and references are so heavily culturally laden (e.g., using references from movie scenes or quotes to generate layered meaning). However, the effectiveness of using metaphors therapeutically is impacted by dynamics of language and of acculturation (i.e., a two-way process of change stemming from the interaction of aspects of two cultures [Berry, 1997]). Research in the field of crosscultural psychology indicates that individuals in a new cultural setting will maintain aspects from their culture of origin, yet they will adapt to fit into the new culture. Thus, I need to recognize that international students may be at differing levels of acculturation, and subsequently my decision to employ therapeutic metaphors and other nuanced uses of language needs to take this into account.

Part of being a multiculturally competent counselor is having an awareness of the acculturation process from both sides; thus, it is also helpful to think about how their culture is impacting my intervention choices, what I choose to focus on, and how I process in session all the while keeping in mind what kind of complex interaction of maintenance or adaptions of behavior are happening for the student-athlete. As I prepare to use metaphors with international student-athletes, at times I find myself overcompensating and simplifying the metaphor to the point where I wonder if they have become so simplistic that they are ineffective or even insulting. I find myself going into my teacher mode often and asking if they understand. This is not the kind of counselor I desire to be, so I have to back up and monitor when metaphors are appropriate with certain clients and when I just use them for my own comfort or edification. As with any intervention, it is important to use metaphors appropriately (and, at times, sparingly) so I can meet the clients on their level. While this dynamic is applicable to domestic students as well, acculturation processes suggest that international student-athletes represent a group that requires extra attention in this regard. However, I have found that even if a metaphor does not work, this presents an opportunity to process what was missing for the exchange to be understood. Usually that leads to a better understanding of language, a better understanding of how the student-athlete makes meaning of the world, and a better therapeutic relationship.

Issues to Consider When Working With LGBTQ Student-Athletes

While research into the application of sport psychology practices with lesbian, gay, bisexual, transgender, and questioning (LGBTQ) individuals is relatively scarce, it has been recognized that this is an integral component of a multiculturally effective approach. LGBTQ athletes may be discriminated against because of their sexual orientation or gender identity. For example, a gay male athlete may be perceived as a threat to the normative view of male athletes being "tough" or "manly" (e.g., the hegemonic masculine stereotype in sport), and a gay male who does not conform to this norm may be perceived as a less effective athlete. However, although it may also have a negative impact, the same stereotype may result in a lesbian athlete being perceived as tough and possessing greater athletic skill. Regardless of the impressions of that stereotype, lesbian athletes may experience discrimination from heterosexual teammates who feel threatened and express overt or covert manifestations of homophobia through microaggressions and/or explicit expressions of exclusion. Furthermore, the dynamics of intrateam dating among gay athletes is another dimension of LGBTQ considerations, since teams at the high school competitive level and beyond are almost always separated by gender, and there exists a stigma against amorous relationships among teammates. Additionally, the experiences of transgender athletes are underrepresented in the sport psychology literature. Further research is needed in these areas, but in this section we will attempt to elicit thought into how a sport psychology consultant can be sensitive to sexual orientation and gender identity issues when working with athletes, teams, and coaches.

Vignette (LGBTQ Student-Athletes): Hanna

Hanna is an 18-year-old White female soccer player at a large Division I university. Hanna was a walk-on to the soccer team and has not been receiving any playing time. Hanna came into the office because she was struggling with her parents' opinions of her current relationship. Hanna identifies as bisexual and has been in a relationship with her girlfriend from back home for more than six months. Hanna describes how she had to sneak around her parents in order to see her girlfriend over the summer. Now that she is at college, Hanna feels she has more freedom to make her own decisions; however, when her girlfriend came to visit her at college, her parents found out and demanded that Hanna cut off all contact with her girlfriend, since they don't believe that Hanna should be with a woman. Hanna is struggling with the transition to college and feels as if she has no one to confide in. She is also unsure whether being a soccer player at a large university was the right choice for her and is thinking of quitting the team to join a sorority.

Making the transition from high school to college can be difficult for any student, especially an athlete who is facing adjustment to a new team, coaches, social network, and geographical area. In my (Nicole) work with Hanna, she was able to explore and continue to develop her identity as an emerging adult, outside of her family influence. She was faced with a difficult decision because her parents did not understand her sexual orientation, and they had spent most of Hanna's high school years trying to change it. Although Hanna was far away from home and had more freedom to make her own decisions, her parents still had financial influence over her and threatened to withdraw funds if she did not comply with their wishes for Hanna to stop dating a woman. Hanna reported that her parents had previously read her text messages and emails, and she was worried that if she continued her relationship, her parents would threaten her girlfriend. I spent a lot of time validating Hanna's feelings, especially her parents' lack of acceptance of her sexual orientation and her lack of privacy.

I hoped to convey that my office was a safe place where she could feel validated, and together we spent time discussing how to cope when loved ones do not accept our identity or our decisions. Hanna was conflicted because she still felt love and respect for her parents, even though she hated them for how they were treating her and her girlfriend. During our sessions together, Hanna's mother came out to visit her at college. Prior to and after the visit, we spent a lot of time processing her feelings toward her parents, including frustration, resentment, dependency, and anger. Hanna also found it difficult to discuss her relationship with teammates because she was a freshman and she was not out to her team—not everyone on the team knew she identified her sexual orientation as bisexual. We discussed the coming-out process and the importance of her exerting a level of control over that decision.

In addition to these issues, Hanna also faced a dilemma of whether collegiate sport was right for her. In an example of a compensatory strategy that elicited a sense of gender stereotype threat, Hanna's mother thought it would be a good idea for her to rush for a sorority. Hanna eventually began to consider the possibility of quitting the team, and we spent a lot of time discussing the pros, cons, and potential effects of that decision. Oftentimes, big transitions in one's life affect multiple aspects of identity. For Hanna, her sexual, familial, athletic, social, academic, and personal identities were affected by the transition to college. Many LGBTQ athletes may face serious discrimination or lack of support from family members, which could affect their ability to cope with stressors in other domains. It is important to explore the athlete's support network, while validating his/her experience as a person of worth who is also a member of a marginalized group.

Questions for Consideration

1. How would you work with Hanna to help her cope with her parents' attitudes and behaviors toward her sexual identity?
2. If Hanna were to openly disclose her sexual identity to her teammates, what might be some potential reactions and how would you help Hanna prepare/process these in session?
3. As sport psychology consultants, we have a professional duty to see the athlete as a holistic individual and not only a performer. If Hanna were to decide to quit the soccer team, how would you help her through this transition? What are your institution's policies on providing services to former athletes?
4. If Hannah expressed amorous interest in one of her teammates, how would you handle that situation?

Issues of Gender

In my (Aaron) multiple years of providing sport psychology services within athletic departments, I have had a four-to-one ratio of female-to-male clients. One thing that I have noticed in working with female athletes is that at some point, most of them have had an experience with a male coach. In fact, most of the female athletes I have worked with have reported that they got along better with male coaches. When asked about the best coaches they ever had, they often cite male coaches over female coaches. As a caveat, this anecdotal assertion is specific to my practice, and I am not trying to make a generalized claim about all female athletes. I am saying this because my knowledge that female athletes have previously worked well with men gives me a level of comfort in thinking that I too can be effective in helping female athletes within our crossgender dyad.

One area of concern for me in thinking about my own experience working with young athletes is being aware of my own feelings and my female clients' feelings in sessions. At times I have had clients share information about relationships, sometimes being explicit about sexual aspects in these relationships. As a heterosexual male, it would be possible to misconstrue this interaction as a young woman sharing this information for my benefit or even directing this information flirtatiously toward me. Another concern to acknowledge is when clients do become overly flirtatious, not necessarily in the unambiguously unethical manner of wanting to sleep with you, but more so in the kind of flirty way of attempting to pull you into their attachment style or personality. Being married and much older (by more than 10 years in some instances) than the female student-athletes I saw, I initially thought I would be immune to such flirtations in session. However, it was not until supervision that I had it brought to my attention that my client could be engaging with me in such a way. It felt like a taboo subject to even broach in supervision, like if I raised the issue, then I was implying that I was trying to sleep with my clients. This shameful misperception was dispelled through honest dialogue in supervision. When I discussed one particular flirtatious experience with my supervisor, we discovered that in these instances, it was not about me, but rather it was about my client's way of understanding the world and attempting to get what the client needed from men. All behavior has purpose, and sometimes a client's presenting concern (e.g., primarily eliciting attention through sexual expression) may emerge within the therapeutic alliance, which should be a safe place to discuss, process, and explore this potentially maladaptive dynamic, especially within a crossgender dyad.

Vignette (Gender): Female Sport Psychology Consultant Interacting With Male Coaches

You are a female doctoral student working in a large Division I athletic department. One of the coaches from the men's lacrosse team contacts you in hopes that you might be able to provide insight into his coaching style, specifically how he can better reach his players. You agree to meet with him in your office. After the meeting, he mentions that you two should get lunch or dinner sometime to discuss these topics further. You shrug his comments off, but can't help but feel like he is coming on to you because you are a woman. In supervision that week, you discuss your experience with your supervisor, who is also a male. He validates your feelings that these comments may be directed by intentions driven from personal interest rather than professional consultation purposes. As a female sport psychology consultant, you want to be taken seriously, but you also do not want to burn any bridges with the coaching staff. You are worried that your credibility may be undermined. You are also struggling to find a woman's perspective since most of your mentors in athletics are males.

In this vignette, I (Nicole) have presented a specific situation where I felt my gender identity intersected with my professional role as a sport psychology consultant. My response intends to provide suggestions for responding to gender bias/discrimination, and to propose questions for consideration. As a female working in the field of sport psychology, I have often encountered situations in which I experience confusion regarding my gender identity and how it affects being taken seriously as a practitioner. Working in the male-dominated domain of athletics, I have occasionally felt "lesser-than": less knowledgeable, less competent, and less qualified, based on my gender. While the field of sport psychology attempts to be mindful of gender dynamics from a multicultural perspective, the world of athletics is not always as kind. Both female and male consultants may experience either favoritism or discrimination based on their gender; therefore, it is important to consider how gender dynamics play out in interactions between coaches, athletes, teams, supervisors, and sport psychology colleagues alike.

While the previous vignette is written from a woman's perspective, I want the reader to be able to consider the same scenario as if it was written from a male student's perspective as well, because this situation is likely to be faced by both men and women and coaches from either gender. This may play out between consultants/coaches of the same gender as well. For the purpose of personal reflection, I will be speaking solely from my own (female) experience, but that doesn't mean that this cannot be applicable to male student consultants in a similar way.

In my experience of feeling placed in a compromising position due to my identity as a female, I have found that one of the most important things to consider is the establishment of personal boundaries. If I ever find myself in an uncomfortable position with a coach (or athlete), I usually "go with my gut." If something doesn't feel right, it usually isn't. During these times, the most helpful thing you can do is to discuss your concerns with a supervisor whom you trust. While it may be helpful to consult a colleague or supervisor of the same gender who may be more likely to see things from your gender perspective, this is not always necessary. In the case mentioned previously, I set clear boundaries between what I do as a sport psychology consultant and what is professionally acceptable in terms of interpersonal relationships. In this situation, I thanked the coach for his offer but informed him that consultation usually takes place in the office or on the field. There are certainly conditions where meeting in a less formal setting would be appropriate, but, in this situation, I had to trust my intuition.

Perhaps driving this decision, one of my biggest fears as a female sport psychology consultant is that I will not be taken seriously in comparison to my male counterparts. On the flip side, I am also aware that coaches or athletes may be more inclined to work with me *because* I am a woman (just as coaches or athletes may be more inclined to working with a male). While it is unrealistic and unwise to expect that coaches and athletes be "gender-blind" (just as professing to be "colorblind" dismisses the existence and merit of racial differences), it is important not to allow stereotype threat to sabotage one's own self-efficacy and ability to work with clients and coaches. If I shrink when faced with comments or acts of gender discrimination, this hurts others' view of me as a valued and capable sport psychology consultant. Recognizing that gender bias may either work against you or in your favor, I have found that the best practice is to (a) try to be aware when it may be occurring; (b) have a safe place to discuss my concerns and frustrations; and (c) feel confident in my knowledge, skills, and training, even when it can potentially be dismissed or go unrecognized due to the conscious or unconscious gender bias of others. I also accept that if I lose the interest of a particular coach because I do not agree to compromise my own boundaries, I will still be able to sleep at night knowing that I am abiding by reasonable values and expectations of professional practice. There are cases when socializing with the coach(es) is reasonable, well-intentioned, and completely acceptable; however, whenever I feel that it is compromising my professional identity or is done for the purpose of personal rather than professional gain, I make my boundaries known politely yet firmly. Finding mentors and peers of the same gender who have experienced similar situations can be a valuable source of social support and guidance. While the movement toward gender equality is improving, continuing discussion about the implications of gender bias, discrimination, and stereotype is essential to furthering this cause, especially in the sport world.

Questions for Consideration

1. How would you handle this situation with the coach if you would like to continue to maintain your working relationship with the coaching staff and the team?
2. What are the pros/cons and potential implications of agreeing or not agreeing to meet with coach alone for dinner?
3. Do you identify with any aspects of the vignette? How would you approach this with your supervisor if that person is not of the same gender?
4. What are some stereotypes generally associated with being male or female in the athletic context? How might males in the field of sport psychology help to reduce the prominence or effects of gender stereotyping against women?

Issues of SES

For counselors who are not familiar with how collegiate athletics works, it is easy to get caught up in the media hype and stereotypes that all athletes are on scholarship or that they are taking money on the side. This is not the case for the majority of college athletes across the country. Only a select few sports give full scholarships, depending on school and division. The other athletes might be on partial scholarships (e.g., a percentage of tuition is covered; possibly only books are covered). Other athletes get nothing in terms of athletic-based financial aid from the university. These student-athletes may get only the same gear (e.g., sweatshirts, T-shirts, workout clothing, shoes) that everyone on the team gets. Working with both scholarship and nonscholarship athletes has reminded me that not all athletes come from a place where they can afford college. I have had walk-on athletes tell me how they see their scholarship teammates "pissing away their opportunities" due to lack of caring in school, constant drinking, or doing drugs. They often share what it took for them to get to college and what kind of loans they have to take out to continue to be there. There have been times in consulting with coaches that I have felt the urge to remind them about the disparity between scholarship and nonscholarship status in how they interact with their players. That is not to say I think they should hold someone to different expectations or standards; rather, it is important to have an understanding that some of their athletes are working a job outside of being an athlete just to be at practice and contribute.

In addition to SES, there are often multiple additional factors that can intersect with this aspect within athletes. Student-athletes with learning disabilities or other types of disabilities can present unique considerations in both the academic and the athletic domains. In this final case, we will discuss an athlete's experience by integrating race, SES, and learning disability.

Vignette (SES): David

David is a 22-year-old Latino male on the men's rowing team. David was diagnosed with dyslexia and ADHD at an early age, and he has received tutoring services since middle school. David is from a middle-to-high socioeconomic background, and both parents have been diagnosed with ADHD as well. Additionally, David's mom also has dyslexia. David's parents have always provided him with the resources to succeed academically despite his learning disabilities. When David came to college, he decided to pursue a premed degree. Now as a senior, David is a direct admit to the university medical school, but he worries that his learning disabilities will keep him from succeeding at this level. In addition to academic concerns, David is also struggling with his rowing performance. He feels as if he is unable to concentrate in practice, especially when he is working on his technique. David states that he only takes his ADHD medication when he is in class during the week, and he does not take it on the weekends. Since it is the spring season and the rowing competitions take place on the weekends, David is wondering if he should start taking his medication on the weekends in order to improve his athletic performance.

In my (Nicole) work with David, we spent a lot of time exploring family dynamics and how David's childhood experience of growing up with ADHD and dyslexia affected his self-concept and identity development. This case also highlights how sport psychology consultants need to consider medication decisions and the potential implications of such decisions. David seemed to have a fixed understanding of his intellectual ability. He felt that, because he had learning disabilities, he was not "born smart" and therefore only deserved his academic merits due to his effort and the support of others. While David acknowledged his work ethic, he did not consider himself to be intelligent and therefore had a fear of failure in the academic realm. This was a somewhat complex case for me, since I wanted David to feel confident in his own intellectual ability regardless of his learning disabilities, while also validating the struggles he had faced due to his learning disabilities and acknowledging that he dealt with challenges that many of his peers did not have to overcome.

Overall, I took a Strengths-Based approach, helping David to consider a more malleable view of his own intelligence. I drew on Gardner's Theory of Multiple Intelligences (for more information, see Gardner, 2011), as well as Dweck's work on Fixed vs. Growth Mindsets (for more information, see Dweck, 2000). Additionally, David and I explored his Latino heritage and how this impacted perceptions of him in rowing, a sport populated largely by White student-athletes. We also explored how his culture, family, and SES impacted his father's expectations of David's academic and athletic endeavors. David described his father as a "self-made man" and said that, despite his minority status and ADHD diagnosis, he had worked hard to establish a comfortable lifestyle for his family. David seemed afraid that he would disappoint his father if he was not able to succeed in medical school. Together, we explored how the expectations of others including his father, mother, coaches, and teammates affected his feelings about his own academic and athletic ability, as well as his self-efficacy in school and sport. David felt that his coach had pegged David as "not being able to focus" since freshman year, and that stigma followed him throughout his senior career. In the case of medication, David admitted that taking his ADHD medication to help him focus in practice/competition was often tempting, but he wasn't sure if it would even make a difference.

While David's decision about his medication did not change, it is important to consider that decisions and uncertainty about medication recommendations will often come up in sport psychology consultation. In these cases, it is important to keep an open mind and gain a thorough understanding of the medical history, including how the athlete feels about medication as well as recommendations from the prescriber. Since David had decided to take medication only during times he would be attending class, I respected that decision and worked with him to foster focusing skills that could be utilized in practice. It is important to consider that learning disabilities in the classroom will also bleed over into the athletic domain. Keeping the athlete's holistic well-being at the forefront of treatment, not just as an athlete but as a person, is of the utmost importance.

Questions for Consideration

1. David has a tendency to be a perfectionist and is generally hard on himself. How might you help him to develop a greater sense of self-compassion and tolerance for ambiguity?
2. What are some additional directions you might explore with David in terms of his family dynamic and educational background?
3. If David's rowing performance during his senior year of college is disappointing to him, how might you reconcile his feelings of failure knowing that he will be graduating soon?
4. How might you help David identify transferrable skills between his athletic and academic identities, both during the remainder of his senior year and upon graduation?

Conclusion

An intentional incorporation of multicultural perspectives can help sport psychologists be effective in helping their student-athlete clients. Given that student-athletes face unique sport-related pressures in addition to the typical challenges of other college students, sport psychologists must be mindful of the intersection of multicultural issues that appear in the identity development of the student-athlete. College is often the first time athletes have been away from their homes, parents, siblings, or typical support networks. It can be extremely difficult to be placed in a new geographical, academic, athletic, and social environment where most others have no knowledge of your background and experiences. Unfortunately, assumptions are often made based on observable or assumed demographic factors such as race, international status, gender, sexual identity, or SES. Sport psychologists need to be multiculturally competent in order to help athletes understand the potential dynamics of stereotyping, discrimination, and marginalization that are present in the college athletic environment and beyond. Additionally, helping student-athletes develop a balanced sense of identity requires an exploration of many factors, including cultural dimensions of the self, in order to impact the many intersecting individual components of multidimensional identity development. With proper training and supervision, sport psychologists can incorporate multiculturalism into their work with athletes, teams, and coaches, so they can provide services that can help student-athletes be successful both on and off the field.

Supervision is a valuable tool in cultivating these multicultural competencies and developing a better understanding of the complex nature of sport culture. In fact, supervision is one of the most valuable educational experiences available to us as sport psychology graduate students. Having an experienced professional available to guide discussions of difficult and challenging issues is vital to one's growth and development as a psychologist. In addition to broadening my theoretical approach to counseling, I (Aaron) have gained a better understanding of my own personal identity through the supervisory experience. This has been a place for me to explore those aspects with which I have less knowledge or experience. The best way to learn is through personal experience, which can be both scary and rewarding. Having the guidance of a trusted supervisor has allowed me to explore and process my own personal biases by giving me a more objective assessment of my work with athletes. I would like to reemphasize a valuable piece of advice previously mentioned in this chapter: "If I am uncomfortable or think this could make me look bad, then this is what I need to be discussing the most." While it can be difficult to be honest with yourself and your supervisor, these are by far the times when I have grown the most in my supervision experience. That is the benefit of being in the field of psychology: you get to process, process, and process, and, in doing so, you can make the implicit explicit. That is where real growth exists, and I am grateful to have the opportunity to explore this, particularly while I am working with student-athletes.

References

Berry, J. W. (1997). Immigration, acculturation, and adaptation. *Applied Psychology, 46*, 5–34.

Crocker, J., Major, B., & Steele, C. M. (1998). Social stigma. In S. T. Fiske, D. T. Gilbert, & G. Lindzey (Eds.), *The handbook of social psychology* (4th ed., pp. 504–553). New York: McGraw-Hill.

Duda, J., & Allison, M. (1990). Cross-cultural analysis in exercise and sport psychology: A void in the field. *Journal of Sport and Exercise Psychology, 12*, 114–131.

Dweck, C. S. (2000). *Self-theories: Their role in motivation, personality, and development*. Philadelphia, PA: Taylor & Francis.

Gardner, H. (2011). *Frames of mind: The theory of multiple intelligences*. New York, NY: Basic Books.

Leung, S. A., & Chen, P. H. (2009). Counseling psychology in Chinese communities in Asia: Indigenous, multicultural, and cross-cultural considerations. *The Counseling Psychologist, 37*, 944–966.

Martens, M. P., Mobley, M., & Zizzi, S. J. (2000). Multicultural training in applied sport psychology. *The Sport Psychologist, 14*, 87–91.

Parham, W. (1996). Diversity within intercollegiate athletics: Current profile and welcomed opportunities. In E. F. Etzel, A. P. Ferrante, & J. W. Pinkney (Eds.), *Counseling college student athletes: Issues and interventions* (2nd ed., pp. 27–53). Morgantown, WV: Fitness Information Technology.

Pedersen, P. (2001). Multiculturalism and the paradigm shift in counseling: Controversies and alternative futures. *Canadian Journal of Counselling, 35*, 15–25.

Sue, D. (2010). *Microagressions in everyday life: Race, gender, and sexual orientation*. Hoboken, NJ: John Wiley & Sons.

Waterman, A. S. (1985). *Identity in adolescence: Processes and contents*. San Francisco: Jossey-Bass.

Wirtztum, E., van der Hart, O., & Friedman, B. (1988). The use of metaphors in psychotherapy. *Journal of Contemporary Psychotherapy, 20*, 1–11.

12 Frequently Asked Questions

Jamie L. Shapiro, Mark W. Aoyagi, and Artur Poczwardowski

This chapter will briefly address and provide guidance on a wide range of common questions that consultants in training may have. Analogous to SPP consulting, there is rarely a right or wrong answer to these questions, and where possible, we have tried to include multiple perspectives. Thus, the information here is meant not to answer the questions but rather to stimulate your thinking and reflective process and offer guidance as to what possibilities may be the best fit for you.

1 In My Applied Work, Should I Focus on One Team/Individual and Go for Depth or Seek Out Many Teams/Individuals and Go for Variety/Breadth?

JULIA CAWTHRA, M.A.; PH.D. STUDENT, COUNSELING AND EDUCATIONAL PSYCHOLOGY, INDIANA UNIVERSITY, BLOOMINGTON

A PERSPECTIVE ON WORKING WITH MULTIPLE TEAMS

"Less is more" is one of those cliché sayings that applies to graduate students when it comes to sleep, but not much else, including opportunities. I struggled to find my balance between biting off more than I could chew and challenging myself while still doing a good job with every client. Finding your balance is difficult, but essential, if you take the path of "the more, the merrier." In all seriousness, the answer depends on what you want to continue doing after your time in graduate school is over. My experience was tailored toward admittance to a Ph.D. program and gaining experiences that would help me feel competent working with a variety of athletes and sports; therefore, I wanted as many open doors as possible.

Focusing on one team or individual and learning the nuances of an extended relationship is valuable but vastly different from working with multiple teams and reaching your arms as wide as possible. Going with the latter route enabled me to discern what was a productive and efficient use of my time and did not necessarily mean sacrificing depth. Seeking out various teams and individuals allowed me to see a wider range of presenting problems, learn to work with many different coaching styles, gain entry in varying ways, and build strong rapport quickly. Working with several teams also helped me learn the skills of having direct conversations with coaches to gather more information in less time, increased accountability and investment in the relationship, and creating an effective session. At times, I had to navigate multiple teams in one season, which meant being intentional and diligent with all clients. Looking to peers and mentors for help is an important piece of this puzzle—processing and consulting with trusted colleagues can bring clarity and confidence to a young professional. Going for variety is hard work and will be depleting at times, but asking for suggestions promotes community and elevates your work. The most important aspect of seeking out many different applied opportunities: do good work . . . always. Being a professional and giving your best with your clients promotes the field of sport and performance psychology, gives stakeholders a better experience with the service, and is likely to "pay it forward" in multiple ways (e.g., strengthened relationship with clients, word of mouth referrals from clients, and unique opportunities from colleagues who trust your quality of work).

SCOTTY MARIE HANLEY, M.A.; PSY.D. STUDENT, CLINICAL PSYCHOLOGY, UNIVERSITY OF DENVER

A PERSPECTIVE ON WORKING WITH FEWER TEAMS

In my training and career, I have had the opportunity for both of these options. Though it is exciting to work with multiple groups at once, I have found that I have done my best work when I have committed time and energy to one or two teams instead of multiple teams. The first reason is the quality of the relationship that you can build with a client. A sustained presence will help to gain entry and build trust with a team, and a better relationship means that more rewarding work can be accomplished between a consultant and team. When I was in graduate school, I chose to work with a roller derby team for the duration of their season, nine months, instead of the duration of our school quarter. By the end of our season together, we had worked on communication, energy management, emotional regulation, and burnout prevention, and I was considered part of the team. I also like to think that the referrals for individual clients I got from the coaches were due to the effort and attention I gave to the team.

Another reason to go for depth with fewer teams is the opportunity for your personal growth and learning. I worked with a diving team, and they loved the session I ran on the mind–body connection. They were genuinely curious about the research and the different ways to demonstrate the connection between our minds and our bodies. Their interest exceeded my materials, and, as a result, I took the opportunity to increase my knowledge and understanding of the topic. If I was working with 10 teams, I could have taught mind–body connection 10 times and never learned anything new myself. It is my belief that focusing on quality time with fewer clients is the best way to maximize my clients' experiences as well as enhance my professional growth.

2 In My Applied Work, Should I Work With the Sport/Performance Area That I Perform(ed) In?

KAELENE CURRY, M.A.; ASSISTANT SOFTBALL COACH, SONOMA STATE UNIVERSITY

It can be an advantage for consultants to have a performance background in the sport they are consulting with. The consultant not only has a stronger understanding of the sport and language but can also work from an empathetic perspective. The consultant can be seen as more relatable in initial interactions and throughout the consulting process. There is also the potential to gain entry and buy-in by utilizing the consultant's background, knowledge, and experiences.

I was fortunate to have experiences with men and women in my area of performance. Having the ability to speak the common language known to baseball and softball players and coaches expedited the buy-in process for the baseball team. I was able to "talk baseball" with the coaching staff, which helped with their trust and desire to utilize my sport psychology skills. Eventually the coach gave me the freedom to conduct team sessions, individual sessions, and impromptu brief interventions with the topics and tools that were ultimately set by me. He had developed a trust in my abilities, which was backed by my life in the game and eventually by my knowledge and abilities in the field of sport psychology.

The opportunity to consult with a collegiate softball team was afforded to me by my participation in collegiate softball. A relationship was already formed with the college coaching staff, so my biggest challenge was attaining buy-in from the players. My ability to empathize with the collegiate schedule, stresses, and competitive environment helped to gain respect from the athletes. "No one cares how much you know, until they know how much you care." This quote drove my consulting approach with this team; since I did possess softball knowledge, I needed to use it tactfully so the athletes knew I was there to empathize with them and be a resource for them, rather than seeing me as another critical coach. Surveys were an integral component to my consulting style. It was important to learn what the team and individuals needed from me before adding my mental skills goals. It was then easier to compile the team and individual needs into a tentative curriculum for fall and spring seasons. I was able to plan sessions using their self-assessments and also by understanding the ups-and-downs of the season, since it was something I had previously experienced. For example, I planned multiple educational sessions on topics throughout the fall that I wanted to be able to review again in the spring. Come spring, I could plan a more advanced confidence review session right before the toughest opponent in the conference. I also conducted a similar session regarding energy regulation and relaxation in the heart of the season when I knew the players would be feeling the grind of the season. As a final example, I scheduled a team chemistry session right before the postseason, when exhaustion and tension among athletes may be present, and they often need to be appreciated by one another and brought together again as a unit.

BROOKE LAMPHERE, M.A.; PH.D. STUDENT, COUNSELING PSYCHOLOGY, UNIVERSITY OF DENVER

Many novice sport psychology professionals with specific performance backgrounds enter the field with the intent of working with the sport or performance domain where they have the most experience. Often, students that I encounter believe that because they have gained expert understanding and competency in the physical and technical aspects of a certain activity, they are then more qualified to work on the mental aspects of the game because they have lived it—they have been in the performer's shoes, and they can walk the walk and talk the talk. Reflecting on my personal experiences as a novice professional, I found the exact opposite to be the case. My experiences (a) working with populations that were culturally or socially different from me and my background and (b) participating in an activity with which I was completely unfamiliar, while challenging and uncomfortable at times, proved exponentially more rewarding than working within my familiar sport bubble of soccer. According to Schinke and Hanrahan (2009), building the competency to work with diverse clientele requires not only adequate educational training but applied experiences and exposure to multicultural populations as well. Thus, building experience with diverse clientele is an essential process in attaining competency as a sport psychology professional.

Take the following scenario as an example: Student S, a graduate student in a sport psychology master's program, played college soccer at a well-known university. Student S decided to work as a sport psychology consultant with a 5A high school soccer team as her primary field placement, as she felt most comfortable and competent in this environment. The coaching staff for this team knew of Student S's expert background in the sport and often sought her out for technical and tactical advice. Student S was grateful for the chance to build rapport with the coaching staff, and she relished the role of expert in this context. Student S believed that her tactical expertise was helpful not only in establishing rapport with the coaches but also building trust and credibility with the players. Slowly, Student S began to integrate into the team culture and was thrilled to work with many of the team's starters on mental skill building. It was not until just before playoffs that she realized that many of the players considered her a member of the coaching staff and not a consultant—that those struggling to earn playing time or with injuries were hesitant to speak with her for fear of what would be relayed to the coach. Student S then realized that in her hurry to prove her expert status and familiarity with the sport, she had undermined the intentions of her original role, thereby limiting her potential effectiveness by not maintaining clear boundaries or honoring the unique experience of every member of the system.

Andersen, Van Raalte, and Brewer (2000) identified several mistakes commonly made by graduate students in sport psychology, including the following: presenting psychoeducational topics or skills training with too much information, missing information that the client (e.g., athlete) tries to communicate, failure to establish and maintain adequate and clear professional boundaries, and becoming involved in situations that are beyond the scope of their training or expertise. Student S's decision to work with the same population in which she had performed unfortunately contributed to the occurrence of several of these issues—most importantly, issues with establishing appropriate boundaries and missing information about client experiences. Choosing to take the risk of working with unfamiliar and diverse populations not only creates developmental experiences that circumvent many of the above identified issues but pushes novice professionals to practice what we preach, and get comfortable with being uncomfortable. Taking into account the experience of Student S, many novice professionals struggle to set boundaries and differentiate themselves from the coaching staff. Orchestrating my first few consulting experiences with unfamiliar populations allowed me to practice valuable skills in gaining understanding of the role of a sport psychology consultant, as well as effectively establishing the parameters of my role in a social system.

While working with youth and adolescent adaptive athletes and incarcerated young women in particular, I found that working with unfamiliar and diverse populations enhanced learning processes and outcomes for all involved parties. In these settings, I discovered that my lack of knowledge of the nuances of these performance domains was not a weakness but the foundation for building rapport and trust with clientele who rarely have the opportunity to share their stories. Showing up authentically as a professional allowed me to get to know the individual experiences of each of my athletes without attaching preconceived biases. My decision to share my vulnerabilities, ask questions, and genuinely seek to understand a lifestyle and identity that I have not personally experienced allowed me to connect with many clients who otherwise may not have been interested or open to services. As such, I believe that growing into the role of a sport psychologist through a mindset of curiosity and awareness is the path that is most conducive to honoring the humanistic assumption of the therapeutic relationship as a meeting of two experts—the sport psychologist as the expert on the mental aspect of performance and each client as an expert on his or her own performance experience.

3 I Have a Lot of Contacts From the Community in Which I Used to Perform; Is It Okay for Me to Consult With Them as Clients?

TARYN BRANDT, M.A., CC-AASP; PSY.D. STUDENT, COUNSELING PSYCHOLOGY WITH A CONCENTRATION IN ATHLETIC COUNSELING, SPRINGFIELD COLLEGE

Many sport psychology graduate students, like you, were inspired to enter into the field based on their own athletic experiences/interests. This means that you probably have a number of contacts from the community in which you used to perform. For example, I was a competitive figure skater, and, as I have pursued graduate training in sport and performance psychology, I have maintained contact and connections with many coaches, athletes, and significant members of the figure skating community. It is not uncommon for these individuals to ask you for advice or consulting once they know what you are studying and the value of the services you are educated to provide. As much as it is tempting to offer your services, this presents some ethical concerns—particularly with those individuals you know directly. By consulting with individuals you have a prior relationship with, your objectivity is compromised. Multiple relationships can create ethical concerns related to lack of objectivity, difficulty maintaining confidentiality, blurry boundaries, and role definition, and they may not be in the best interest of the client. In situations where you have a prior relationship with an interested client, it is probably best to refer to a colleague or other professional in the field. I do want to emphasize that having connections within a sport community is not always an issue; there may be times when your connections are advantageous to creating consulting relationship; however, it is important to use good ethical judgment when objectivity may be difficult to maintain.

During my graduate training, I did a large amount of consulting work with figure skaters within the community I used to perform. Prior to reaching out to advertise my services, I took the time to define my boundaries with regard to the athletes it would be appropriate or inappropriate to provide services to. This led me to make the decision that it was okay to provide workshops to visiting skaters participating in a summer training program and to students I had no prior communication with despite having a formal, collegial relationship with the skaters' coaches. I made the decision to offer referrals to any skater who approached me who I had either competed with, trained with, or had socialized with in a nonprofessional capacity. Being significantly older than many of the up-and-coming young skaters was helpful in my situation as many of the skaters who were at an age where sport psychology consulting might be beneficial were far removed age-wise from the group of skaters I may have trained with. Overall, I recommend that you take the time to reflect on the sport communities you have connections with and to define the boundaries you feel are ethically appropriate for providing consulting services within these communities.

4 What Should I Consider When Creating a Session Plan?

DOLORES A. CHRISTENSEN, M.A.; PSY.D. STUDENT, COUNSELING PSYCHOLOGY WITH A CONCENTRATION IN ATHLETIC COUNSELING, SPRINGFIELD COLLEGE

There are two primary factors to consider when creating a session plan. First, you want to consider the team or group's prior experience with sport and performance psychology (SPP) services. A team that has had established consultants work with them every week during their competitive season for the past few years requires a very different approach than a team that has just one preseason team-bonding workshop per year. For the former, it would be important to communicate with past consultants or review your case notes if you have worked with the team previously, in order to ensure that you are not inadvertently repeating sessions with the same group of athletes or performers. For the latter, you have more leeway in creating the session plan because the team has less experience with SPP services, and the odds of duplicating session topics or activities are much lower. Along this vein, it is important to note if the team makeup changes year to year. For example, you could repeat activities each year when working with first-year athletes during an SPP orientation because, annually, there would be a different group of participants. However, if you were creating a session plan for a college baseball team, you would have some of the same athletes over the course of several years as athletes progressed through their education.

The second important factor to consider is the team's goals. It is crucial that you get a clear picture of what the coach *and* the athletes are looking for in a session, especially because those two ideas can be very different. Some goals can be as broad as "working together" or "communication," while others can be much more complex. A coach may desire that the quiet, newer players are given more opportunities to lead, while simultaneously asking that the strong, confident leaders are put in secondary roles. This knowledge changes the type of activity a consultant may choose, rules and restrictions that can be applied during the activity, and the way in which it will be debriefed. It is also important to think about the developmental aspects of participants (e.g., females? coed group? sixth graders? elite athletes?), history of the team or group (e.g., conflicted? successful?), and if there are special requirements to keep in mind while selecting activities (e.g., necessary physical adaptations, trauma histories that contraindicate some activities). Finally, it is critical to remember that it is *not* up to the team or the team's goals to fit the activity. Rather, the consultant has a responsibility to fit the *session* to the team and their goals. These considerations will assist in sequencing the proper outline of activities to ensure that goals are met and the session is engaging and fun.

As an additional logistical consideration, it is important to be skillful at managing the time of the session itself. It is recommended that you plan the approximate amount of time you want to spend on each component of the session in advance, while remaining flexible during the session. It can be helpful to "overplan" when preparing for a session, meaning that you have one or two activities that you *could* include, but due to time constraints might not actually be able to fit in. As such, these activities serve more of a "supplementary" role to the overall program. Overplanning also provides a safety net to avoid any dead space during the session that can stall group momentum and energy. As a parallel process to this idea, it is vital for facilitators to remember that *processing*, or debriefing, the activity is always going to be more important than fitting in *more* activities. This means that if the debrief is running long—but has been productive and engaging for group members—you might need to cut the next activity to afford room for the important discussion. Flexibility is always key in making these impromptu decisions.

The final logistical consideration is pertinent when cofacilitators are running a session together. Once the activity sequence has been created, it is important to assign roles for each section of the session to ensure smooth transitions and efficient use of time. For example, the facilitator who explains the setup of the first activity might also debrief that activity. Other times, the cofacilitator could serve in the debrief role instead to give more voices to the activity. Who takes the lead on which part of each activity is dependent upon facilitator comfort level and training, desire to explain a new activity for the first time, or the need to balance the leadership of the session (e.g., ensuring that one facilitator does not lead four activities in a row). These decisions should be discussed thoroughly beforehand so that each facilitator knows their role and can plan accordingly, while simultaneously preventing an overload of "too many cooks in the kitchen" during activities.

5 I Enter My Sessions With a Plan, but the Team Wants to Talk About Something Else—Do I Go With My Plan or Follow the Team's Wishes?

CHRISTOPHER E. BILDER, M.A.; PSY.D. STUDENT, COMBINED-INTEGRATED CLINICAL AND SCHOOL PSYCHOLOGY, JAMES MADISON UNIVERSITY

When I was receiving my graduate training in sport and performance psychology at the University of Denver, I was given advice that has benefited me numerous times in my applied work: "have a well-developed plan, but be prepared to immediately throw it out if something more important arises." Taking this advice to heart has allowed me to be flexible in my consulting work and to focus on what is best for the client. When posed with this question, I am also reminded of the quote by boxing legend Mike Tyson, who stated, "Everyone has a plan, until they get punched in the face."

I have received the proverbial punch in the face a few times in my young consulting career. The most salient instance occurred when I was working with an elite-level roller derby team. The team had recently come from a disappointing finish at the world championships, and the coaches, captains, and my coconsultant and I had developed a plan to systematically integrate desired mental skills into practice. Our sessions with the team consisted of introducing each skill and working with the players on the ideal way in which to use the skill in each drill. The planning for the season, and for each session, took a lot of work, and the end result was something that we were extremely proud of. Immediately prior to the first practice of the season, my coconsultant and I discovered that one of the leaders of the team, who was also one of the top players in the world, would have to leave the team to assist with a loved one who had been recently diagnosed with a life-threatening condition. When we found out about this situation, we immediately threw out our previously planned session to start to work through the thoughts and emotions the team was experiencing, and we began creating a plan with the team on how to most effectively move forward. Our time, effort, and pride were instantaneously put on the backburner so that we could do what was best for the team.

As is the case with most questions in the profession of psychology, the ultimate answer is, "it depends." Several aspects must be taken into account before deciding whether to stick with the prepared plan or following the team's wishes, the first being the reasoning behind the request to talk about something else. Several questions you may want to ask yourself are: (a) What is my role within the team? (b) What are my ideas of the most pressing issues within the team? (c) Do my ideas of the most pressing issues match the team's belief of the most pressing issues? (d) Have we followed my plan in the past? (d) Is there something about my proposed topic that could cause some resistance within the team? (e) What is best for this team right now and in the future? I would recommend throwing out your plan if the new topic is relevant to the team, and it appears to be a significant factor to the team's success or well-being. If this continually happens, however, then you run the risk of having a reactionary rather than a proactive role within the team. Being reactive rather than proactive with team issues is not necessarily detrimental, but it is something you would want to discuss with the important stakeholders within the team (i.e., coach, captains, general manager, president). You also run the risk of having the team think that you will drop your plan at a moment's notice to placate their every whim. This could become a significant issue within the relationship, and a neophyte consultant should be at least aware that this could happen. Finally, one must be cognizant of the possibility that the team is avoiding a topic that may be difficult to tackle. It should be addressed with the team if a consultant notices that the team consistently moves away from a certain topic. Some issues are uncomfortable, but working through those issues may ultimately be what is best for their performance and well-being.

A consultant in training may not have a lot of time to process this curveball in the moment, but the decision to either stick with your plan or drop it should be reflected upon in depth at the conclusion of the session. This would be an ideal time to utilize a coconsultant or shadow to gain his or her perspective on the process. After consulting with peers, one should take advantage of any and all supervision offered. I have had multiple instances where consulting with peers and utilizing supervision have tremendously assisted in conceptualizing how to work with a team under these circumstances, and I will continue to employ this tactic for the rest of my career. I encourage any sport psychology consultant to do the same.

6 How Do I Write a Good, Concise Note About a Consulting Session?

RYAN MARSHALL, M.A.; MASTER RESILIENCE TRAINER-PERFORMANCE EXPERT, COMPREHENSIVE SOLDIER AND FAMILY FITNESS (CSF2)

Writing an efficient and effective note following a consulting session is a simple yet difficult task. To reduce errors and increase accuracy, try to write the note as soon as possible following a consulting session: within 24 hours is good; on the same day is great. To optimize writing a note, use the following five steps: (a) cover the logistics, (b) describe the session, (c) assess the session, (d) create a plan for future sessions, and (e) write a personal reflection.

Cover the logistics by laying out all the facts in their simplest form. This is the date of the session, number of attendees, client age, client skill level, etc. Next, describe the session by concisely explaining the session's purpose, presenting problem, and important points. Use simple terms here, and try to use the client's exact language when possible. Then, move into assessing the session by conceptualizing the "why" or the issue behind the issue. Connect the dots from the facts to conceptual understanding by incorporating sport psychology theory and empirically based practice into the assessment. After completing the assessment, create a plan for future sessions by writing out the focus and actions for the next session. Try to schedule a concrete date and time in your calendar to go along with the plan. Lastly, use a separate document (for legal purposes) to write a personal reflection including thoughts, feelings, and general ideas about the session. These can be shared with a supervisor or peer supervision group for increasing self-awareness and creating personal growth as a student-consultant.

Editors' note (JS and MA): The client note itself is commonly called a DAP or SOAP note. A DAP note consists of (a) **D**ata or **D**escription of the session, (b) **A**ssessment, and (c) **P**lan. A SOAP note includes (a) **S**ubjective information about the client, (b) **O**bjective information about the client, (c) **A**ssessment, and (d) **P**lan. You are encouraged to use the format that feels most comfortable to you or that your supervisor prefers. It is important that all case notes are kept confidential by having two layers of security (e.g., locked file in a locked office, password protected notes on a password protected electronic device). For more information on writing a SOAP note, see the following reference:

Cameron, S. (2002). Learning to write case notes using the SOAP format. *Journal of Counseling and Development, 80,* 286–292.

Building on Ryan's excellent summary, I (MA) often advise students to follow a slightly different order when conceptualizing and writing their DAP (or SOAP) notes. While the order of Ryan's summary follows the format of the note, I recommend students begin with the Assessment section. This forces the students to start with their conceptualization: How do you understand what is going on for the client, and what is going to be helpful for them moving forward? After developing your Assessment, then go back and include the information from the session that supports your Assessment in the Data section. There are two primary benefits to this method: (1) the process emphasizes case conceptualization, which means applying one's theoretical orientation to performance excellence and is perhaps the most important skill for neophyte practitioners to develop, and (2) one of the challenges for young consultants is writing a concise note, as many have the temptation to write a moment-by-moment summary of the session. Beginning with the Assessment dictates what the important information (i.e., key points influencing the conceptualization) from the session was and then allows the student to include only this information in the Data section.

7 Any Advice for First Sessions/Gaining Entry?

MARK A. LAIRD, M.A.; M.F.A. STUDENT, ACTING, REGENT UNIVERSITY

The best ways to gain entry with an individual or group are to gain the trust of others and confidence in yourself. Establish your role specifically as a graduate student of performance psychology because it will negate any ambivalence in why you are working with the team. Confidence comes from preparation too, and the more preparation you have when it comes to knowing the population, often learned through interactive observation, determines how confident you will be as a consultant (things that I looked out for in my field placements were performance domain rules, the coach's orientation, role of my gender and sexual orientation on the team, and how I could tie in technology). This knowledge, along with honesty about a graduate student's competencies, lets the trust develop. When first working with a sports team, it was important for me to do at least two assessments: one with the coach to evaluate her/his needs and one with the players. They often are different when first discussed, but, broken down, they may have elements that both parties could grow from with future sessions.

Within field placements, it depends on whether it is the individual's/group's first time with performance psychology or whether they have already had experience with psychology. It was important to teach to the individual with the least level of experience while still utilizing the advice and feedback of peers within the team who already have expertise. You must also respect the consulting work of previous practitioners by using that work as building blocks for your own collective goals.

My master's project was called *Revisiting Gaining Entry With Athletic Personnel for Season-Long Consulting*, which was an empirical study that added validity and new information to an article originally published more than 25 years ago (Ravizza, 1988).

According to our focus group of experienced consultants, much of the original article was still relevant to the gaining entry process, while augmented and new considerations were also found. A few augmented issues found were that the stigma of psychology, the time that consultants must spend with their teams, and the way a consultant shows respect to a team all changed. New considerations involved the pressures and safety nets put upon graduate students working with teams: financial stresses, professional competencies, and having a fan mentality. New considerations also raised multicultural issues within the team/consultant relationship that I easily related to as a practitioner. Along with knowledge learned from my master's project, I found it best to work with multifaceted populations to build my practice beyond athletics, and I encourage any graduate student to do the same to better understand first sessions/gaining entry.

8 What Do I Do When Feeling "Stuck" With a Team or Individual—Either Not Knowing Where to Go Next or If the Client Is Not Progressing?

KIRSTEN ALLEN, M.A.; PSY.D. STUDENT, CLINICAL PSYCHOLOGY, UNIVERSITY OF DENVER

When I have felt stuck with a client, I have found that there are many potential factors that might be contributing to this "rut," such as insufficient rapport between the client and myself; a break from consulting may be needed, as the client no longer feels engaged or motivated to receive the services, or he/she (or the team) may be overwhelmed by his/her phase in physical training; or session topics may not be focused on addressing the real issues. To facilitate progression, I revisit the goals that were set for sessions at the beginning of the season, review what has been discussed and what services have been offered thus far, and check in with the clients, coaches, athletes, trainers, etc. to gain their insight into the current situation. After gathering such information, I reflect on the overall situation and often consult with others in our field for support and collaboration. What do they notice? What do they think may be contributing to the rut? (Gaining an outside perspective and bouncing ideas off others is always very helpful.)

I have found that there are sometimes issues that are too powerful to ignore and "interfere" with the season's original goals (e.g., team dynamic struggles, individual client family issues, coach–athlete issues, etc.). These issues therefore need to be addressed before you can refocus on (and potentially adjust) the consulting goals. However, other times, as mentioned previously, I have found that a simple break from sessions refreshes the athletes, and we return reinvigorated. Every situation is different, and conversing with others will help clarify what can (and needs to) be done.

9 How Do I End Consulting/Terminate?

KEVIN O'CONNOR, M.A.; PSY.D. STUDENT, CLINICAL PSYCHOLOGY, UNIVERSITY OF DENVER

Termination is an inevitability of any and every consulting relationship. It is not a singular event but rather a process. The moment a consulting relationship is born, termination is a reality that we must begin preparing our clients for. Some consultants would argue that it is our task to eventually render ourselves obsolete; that is to say, we strive to equip our clients with the skills necessary for success without using us as a crutch. For that reason, termination is something that should be discussed early and often.

A termination session with a client (individual or group) could include the following: summary of lessons learned, client evaluation of consulting (e.g., Partington & Orlick, 1987), referral sources for the future, and a discussion about application of skills inside and outside of sport. In my experience, sport and performance psychology transcends the realm of performance. Skills that I may teach my clients in an athletic setting can and should be utilized in all areas of an individual's life. By encouraging performers to apply SPP principles outside their performance domains, I am in essence training them to use those skills in my absence. In the short term, my absence may only last one to two weeks. Eventually, though, that absence becomes permanent. Reminding clients that the knowledge I share with them will live far beyond my physical presence provides them with the responsibility and the freedom to grow and thrive for the rest of their careers and lives.

Editor's note (JS): We now prefer to use the term "consolidation" instead of "termination" when referring to the process above. We feel that this term is a more accurate reflection of the processes that occur (e.g., summarizing the consulting work, applying the skills inside and outside of sport, reflecting on improvement) to transition someone out of formal consulting. "Consolidation" also has a more positive connotation than "termination" and fits well with a strengths-based approach. For more information on the rationale for changing this terminology, see Maples and Walker (2014).

References

Andersen, M. B., Van Raalte, J. L., & Brewer, B. W. (2000). When sport psychology consultants and graduate students are impaired: Ethical and legal issues in training and supervision. *Journal of Applied Sport Psychology, 12*, 134–150.

Maples, J. L., & Walker, R. L. (2014). Consolidation rather than termination: Rethinking how psychologists label and conceptualize the final phase of psychological treatment. *Professional Psychology: Research and Practice, 45*(2), 104–110.

Partington, J., & Orlick, T. (1987). The sport psychology consultant evaluation form. *The Sport Psychologist, 1*, 309–317.

Ravizza, K. (1988). Gaining entry with athletic personnel for season-long consulting. *The Sport Psychologist, 2*, 243–254.

Schinke, R. J., & Hanrahan, S. J. (2009). *Cultural sport psychology*. Champaign, IL: Human Kinetics.

Index